THE GREAT
IRON SHIP

THE GREAT IRON SHIP

JAMES DUGAN

SUTTON PUBLISHING

This book was first published in 1953 by Hamish Hamilton Ltd

This edition first published in 2003 by
Sutton Publishing Limited · Phoenix Mill
Thrupp · Stroud · Gloucestershire · GL5 2BU

British Library Cataloguing in Publication Data
A catalogue record for this book is available from the British
Library

ISBN 0 7509 34476

Printed and bound in Great Britain by
J.H. Haynes & Co. Ltd, Sparkford.

FOR
JOHN DUGAN
IRON MOULDER

CONTENTS

LIST OF PLATES

ACKNOWLEDGMENTS

I THANK the following for information, clues, pictures, and advice on this book. Much of the British material was gathered by Kathleen Taylor of London, who nearly became the *Great Eastern*'s latest victim from exposure in the vaults of the British Museum. Important data came from Daniel P. Costeau of Paris; Jack McNaught, Toronto; Mrs. Sturges Turner, Washington, Connecticut; J. S. Paton, Liverpool; Robert Kempner, New York; and Karl V. Lellman, Port Stanley, Falkland Islands.

Britons who helped include L. C. Johnson, archivist, British Transport Commission; V. C. Frank of the Telegraph Construction & Maintenance Company; and L. E. Hallet, Royal Photographic Society. The Cheshire delegation, captained by David Duff, M.B.E., numbered Ancill R. Dauber, Mrs. F. G. Cull, and Margaret Corbett, all of Wallasey; two men from Wirral, W. A. Phipps and James V. Knox; Richard Lane Anderson of Marple; Nigel Kennedy, Lower Bebington; C. C. Bennett, Northwich; and Mrs. Anne G. Bell, Birkenhead. Lancashire people included the Liverpudlians A. D. Lobley, Cunard Steam-Ship Company; R. H. Thornton, Blue Funnel Line; G. Williams; J. H. Downing; Mrs. M. L. Brown; J. M. Lamb; E. Smith; J. V. Carlisle; and T. Atherton; Miss L. Roberts, Bootle; Mrs. Gertrude Bingham of Wigan; Alan T. S. Holt and Mrs. Charlotte M. Hindle of Manchester. I thank also R. Andrews, Harrow, Middlesex; Mrs. Margaret E. Pierce of Rhyl, Flintshire; and S. E. Barrett, Weymouth, Dorsetshire. From Wicklow, Eire, I received the help of P. J. Noonan, Miss Belle Halpin, and Seán S. Ó. Ceallaigh, Town Clerk. These English firms and institutions provided material: the British Museum; the Science Museum, South Kensington; the Royal Photographic Society, Kensington;

C

11

British Railways Executive, Western Region; Lewis's Ltd., Liverpool; Associated Newspapers; Reuters Ltd.; the *Manchester Guardian* and the *Liverpool Echo.* The French Telegraph Cable Company was courteous.

United States sources were the National Archives, the Library of Congress and the General Services Administration in Washington; the New York Public Library; Harvard University Library; the Public Library, Easton, Pennsylvania; the American Antiquarian Society, Worcester, Massachusetts; the Museum of the City of New York; and the *New York Times* Information Bureau. Individual concern was shown by John L. Lochhead, Librarian of the Mariners Museum, Newport News, Virginia; U. E. Baughman, Chief, U.S. Secret Service; Edwin A. Patt, Steamship Historical Society of America; Osgood Williams, Peabody Museum, Salem, Massachusetts; Eugenia M. Southard, Public Library, Portland, Maine; Frank B. Laughlin, Acting Collector, Port of New York; William Williamson, Marine Museum of the City of New York; Mrs. M. B. Figmic, Duxbury Free Library, Massachusetts; Robert A. Hug, New York Public Library; and Beaumont Newhall, Curator, George Eastman House, Rochester, New York. Dr. G. L. Howe of Rochester gave from his notable collection of stereo-photographs.

Individual Americans who advised on details include Edward Rowe Snow, Marshfield, Massachusetts; the York Staters, Douglas Gorsline, Blauvelt, and Mrs. Beatrice L. Munro of Bedford; and the New Yorkers, Mrs. Lucille Liebling, Mrs. Loraine Dexter and Noel McLean. In New Jersey advice was given by James A. Leftwich, Lambertville, and Martha C. Whittingham, Milburn. Supervising this launching were Robert Carse and Ruth Lonergan Dugan.

Literary sources are mentioned in the text, but in addition I thank Mrs. Celia Brunel Noble for her double-header biography of Sir Marc and Isambard, *The Brunels*, a book which did not reach its proper audience because the plates were destroyed in Hitler's blitz of London.

J. D.

CHAPTER ONE

THE WONDER OF THE SEAS

A HUNDRED years ago, in the Iron Age, the world watched a wonder grow at the Isle of Dogs on the Thames. It was a steamship five times the size of the biggest vessel afloat then, in the morning of steamers. The colossal hulk was the *Great Eastern*, mother of ocean liners, the first work of marine architecture to surpass Noah's Ark and the Rhine timber rafts of the Dark Ages. The ship was designed to carry four thousand passengers, almost twice as many as her great-grandchild, the *Queen Mary*, launched seventy-seven years later. The *Great Eastern* was 692 feet long.

Poets, engineers, peoples and kings stood in common awe of the iron grandeur rising on the muddy strand of the London river. Two thousand workers scuttled like insects among the exorbitant parts of the ship—a screw which reminded one writer of 'the blade bones of some huge animal of the pre-Adamite world', hull plates that would have 'formed shields for the gods', and paddle-wheels larger than a one-ring circus. Americans were told that 'the human intellect expanded at the sight'. In Massachusetts, Professor Henry W. Longfellow mused on the monster in England:

> Sublime in its enormous bulk,
> Loomed aloft the shadowy hulk.

She was to be 'The Wonder of the Seas', 'A Mighty Home on the Deep', the equivalent of five capital hotels. The ship had six masts and five funnels, more than any other ship has ever carried. She had two sets of engines, indicating the then inconceivable strength of eleven thousand horses, 'enough to run all the cotton-mills in Manchester'. One power plant turned the fifty-eight-foot paddle-wheels and the other motivated the twenty-four-foot screw, still the largest a ship has carried. Fully laden, the *Great Eastern* was to outweigh the combined tonnage of the 197 English ships that fought the Spanish Armada.

The only size analogy was Noah's Ark. Somebody remembered that Sir Isaac Newton had calculated its dimensions. He had determined the Biblical cubit at 20½ inches, which produced an Ark 515 feet long and 86 feet wide with a tonnage of 18,231. The *Great Eastern* was a vessel of 22,500 tons displacement.

The *Great Eastern* carried 6,500 square yards of sail, an impressive figure even at the height of the clipper ship period. The big ship carried twenty lifeboats. She was to have a feature still unmatched, a pair of hundred-foot satellite steamers hanging from her sides. Passengers privileged to voyage on her were to find gas illumination, an electric light on the mainmast 'bathing the ship in perpetual moonlight', and air trunks ventilating the inner cabins, which were three times the size of the finest staterooms afloat. The great ship was to grant the ocean traveller the final boon: she would abolish seasickness. She was longer than the trough of the largest storm wave measured by Sir William Scoresby, the oceanographer, and would ride so stably that regiments of raw recruits could be drilled on deck while on their way to war, and Americans could duel without having their aim disturbed. She was 120 feet wide, too broad for the Panama Canal opened a half-century later. Her displacement was not exceeded for forty-nine years after her launching.

The behemoth was designed to steam nearly round the globe without refuelling. She had capacity for fifteen thousand tons of coal, a supply that transformed her nether regions into an ocean-borne coal-mine. Coal was bunkered around and over her ten boilers, so that the crew passed fore and aft through a six-foot iron tube buried in coal. To appraise the ship poets and pamphleteers exhausted the glossary of hyperbole. She was 'The Floating City' and 'The Crystal Palace of the Sea'. 'Like the old mythological heroes', the ship was 'ushered into the world amid signs and portents'. Currier and Ives published five lithographs of the *Great Eastern* before she went to sea. The potteries of Staffordshire turned out *Great Eastern* dishes, and stereo-photographs of the marvel were common pleasures of the Mid-Victorian parlour. A champion American gelding was named 'Great Eastern'. Music halls offered 'the Leviathan March' and 'The Leviathan Gallop', using the short-lived name given her at the launching.

As the poets sang, the shipyard workers toiled. The ship was constructed of thirty thousand iron plates, seven-eighths of an inch thick and averaging a third of a ton. The hull sections were cut over individual wooden templates by powerful steam shears and each then rolled to a unique curvature. The ship was hydro-dynamically designed on the 'wave-line' principle, inspired by Hogarth's line of beauty. She was the first ship without ribs, a daring fabric of plates, raised like a house of cards. She had two hulls, one inside the other, three feet apart and heavily braced, extending to six feet above the waterline. Inside these she had both longitudinal and transverse watertight bulkheads, forming sixteen compartments. The *Leviathan* was as nearly unsinkable as engineering genius could make her.

Prominent engineers, however, predicted that when a big wave lifted her amidships, the great structure would snap like a twig over a stone. Or when waves lifted the bow and stern, she would break down in the middle. One of her detractors was Herman Melville, who passed the ship on the Thames on his return from Holland in 1857. He wrote in his journal: 'Vast toy. No substance. Durable materials but perishable structure. Can't exist a hundred years hence.'

The ship required three million rivets, each an inch thick, all driven by hand by two hundred rivet gangs in a thousand working days from May Day, 1854. Outside two 'bashers' hammered alternately at the white-hot tip, which was held by a man inside. The latter was served by three boys and a candle. One child tended the forge, another passed the rivet and the third stuck it in the hole. The inside gang remained in the cramped dark between the hulls, in the hellish reverberation of four hundred hammers, during a twelve-hour day, six days a week. During construction a worker fell to his death, another died between the hulls, and a riveter fell on a man and killed him. A workboy fell head first from the structure and was impaled on a standing iron bar. 'After he was dead, his body quivered for some time,' said a witness. Another casualty was a visitor, who, 'in prying about, was bending over the head of a pile, when the monkey came down, flattening his head'. The builders were proud of the low casualty rate.

The reason for the ship was grandly simple. Her designer, Isambard Kingdom Brunel, the renowned 'Little Giant', declared, 'Vessels much larger than have been previously built could be navigated with great advantage from the mere effect of size'. He persuaded a group of capitalists to raise £600,000, the largest ship shareholding investment up to that time, on the theory that 'Nothing is proposed but to build a vessel of the size required to carry her own coals on the voyage'—a 22,000-mile round trip to Trincomalee, Ceylon. The big ship would seize and monopolize the imperial trade to the Orient and Australia. The merchant fleets of the Eastern Hemisphere were to become slaves to *Leviathan* by shuttling goods and passengers to and from Trincomalee. Brunel showed that 40 per cent of the capital investment would be earned each year.

The great ship was conceived in 1851, the year of the Great Exhibition, when mechanical engineers emerged as the cadre of human progress. Brunel was the most brilliant and daring of them all, with prodigious achievements in bridges, railways and steamers. The capitalists were led by Henry Thomas Hope, son of James Hope, author of *Anasta-*

tius, 'the novel that made Lord Byron weep because he had not written it'. In 1851 Henry Thomas Hope had organized the Eastern Steam Navigation Company to win the lavish Royal Mail subsidies for the Orient. He lost the contract to the Peninsular & Oriental Line and was susceptible to the Little Giant's scheme.

A consortium (or as it seemed later to the capitalists—a cabal) of renowned engineers was involved in the building of the great ship. The famous James Watt Company would build the screw engine; Professor Piazzi Smyth, the Astronomer Royal for Scotland, would devise the gyroscopic navigational instruments; more sub-contractors than had ever been engaged were standing by; and the hull and its paddle engines would be built by the brilliant Professor John Scott Russell at his shipyard at the Isle of Dogs. It was an engineering and financial venture that plunged far ahead in time. A steam historian who later tried to explain it said, 'The *Great Eastern* was the child of the Mechanical Section of the British Association for the Advancement of Science'. His mind was too tidy. The ship was a technological explosion.

Unlike her descendants, the ship was not built in dry dock. There was none in existence large enough. She was erected on the soft riverbank under West Ferry Road on a promontory reaching into a two-hundred-degree bend of the Thames, where the river takes two reversals, like an S tipped over on its side. The yard was located inside the left loop, on the misnamed Isle of Dogs, part of the dejected Millwall quarter of London Dockland. For three years her fifty-eight-foot height dominated the huddle of riverside dwellings, and was advertised to the world's shipping in the stream. She was raised parallel to the river, which is little more than a thousand feet wide at Millwall, too narrow to receive a seven-hundred-foot ship head on. The *Great Eastern* was to be launched sideways, a scheme then contrary to all precepts of large shipbuilding, and one which drew many warnings of failure.

Early in construction the price of iron-plate increased,

despite the fact that her demands were expanding the northern mills like a gigantic contemporary war order. Several
directors resigned when the cost of iron went up. The others
became agitated and timorous and blamed I. K. Brunel and
John Scott Russell for getting them into the scheme. The
directors were divided on which of the engineers was the
more dangerous and jockeyed for newspaper space to praise
one and defame the other. Sixty thousand shares had been
sold to three thousand people for a goodly proportion of the
venture money in England. Brunel and Scott Russell maintained mutual trust and added to their technical problems
that of recruiting more directors and money. They were
aided by a lively young director named Charles Geach. He
took a fatal chill from his selling exertions, and became the
first victim of the great ship, the unappeasable whale that
ate men and gold.

Brunel defended himself in windy memoranda to the
directors. If the ship succeeded the directors would share the
honours, he said, but if it failed, 'There is no doubt that I
should have to bear solely and very heavily the blame'.
After two years of construction the company ran out of
money, and work was suspended. Brunel was removed from
his post as resident engineer. He responded by raising more
money and renting a house near the yard. When work was
resumed after three months, he continued to direct without
pay and without an official connection with the Great Eastern Steam Navigation Company.

Each hull plate bore a code number, beginning with 'X' so it
could take its proper place in the complexity of curves. The
plates rose like a demon's noughts and crosses in the fogs of the
river. The ship seemed in her long, long gestation like a vast
building, a London landmark to rival St. Paul's. Sailors went
down the stream to the ports of the world and returned past
her with sarcastic remarks. They hated the iron moloch, the
big 'smoke-box', that would turn seafaring into foundry
work.

Two well-born apprentices stood by Brunel, Ernest Benedict, son of Sir Julius Benedict, a noted Victorian musician, and William Walker. They went to work with the shipwrights at 6 a.m., breakfasted at eight, and had dinner at one. They knocked off at five-thirty, except on Saturday, when quitting time was three o'clock. The bright boys identified a strange workman, who called himself 'Mr. Oakum'. He had a nasty job, that of filing down the roughcast cogs of the huge paddle-wheel rack. He was really Viscount Ockham, eldest son of the Earl of Lovelace, and grandson of Lord Byron. The Viscount was not an apprentice, but a common labourer. What were his reasons, no one knew. He was one of the intriguing Victorians lost to us.

The ship lay on two timber cradles, which rested on 120 iron rollers, placed across 160 railway rails, supported on a two-foot layer of concrete, in which were embedded 2,000 timber piles driven thirty feet through mud to the gravel base of the Thames. She lay 330 feet from the high-tide mark, on an incline of one in twelve feet. As the last plates were riveted in September, 1857, there arose a speculation and a clamour for the launching date. Brunel reminded the directors that he would have to have adequate power to get her into the water. The *Great Eastern* was the heaviest object that man had attempted to move.

To overcome her twelve thousand inert tons, Brunel would need sufficient hydraulic rams to push her, steam tugs on the river to pull her, gigantic steam winches on shore to let her down the ways and huge windlasses to check the mass when it slid too fast, operations which would require miles of massive chain cable. The directors borrowed chains from the Admiralty and gathered tugs and winches, but gave Brunel only two small hydraulic rams. Despite misgivings, Brunel announced the launching for November 3, 1857, when the ship could be floated on a rising tide. *The Times* tried to quiet public excitement by saying, 'The launch is likely to be a long and tedious affair, which will probably occupy eight to ten hours'. The day before, Brunel supervised the attachment of scrap-iron weight to the wooden cradles on the river sides, so they would sink and not foul the paddle wheels when she entered the water. He enjoined all hands, 'Nothing is more essential than *perfect silence*, so that everyone can hear the simple orders quietly and deliberately given by the few who will direct'.

He did not know that company directors had issued thousands of tickets, that grandstands were being built on nearby houses during the night and that Thames watermen were booking hordes to watch from the river. In fact the shipyard workers were going to bring their families into the yard. In the middle of the night young N. A. Woods, of *The Times*, who had made a name for himself with his Crimean War dispatches, set out from Printing House Square in a brougham for Millwall. The directors had not given tickets to the press and Woods had to pull strings to get one. Then, as now, company directors treated journalists somewhat like writ-servers. Woods drove through a dark drizzle in streets crowded with cabs, country rigs and people on foot, including beggars, tumblers, buskers, and 'swell mobsmen', all pressing towards Millwall. The pubs were alight and blaring with brass bands.

The Times man climbed on the directors' platform among ladies in crinoline, shell bonnets and lemon kid gloves. Flanking him he noticed two cool individuals who wore the loud and unmistakable uniform of the Field Lane thieves' coterie. Everybody was there. Perhaps the two pickpockets were shareholders in the company. In the grey dawn Woods saw ten thousand people in the yard below, including sensible girls with their skirts pinned up to expose brown woollen calves, painters in smeared jackets, stokers in fustian, and shipyard navvies in 'buckish turnouts' of short trousers and tight-laced boots. Children were scuttling everywhere. In the midst of the muddy tumult was little Brunel, 'looking like a respectable carpenter's foreman', rushing around, trying to herd the crowd away from the launching apparatus. The directors had provided four constables, who were charging here and there and yelling at people, quite unaware of which were the critical areas. The Comte de Paris and his suite arrived, and then the Duke of Aumale and retinue. The deafening confusion abated slightly while the crowd goggled at some new arrivals in turbans and printed cotton trousers. They advanced behind a resplendent figure in a sparkling robe of cloth-of-gold. It was the Siamese Ambassador. The Siamese were 'far from being indifferent to the observation they excited among the spectators', said Woods. As the hour of launching approached at noon, he estimated the crowd at a hundred thousand people.

Brunel disappeared under the ship to supervise men lubricating the ways with grease and black lead. Then he took his place on a rostrum high up on the side of the ship and released red and white signal flags, with which he was to direct the launching. The directors chose this moment to climb to him with a list of names proposed for the ship. The chairman's daughter, Miss Hope, was ready with the champagne and wished to have something to say when she swung it. 'You can call it Tom Thumb if you like,' said the exasperated engineer. The directors selected *Leviathan*. Nobody ever called her that. People liked the bassoon note of the double adjective and she was always the *Great Eastern*. Miss Hope christened her. A stupendous cheer echoed through the rainy middens of Millwall.

A clerk stood at each launching cradle with a blackboard to record her movements for Brunel; no voice could be heard above the crowd. The engineer waved his white flag to release the bow and stern fastenings, and to slack off chain on the two drums that were to check the slide. The mighty ship gave a shuddering rumble, and stood and groaned for ten minutes, a convulsion so majestic that people were knocked dumb. The very mud beneath them quaked.

'She moves!' they yelled. 'She moves!' The stern slid three inches. Brunel waved his red flag for the hydraulic rams to push. There was a scraping squeal, the earth shook, and the *Great Eastern* started to slide. Among the thousands who simply stood and sighed was the gang on the sixty-ton stern checking drum. The ship took up the slack of their chain and sent the windlass spinning in reverse. The huge handlebars caught a dozen workers and threw them above the heads of the crowd. Spectators and workers ran in panic, except for Brunel and the foreman of the forward drum crew, Ned Hepworth, a Yorkshire yeoman shipwright, who applied his brake. The ship stopped with a horrible complaint of iron. The crews of the river barges lost their heads and leaped into the river.

Five men were carried off, of whom two died. Brunel couldn't find the frightened barge crews. He ordered the lighters to be cut out of the river organization and went on with steam tugs alone. The crowd was readily cleared from the launching gear as Brunel organized another attempt. A heavy rain began to fall. He signalled the tugs to take up bow and stern tackle, and started the steam winches and hydraulic rams. The ship would not move. The *Great Eastern* groaned and grumbled, inert and motionless. The bow winch stripped its gears. Chains snapped and flailed links as thick as a man's arm at screaming, running people. Brunel signalled the end of the day's effort. The crowd stayed for a long time in the mud and downpour, under the broken wine bottle hanging from the bow.

Brunel walked out of the yard into an outburst of derision. Cockney wits called her 'The Leave-her-high-and-dry-athan'. 'Barnacle Minimus' wrote to *The Times* asking why the ship had not been treated the way his nurse handled him when he would not take a bath. 'She put me in the tub and poured water over me. Why don't clever men make big ships in big holes and let the water in when the ships are finished, instead of trying to make the ships travel on rail-roads?'

Brunel induced the directors to bar the public while he prepared for launching in the next spring tide a month hence. Prince Albert and the sixteen-year-old Prince of Wales were admitted, however. Brunel borrowed two more rams and made a secret attempt in dense fog to push the ship forty feet to a better stance. The wooden abutments of the rams cracked and a mooring chain and the bow tackle parted. The ship would not move. He grappled the river bottom for broken chains and installed heavier timber and pilings. He continued to move the great ship, an inch at a time, for a distance of fourteen feet. He lost two more chains four days before the next launching. He went to the coroner's inquest for the men killed on the big drum and manfully stated, 'I may blame myself, for I did not anticipate that the handles would have revolved so rapidly'.

In the last days before the tide, Brunel applied ten more screwjacks and hydraulic rams, and lost another chain. He borrowed more chain from the Admiralty and the Brown & Lenox Company. He was acutely at a loss for advice from his fellow engineers. The directors regarded him as a dismissed employee who had no right to invite anyone to the yard. He nudged the ship seventeen feet further by the eve of the launching, an effort terminated by an extraordinary event. A ten-inch hydraulic ram burst its cylinder from exertion. Brunel worked all night to replace it and hunt up two more rams for each cradle.

The Prince of Prussia, the Duc de Joinville and the Marquis of Stafford were on hand in the morning, among the select group admitted by the directors. They went away disappointed. The borrowed rams failed to arrive and Brunel could move the *Great Eastern* only fourteen feet. The day was not without its catastrophe. An unofficial sightseers' gallery, erected between two housetops outside the yard, collapsed, flinging a hundred people to the ground. Cartloads of injured were hauled off to Poplar Hospital, but on this occasion the ship exacted no life.

Still trying for the December tide, Brunel moved her thirty feet in the next two days. The Princess Royal and the Duchess of Atholl lent their presences to the effort. He was halted by the explosion of a seven-inch and a fourteen-inch ram. The engineer continued to shove throughout a cold month of rain and fog. His friend, Robert Stephenson, told a common acquaintance that he was hurt at not being asked to Millwall. The friend explained Brunel's peculiar status. Stephenson swore an old-fashioned engineer's oath and got up from his deathbed to go and help Brunel. He found the embattled engineer getting short slips of five and six feet at a time. Stephenson studied the arrangements and recommended more ram power and the abandonment of the off-shore anchors in favour of driving pilings on the other side of the river and stretching chains across. Brunel adopted the suggestion, but the ship would not move.

At the end of 1857, after two months of struggle, the *Great Eastern* lay half-way to low water. For the coming January tide, Brunel had scoured the country to borrow rams, and had twenty-one brutal presses poised at her flanks, including the biggest in existence, the twenty-one-inch giant that had been used on the Britannia Bridge. Brown & Lenox regretfully asked for the return of their chain, which had been lent for a short emergency period. Brunel sent it back and stretched his old repaired chains. He had to rearrange the river system after a bark had collided with one of his steam barges and sank it with valuable windlasses and gear. The engineering progress of the era was at a halt on January 5 as the rams of Christendom butted at the starboard flank of the Floating City. The engineer had assembled a motive force of nearly six thousand tons, half the deadweight of the ship.

The morning was very cold. Fires were built to thaw water in the presses. The ship yielded three inches to the first attack. Then the rams began to burst. 'Hydraulic rams, windlasses and chains, although of the most massive construction, were all broken in regular succession, till scarcely anything of the apparatus was left to continue work,' said *The Times* man, Woods.

It was something unheard of in the history of mechanics. In fact the accident to a windlass, when a side of its massive iron drum round which the chain was coiled, was crushed like a nut, was not only never known to occur before, but until yesterday such a breakage was considered almost impossible. Through the sides of a hydraulic ram ten inches in diameter the water was forced through the pores of the solid iron like a thick dew, until the whole cylinder ripped open from top to bottom with a noise like a dull underground explosion. The iron of this cylinder averaged six inches in thickness and stood a pressure upwards of twelve thousand pounds per square inch before it gave way. The massive cast-iron slab against which the base of another ram rested was split like a board, but this of course, was a mere bagatelle among the other mishaps, which are not only expensive in themselves but by the delays they give rise to, occasion an expenditure in which the cost of their repair is a mere item.

The company was forced to pay for the borrowed rams. Woods said:

> The shareholders stand round in solemn silence, witnessing the awful silent contest for the visible effects of the invisible struggle, as hours and days and days roll on, and small indeed and gradual is the fruit. There she lies on the very bank of the noble river which is to convey her to the ocean, but she will not wet her lips.

The man who made the rams, Sir Richard Tangye, was a Cornish Quaker hardware manufacturer who had introduced the scandalous practice of giving his employees a half-holiday on Saturdays. He enjoyed so much prosperity from the *Great Eastern's* orders that he was able to build his own works in '58. Tangye's Ltd., now one of Britain's great machine tool firms, still boast, 'We launched the *Great Eastern* and the *Great Eastern* launched us'.

The launch had cost a thousand pounds a foot, as the ship stood nearly two-thirds of the way down. The vessel was resting on her bottom in six feet of water. For fear that an unexpectedly high tide would float her off prematurely, Brunel had a fireboat pump tons of water into the hold. Advice poured in from everywhere. G. W. Bull of Buffalo, New York, sent Brunel diagrams on how Great Lakes steamboats were launched sideways, without rams; and a man wrote a description of how the immense statue of Peter the Great had

been erected at St. Petersburg. Brunel sent a printed acknow-
ledgment to his advisers. Some wrote back, complaining at
being lumped in with crackpots. A Sabbatarian paper attri-
buted his frustration to the fact that he had tried to launch
her on a Sunday. But *The Engineer* commented, 'A brave man
struggling with adversity was, according to the ancients, a
spectacle the gods loved to look down on'.

The fourth tide of the ordeal was due on January 30, 1858.
Four steam tugs held the reins, and the fireboat was ready
to flood her should she float prematurely. Brunel had weather
reports telegraphed from Liverpool and Plymouth, to estimate the probabilities.

Benedict and another apprentice named Leslie stayed overnight with Brunel in the yard offices to await the launching.
Brunel lay exhausted on a draughtsman's table, awake and
smoking cigars. He sent the apprentices into the rainy night to
check the river level by inspecting white-topped pegs driven
in the beach. In the morning the two youths were to stand at
blackboards on the bow and stern launching cradles, to chalk
up the descent of the *Great Eastern*.

But Brunel did not try to move his 'great babe' on the
thirtieth because of a stiff southwesterly wind and a spectacular rise of tide. That night, Brunel received a telegram
from Liverpool that the weather was calm on the Irish Sea.
He ordered the fireboat to pump her out and announced he
would launch at eleven o'clock the next morning. It was Sunday. The day came in brilliant sunlight and idle air. No
visitors were present. People were exhausted with attending
launchings of the *Great Eastern*. The Tangye rams hissed
and billy-goated at the iron bluff, which had seemed a part of
Millwall. At one o'clock, Captain William Harrison, who was
to be her master, yelled from the deck, 'The wedges are
floating! She's afloat!' In twenty minutes she was riding on
the Thames.

Brunel hurried aboard and directed the tugs to pull her
upstream so that floating debris would not foul the paddle-
wheels. She was towed across the river to anchorage on the

Deptford shore. The *Great Eastern* began her life afloat by fouling several barge cables. Brunel ordered the barges to be scuttled. After dark, he came down the sponson stairs with his seventeen-year-old son, Henry, amidst the pealing of London's bells.

CHAPTER TWO

THE LITTLE GIANT

THE engineer who conceived the mighty ship, promoted her and built her, Isambard Kingdom Brunel, was a dynamic little man with a high beaver hat full of memoranda scribbled to himself, and a leather pocket-case holding fifty Trincomalee cigars. The jut of a cigar from his olive-complexioned face was a famous sight of the time. He was the most celebrated civil engineer of the middle nineteenth century. When people spoke of the 'Little Giant' in 1858 they meant I. K. Brunel. Senator Stephen A. Douglas, who debated with Lincoln that year in Illinois, wore a nickname borrowed from the world-famous Englishman.

The Little Giant built railways, bridges, dry docks, and steamships amidst salvoes of controversy. He was possessed with grandeur. Everything he did was outsize, brilliant and radical. He built the Great Western Railway from London to Bristol with tracks seven feet wide and a two-mile tunnel near Bath which had conservative peers rising in the House of Lords with cries of doom. (The tunnel is still holding up.) At Paddington, the Great Western London terminal, Brunel kept a private flat car to accommodate his fast horse-drawn britzka, which was popularly known as the 'Flying Hearse'. The carriage contained a full-length bed, or at least one that would accommodate his five-foot four-inch person during the four hours a day he lost in sleep. No engine with a head of steam up was safe from him. One day his locomotive superintendent, Daniel Gooch, puffed out of London in his own requisitioned engine and met a runaway heading for him on the same track. Gooch reversed and sped back into Paddington, ahead of the mad locomotive, hit the buffers and leaped for his life. The runaway braked neatly and down stepped Brunel, looking like a chimney-sweep. 'Taking Lady Holland on her first ride tomorrow,' he remarked. The next day Brunel held the aged lady's hand during her maiden steam journey —to a country whist party.

He and Gooch drove the engine for Queen Victoria's first rail journey in 1842 from London to Windsor, amidst prayers for Her Majesty's safety. Before the trip the Queen's Master of the Horse went to Paddington, examined the locomotive according to the Manual of the Horse, and climbed in the cab in his scarlet livery, white gloves and wig. Brunel asked an equerry what this portended. 'The Master of the Horse will, of course, drive the locomotive,' he was told. Brunel lured the dutiful courtier to the pilot engine, which ran ahead of the royal special. The Master of the Horse arrived in Windsor covered with soot and beating away at his wig which was smouldering from sparks. Although the iron horse never succeeded in unsaddling the Master as a court functionary, he has been permanently discouraged from operating H.M. locomotives.

Brunel was famous at twenty, when he carried out the construction of the world's first shaft under a river, the Thames Tunnel. When he was thirty-two he launched the first steamship designed for ocean crossings, the *Great Western*, which antedated the original Cunard steamers by two years. Brunel's ship narrowly missed making the first crossing of the Atlantic entirely by steam. She started for New York in March, 1838, and suffered a paint fire. While the *Great Western* was being repaired, a Yankee named Junius Smith chartered a small Dublin mail packet, the *Sirius*, and set out on a foolhardy bid to reach New York first. Brunel's ship left three days later and arrived in New York six hours after the bold packet had hobbled in, out of fuel and burning spars, furniture, and even a child's doll.

In 1843 Brunel launched the 336-foot steamer *Great Britain*, the first iron-built ocean ship and the first to reject paddle-wheels and rely entirely on a propeller. The ship was an anthology of advanced features: she had a clipper bow, hydro-dynamic lines, a flat double bottom and watertight bulkheads. Few improvements other than the Bessemer process, oil turbine power and electricity have been added to ocean liners since the *Great Britain*. For decades she carried emigrants to Australia round Cape Horn. In 1882 her worn-out engines were removed and she was converted to a three-masted sailing ship, with her hull sheathed in greenheart wood. She was partially dismasted in a gale off the Horn in 1886, and made Port Stanley in the Falklands, where she was moored as a wool and coal storehouse for a half-century. In 1933, the age of coal had passed, and the Falkland Islands Company condemned her. The Royal Navy refused an offer to sink her in gunnery practice, out of respect for the nonagenarian vessel. *The Times* tried to raise a public subscription to bring the *Great Britain* back to the Thames as a national monument, but there was little sentimental money loose during the depression. The company beached her in six feet of water in the outer harbour. In 1943 the lonely islanders celebrated her centenary.

Brunel's *Great Britain* was visited in 1952 by Karl Lellman, the town clerk of Stanley, who was out gathering penguin eggs. He climbed the starboard mooring-chain and reported in a letter to the author:

> The greenheart sheathing is still sound. On removing two dowels the heads of the galvanized bolts were as new. The frame of the deckhouse remains. Between decks the iron plating is very rusty and holed. It seems much better lower down. She is still an impressive sight and at close quarters her curves are amazing. I don't know that there can be a straight line in her hull. When towed out in 1936, the rudder and tiller were used to steer her. Her wheel was put into the *Pengwern* in October, 1899.

After 110 years the *Great Britain* remains in Sparrow Cove, a resort of gentoo penguins and mollymauks, who stroll the deck upon which Victoria walked as a young queen.

The Little Giant built twenty-five railways in England, Ireland, Italy, and India, and the precipitous Taff Vale line in Wales, considered a choice collector's item by contemporary rail fans. He built eight piers and dry docks, five suspension bridges, and 125 railway bridges. He invented the compartmented freight car, an innovation reinnovated a century later by U.S. railways. He introduced railway telegraphy in 1839. In 1825 he published an argument for a canal through the Isthmus of Panama. During the Crimean War he designed an armoured gunboat which would launch amphibious tanks to attack the Russian forts at Kronstadt. The vehicles were to be powered by jet propulsion. The idea was ninety years too early for the Admiralty. The War Office, however, carried out another Brunel design, a fifteen-hundred-bed military hospital, prefabricated in England (no part was too heavy for two men to carry) and erected at Renkioi, Turkey, by eighteen men in ten weeks. The hospital had excellent plumbing, and pumped thirteen hundred cubic feet of cooled humidified air per minute around each bed. While he was building the *Great Eastern*, Brunel was also managing the big railway hotel at Paddington Station, 'a very agreeable relaxation from his more important duties', said his son.

Brunel was a friend of Felix Mendelssohn and a skilled water-colourist. He designed dozens of Roman- and Egyptian-influenced tunnel entrances and viaducts which may still be seen along his railways. He not only engineered the rail routes, but supervised construction, selected the colour schemes of the passenger coaches and flew around the countryside in the britzka, buying the right-of-way. Brunel's persuasive powers were severely tried in testimony before the House of Lords, where he carried the brunt of railway lobbying. Certain antediluvian peers reached for ingenious arguments to fend him off. One noble lord asserted that the Great Western Railway would befoul the Queen's water supply at Windsor, another said Brunel would choke up the Thames with weeds, and a third maintained that the railway would carry abandoned Londoners out to Eton to corrupt the boys.

Brunel lost his biggest parliamentary battle, for the adoption of seven-foot railway tracks, in the famous Battle of the Gauges in 1846. Most British lines were four feet eight-and-one-half inches wide simply because that had been the width of mine carts, for which the first rails were laid. Brunel and Daniel Gooch proved that trains ran faster and more comfortably on rails seven feet apart. But they were outnumbered by lines using the conventional width. Today, we are still riding on the mine-cart gauge.

Brunel was also a parlour magician who enjoyed exposing spirit mediums by duplicating their table-rapping and trumpet tricks. One time he was entertaining his children by pretending to pass a gold half-sovereign from his ear to his mouth. He accidentally swallowed the coin. It fell into his right bronchus. He bent his head and felt the coin drop towards the glottis. When he straightened up he suffered a paroxysm of coughing. He repeated the painful movement to confirm his auto-diagnosis before calling in his brother-in-law, Sir Benjamin Brodie, a leading surgeon. He told Sir Benjamin where the coin was located and how to remove it. Brunel designed an apparatus consisting of an almost vertical board, swinging on a horizontal pivot like an old-fashioned looking-glass, upon which he proposed to invert himself and be slapped on the back to eject the coin in a coughing fit. Distinguished surgeons and friends gathered to watch the little man hanging upside down, hacking and choking. The torture went on for weeks, with the country waiting on the daily bulletins. After six weeks, the medical panel forbade him to continue, for fear he would kill himself. They advocated a tracheotomy. Brunel sketched the special forceps they used to reach through the throat incision. (The instrument, still used today, is called the Brodie forceps.) Sir Benjamin opened his throat without anæsthesia and inserted the forceps. The attempt failed. The incision was kept open and another unsuccessful probe made the next day. Sir

Benjamin was then at the end of his resources. On the third day, Brunel, with the wound still open, got head down on the coughing machine, barked, and the coin fell into his mouth. Thomas Babington Macaulay, who was present, dashed to the Athenæum Club and yelled, 'It's out!' Everyone knew what he meant.

Brunel came of a father quite as extraordinary as himself. Marc Isambard Brunel was an eighteenth-century character who shared with Tom Paine the distinction of legal citizenship in Britain, France, and United States. He was born of Norman peasants, talked his way into a Navy commission, and served with the French West Indies squadron in the American Revolution. As an outspoken monarchist, he fled the French Revolution and settled in New York as a civil engineer. He built the defences of Long Island and New York's first cannon factory. His great-granddaughter asserted that his design won the architectural competition for the U.S. Capitol, a matter difficult to check because several sets of plans have been lost. However, the Commission dropped Brunel's plan when they found what it would cost. All Brunel schemes were expensive.

Marc Brunel built the notable Park Theatre in the Bowery at the unheard-of cost of £26,000. It opened unfinished in 1798. The Brunel touch was evident in the special second-tier box for dramatic critics. It seated 267 critics. During the first performance, Brunel hid in a windmill on the stage, and stopped the show with jokes about the fashionable audience. The next day he was advised to remove to Philadelphia. There he was dining with Alexander Hamilton, when the talk turned to the problem of supplying wooden blocks for the ever-increasing rigging of ships. Brunel went home and designed a practical machine for carving several pulleys at once. He sailed for England, which was a bigger market for blocks. The Admiralty took up his machine and built him a block-making factory. The Franco-American wizard promptly anglicized himself. He married an English orphan named Sophia Kingdom. Their eldest son,

B

Isambard Kingdom Brunel, was born at Portsmouth in 1806.

Marc Brunel converted the block machine to carving multiple boot lasts, thereby establishing his name as the father of shoe manufacture. He shod Wellington's Army in the second Napoleonic War, but its prompt victory over the escaped Corsican left Brunel with contracts cancelled and eighty thousand pairs of boots on hand. He lost his factories and went to a debtor's gaol, where he was joined by his wife. The boy Isambard was then attending the Lycée Henry IV in Paris.

Brunel pondered the ingratitude of the English and wrote to an admirer, Alexander I of Russia, offering his talents to Muscovy, if the Czar would bail him out of the English prison. He let word of the letter leak from his cell. The Regency not only liberated him but voted him £3,800 to stay in England.

Apart from fathering manufactured shoes, Marc Brunel lives in engineering history for the invention of the tunnelling shield. He carried a powerful reading glass through which he was fond of studying the microcosmos. One day he examined the universal shipworm, *Teredo navalis*, which has destroyed more wooden ships than fire, reefs, dry rot, and shot. He saw a tiny elongated animal with two fleshy siphons at the end, through which wood fibre was consumed and passed out behind by digestive processes. The significant aspect of its design for Brunel, however, was two sharpened calcareous plates embracing the siphons. With these the shipworm gouged its tunnels into wood and protected the sucking hoses. He thought he could dig human tunnels by this principle.

He built an iron shipworm in 1826 and organized a company to drive a tunnel under the Thames between Rotherhithe and Wapping. Miners had known since classic times how to dig and prop shafts through dry earth and rock. Brunel's tunnelling shield made it possible to sap the soft, wet beds of rivers. A variation of his shield is still used today. It

was an oval structure thirty-eight feet wide and twenty-three
feet high divided into thirty-six compartments, like so many
doors and sills, upon which workers stood to mine the muck.
They dug through the open doors, and closed them when
the mud became too fluid and when the shield was advanced
by jackscrews. Behind them was wooden scaffolding giving
access for the miners and wheelbarrows. Then came brick-
layers casing the the tube with a three-foot thickness of
Roman-vaulted brickwork as the shield bored in.

Irish sandhogs dug inch by inch for twelve hundred feet
in fifteen years in the Thames Tunnel. They drowned, suffo-
cated and went blind. Above them was the gelatinous mud
of the Thames, an immemorial sewer so foul that when it
broke through it jetted sulphuretted hydrogen, which caught
fire from the gaslights and drifted in flaming swirls on the
watery tunnel floor. 'Fire and water!' the men cried when
the river bed broke in. Sometimes human bones came
through. In the second year the river burst through at the
rate of a million gallons a minute. The last man out as the
tunnel filled was the twenty-one-year-old Isambard, who
was his father's works superintendent. The Brunels plugged
the hole from above by sinking three thousand clay bags
enmeshed in hazel withes, and pumped the water out. On
the next break-through the youngster was standing in the
compartment through which the river came. Unable to force
the iron door shut, he stood aside to estimate the flow. The
platform buckled. He ordered the men out and jumped off
the swaying scaffold to join the general flight. The falling
platform pinned him and the last three men.

'I struggled under water,' he reported, 'and at length
extricated myself.' By swimming with the force of water he
reached the vertical entrance shaft. 'My knee was so injured
that I could scarcely get up the stairs,' the young engineer
wrote, 'but *the rush of water carried me up the shaft.*' His
three companions were lost. Unable to walk, he had himself
carried aboard a barge and placed in a diving bell, to survey
the break-through. The bell dangled short of the river bed.

He tied a rope round his waist, held a breath, and plunged down into the muck. The Brunels dumped thousands of tons of soil into the breach, but the accident bankrupted the company. It was seven years before operations were resumed. In 1841 the Wapping and Rotherhithe shields met. Matching compartment doors were opened for the seventy-two-year-old father, now Sir Marc Brunel, who became the first man to crawl under a river. Today the Thames Tunnel serves the East London Railway. Many tourists visit the 'Prospect of Whitby', a picturesque riverside pub at Wapping Stairs, where they sit a stone's throw from one of the triumphs of engineering without knowing it.

The strangest of all the younger Brunel's works was the Atmospheric Railway, a forty-mile route along the Devon coast at the foothills of Dartmoor. Here he attempted in 1844 to run trains by vacuum power, obtained from stationary pumping engines along the way. Between the rails ran a continuous fifteen-inch tube with a slot through which a leather-cupped piston reached down from the leading coach. The engines siphoned air from the tube ahead of the train and sucked it forward. The slot had a leather flap, opened by the advancing piston and closing behind it to maintain the seal. The Atmospheric Railway not only worked, but attained a speed of seventy miles an hour.

However, as in the case of several Brunel works, the materials available at the time were poorer than his vaulting imagination. The leather flap got cranky, stiffened in cold, mildewed in fog, wore out, and was even eaten by rats. Platelayers plied the flaps with lime soap and fish oil, but after eight months, the vacuum road would not work. The stockholders lost £500,000, part of it the little engineer's own investment. Today travellers on British Railways from Exeter to Newton Abbot ride on the original roadbed of the Atmospheric Railway, beside the waters of the River Exe, along the coast and past the River Teign, and are much taken with the splendid marine views.

The Clifton suspension bridge at Bristol, now 125 years

old, is another Brunel audacity. It is a single 702-foot span, 248 feet above the River Avon. It was made of cast iron and rightfully remains one of the world's wonders.

Isambard Brunel's first skein across the chasm was a cast-iron bar an inch and a half thick. To encourage his workmen, the Little Giant elected to make the first crossing with himself and his wife in the basket car. Half-way across, the car stuck. He removed his high beaver hat and climbed the suspension chains to the swaying bar, freed the jammed pulley and proceeded with his lady to the other pier.

In 1851 I. K. Brunel stood at the top of his profession, in an age of great engineers—Robert Stephenson, James Watt and a new man, the Duke of Devonshire's clever head gardener, Joseph Paxton, who appeared with his one masterpiece doodled on blotting paper, the legendary Crystal Palace. Brunel knew them all. There was a covenant and a camaraderie among the engineers, who stood together to fight for the future. One of their chief obstacles was the aged and oracular Duke of Wellington, who had opinions on each and every public matter, whether he knew anything about it or not. Wellington, when younger, had backed the Thames Tunnel. As time passed him by, he opposed Brunel's railways and steamships. He stated that iron ships would not float.

The Great Exhibition was the Waterloo of the Wellington mind. After 1851 mechanical science was free. The Exhibition cleared the air for the *Great Eastern* steamship and brought Brunel and her other builder together. He was John Scott Russell, a Scotsman of the genuine Brunel stamp. He had been a child prodigy, a graduate of St. Andrew's University at sixteen, and a full professor of physics at twenty-four. He worked out the basic theories of hydrodynamics in his 'wave-line' principle of ship's hull design. Russell operated an iron foundry and engineering works on the Isle of Dogs.

The Great Exhibition was in good part Russell's doing. When an ingenious civil servant named Henry Cole[1] told

[1] The man who invented Christmas cards.

him about the wonders of the Paris Exhibition of 1849, Russell saw the possibilities of a British fair of engineering and manufacturing arts. He discussed it with the Prince Consort. That intelligent and catholically educated German was having a bad time in England. (They made him wear kilts.) The upper classes were suspicious of his erudition and the lower classes abhorred his stiff manners. The Queen, however, wanted Albert to be a success. John Scott Russell weighed these factors and sprang his coup one night in 1850. In the course of handing out medals at an art school prize day, Russell remarked cryptically, 'There is now every hope of carrying out His Royal Highness Prince Albert's plans for 1851'.

Albert summoned Russell to the Palace and they plotted the Great Exhibition. The Queen blessed Albert's hobby. The Old Guard was outmanoeuvred. Today in Kensington Gardens, slightly pocked by the bombs of a later German generation, Albert sits in a granite canopy alive with friezes and allegorical reliefs, a structure exceeded in Victorian high taste only by the Sir Walter Scott Memorial in Edinburgh. In his hand the Prince holds a catalogue of the Great Exhibition. Near by in the Science Museum there is a glass case containing a model of John Scott Russell's paddle-engines of the *Great Eastern*. On Victoria Embankment is Brunel's marble effigy, badly chipped by Hitlerian bombs.

Brunel, Scott Russell and Robert Stephenson were members of the building committee of the big fair. They held a design competition for the main hall and invited the world's architects to submit plans within three weeks. They actually received 245 drawings. None was satisfactory so Brunel drew up a committee plan, featuring a sheet-iron dome two hundred feet in diameter. The building was squatly Romanesque with a whiff of Byzantine.

At this stage Paxton sketched his gigantic greenhouse. Brunel was its first champion and volunteered to design the great water towers to flank the Crystal Palace. Brunel had a generous scientific philosophy. He did not believe in patent-

ing inventions, and protected none of his numerous ideas,
saying, 'Most good things are being thought of by many
persons at the same time. If there were publicity and freedom
of communication, instead of concealment and mystery, a
hundred times as many useful ideas would be generated.'

The Great Exhibition was opened on May Day to
Thackeray's ode:

> As though 'twere by a wizard's rod
> A blazing arch of lucid glass
> Leaps like a fountain from the grass
> To meet the sun!

The engineers were running the world. The capitalists
eagerly tried to keep up with their blueprints. The common
people were prepared to go anywhere with the golden engineers. Royalty deferred to them. The applied mechanical
mind would conquer everything. The Exhibition was the
cachet of machine-age genius. In this triumphant hour,
Brunel and John Scott Russell entered the tragic climax of
their lives. They determined to build the iron leviathan.

CHAPTER THREE

FASTEST VESSEL BEYOND COMPARE

IN SIX prenatal years, the *Great Eastern* had cost £ 800,000. Now that she was afloat there was no comfort for the shareholders. She still wanted funnels, boats, sails, instruments, auxiliary engines, furnishings, rigging, and masts, of which the mizzen was to be a 115-foot pine from Desperation Pass, Oregon. The five other masts were made of hollow sheet iron and served as funnels for the auxiliary engines. The mizzen was made of wood in order to hold the main compass high above the magnetic field of the ship. It projected compass readings to the deck by a beam of light passing through holes punched in the scale of the card.

The jargon of the sea did not have enough names for six masts, so they were called Monday, Tuesday, Wednesday, Thursday, Friday, and Saturday. If you asked a *Great Eastern* sailor, 'No Sunday?' he would reply, 'There is no Sunday at sea, sir'.

The ship could be completed for £ 120,000 more. The debt-ridden company cut its daily maintenance losses by abandoning John Scott Russell's yard. The ship had Brunel's partner almost beaten. A high wind came and snapped the *Great Eastern*'s mooring chains. She was adrift at Deptford for half an hour until tugs arrived to calm her. A ghost story fastened to the great ship: that a riveter had been sealed up alive in one of the hull cells, and his screams could not be heard over the din of hammers. His ghost was said to have brought bad luck to the ship.

Through 1858 the stockholders vigorously asserted the great ship's chief talent, that of filling newspaper columns.

Most wanted to sell her. One hoped in *The Times* that the
First Sea Lord would buy them out. 'As a war steamer she
may be invaluable and irresistible,' the suffering investor
argued. The navy would need only to steam her up to top
speed and ram-sink anything afloat. By autumn *The Times*,
which had kept its nerve throughout the tribulation, was
scratching its head. An editorial said, 'There is some futile
talk that the ship could be sold for a fraction of the investment, then all England might put its head together to think
what to do with the monster'.

No resourceful Drake or miraculous Wellington came forward to seize victory from the national muddle. The directors
opened her for sightseers and took £5,000 in one week from
a cockney crowd which caused a *Times* letter-writer to
grumble: 'The scenes witnessed there would have disgraced
Greenwich Fair, even before the police had shorn it of its
ancient glory.' The visitors chased each other with reverber-
ating whoops through the cavernous ship and courteously
held ladders for enthusiasts to climb aspects of the architecture, then ran away with the ladders. Queen Victoria
arrived in the royal steam yacht and came aboard with her
nose buried in a bouquet. The Thames stank powerfully in
those days. It was London's main sewer.

Even the Little Giant could not solve the ship's dilemma.
The ordeal of the launching left Brunel dazed and sleepless.
He was examined by a specialist, who declared Brunel had
Bright's disease. The diagnosis was irrefutable: the specialist
was Sir Richard Bright, who had first described the disease.
He advised Brunel to take a rest in Egypt, a favourite resort
among prosperous Victorians.

The engineer sailed in genuine Brunel style with his wife,
son, personal physician, a reference library, a carriage-load
of scientific instruments and three hundredweight of hams,
tongues, soap and candles. During a Mediterranean mistral,
the doctor was moaning in his bunk below while the invalid
was braced on the careening paddle-box, measuring the
Beaufort force of the storm and the roll of the steamer. In

B*

Cairo Brunel hired a dahabiya and sailed up the Nile. At the falls, he chartered a date-boat, built cabins on it, and portaged the rapids, disembarking for donkey excursions to sketch and ponder the works of archaic engineers who had transported stones worthy of the attention of the man who had made and moved the heaviest bulk in history. It was Brunel's idea of recuperation.

When he returned to London, the heaviest bulk was still there, and the Eastern Steam Navigation Company was defunct. The shareholders had lost over £600,000. Brunel rallied part of the original directorate, and helped to found the Great Ship Company with a capital of £340,000 in £1 shares. The new company bought the ship for £160,000. The successors disregarded one of Brunel's old memoranda: 'The full advantage of the great coal capacity for long voyages would not be felt in short voyages, for instance, to New York.' The new company harkened to the American demand to see the *Great Eastern*. The directors calculated that she could make eight round trips a year to Portland, Maine, or New York, and return 15 per cent per annum.

The directorial contribution of the second operating company was to fit her out partially for sea. They couldn't afford the two satellite steamers to hang on her sides, or the perpetual moonlight on the peak of Wednesday mast. There wasn't enough money to install her five hotels, but the grand saloon was decorated and staterooms were furnished for three hundred first-class passengers.

There has not been such a grand saloon since. It was sixty-three feet long, forty-seven feet wide and fourteen feet high, predominantly white and gilt in décor, with silver-oxidized ornamental ironwork. A funnel that passed through it was encased in mirrors and decorated with arabesque panels of infants symbolizing the arts and sciences which had contributed to the *Great Eastern*. The sofas and chairs were of carved teak with claret plush upholstery and there were a maroon carpet and red silk portières. The walnut buffets had green marble tops. These effects of Messrs. Crace, the elegant decorators of Wigmore Street, were illuminated by Brunel's inspiration of skylights. Unlike contemporary ocean liners, the *Great Eastern* did not have a superstructure of boat decks, rising above the hull for as many as five storeys. The main deck was an acreage of teak, dotted by skylights and small deckhouses called 'cabooses' that looked rather like railway carriages. The captain's caboose was under the bridge between the paddle-boxes. The others were foyers for the stairs, or cattle pens.

Without a superstructure the *Great Eastern* looked larger than the bigger ships built since. Her five funnels, one more than the later North German Lloyd and White Star behemoths, established her as one of the most thrilling silhouettes ever seen on the sea lanes.

Her staterooms were twice as large as Cunard's best cabins and higher than those of our day. By removing partitions they could be expanded for two, four, six, or eight people. Double-decked berths folded into the bulkheads during the day. Each cabin had a washbasin and dressing-table, a rocking-chair and a turkey rug. A settee concealed a bath with taps for hot fresh or cold salt water.

The company propaganda told prospective second- and third-class passengers: 'In the lower saloon, surrounded by all the substantials of comfort and without any pomp and glitter to put folks on their "best company" behaviour, one seems to feel even more at home than even when lolling on the velvet cushions of the grander apartments.' To allay any suspicion of airlessness in the buried cabins, the pamphlet asked the reader to 'think what a breeze would pour down a windsail from the deck of a vessel tearing across the water at twenty miles an hour!' The issue proved academic. Second- and third-class quarters were not installed for nine more years.

The fitting-out was celebrated in August of 1859 in the Thames anchorage by a banquet for five dozen peers, members of Parliament, engineers and capitalists. Brunel was too ill to attend 'the festivity which marked the successful com-

pletion of his grand idea'. The guests were introduced to
Captain William Harrison who had been chosen from two
hundred competitors to command the great ship. He was a
formidable master mariner of the Cunard Line. Despite the
fact that Sir Samuel Cunard and his shrewd Scots partners,
Charles MacIver and George Burns, seemed to have everything to lose to the great ship, they willingly lent Captain
Harrison. They played the waiting game as they had for an
ill-fated American competitor, the Collins Line on the North
Atlantic in the fifties. So far the *Great Eastern* had boarded
naught but gapers, banqueters and workmen. An Irish syndicate made a twenty-thousand-pound bid for the ship to
sail from Galway Bay to Quebec City and stand in the bay
fifteen days before, to give the Celts a crack at seeing 'the
greatest modern wonder of the world'. The proposal enlarged
the growing suspicion of the directors that they had a
winner. They declined the Irish offer and announced that
the *Great Eastern* would start off from the Thames on September 6, 1859, for Holyhead on the Welsh shore of the Irish
Sea.

The day before she was to leave for her ocean adventures,
a faltering, white-faced man painfully climbed aboard to inspect the ship. His associates were heavy in heart when they
looked at I. K. Brunel. He was fifty-three years old, and had
changed in months from the tough, tanned little engineer
who bossed great manipulations of earth, iron, and minds,
to a quaking ancient. He posed for Nottage of the London
Stereoscope Company against the gigantic mainmast. When
he took off his high beaver, no memoranda fell out and they
saw that his thick brown hair was gone. The twin lenses took
the image. Brunel staggered away and fell with a stroke. He
was carried tenderly through the great ship to a cargo port at
the waterline, placed in 'the flying hearse', and slowly driven
home to his house in Duke Street, St. James's.

The *Great Eastern* did not sail the next day. Bales of bed-
ding, stacks of furniture and barrels of crockery were still
coming aboard in an ant-like procession. Men tried to hang

chandeliers while riveters were still banging away at the bulkheads. The ship waited for more bargeloads of china, sofas, rugs, guns, anchors and cables, received in a vast din of hammers and forges' flares. The ship left a day late under tow to Purfleet with the artificers still aboard. The pilot trumpeted, 'Let slip the moorings!' Six huge chains dropped through the hawseholes with a shower of sparks and a roar heard for miles. The tugs, *Victoria, Napoleon, Victor, Punch,* and *True Briton,* drew her away in a din of orders and counter-orders, which could scarcely be heard down on the tugs. The bridge telegraph, which was to transmit helm orders from the bridge to the afterdeck wheelhouse, was not yet installed. Captain Comstock, an American master who was studying the great ship, stood at the aft wheelhouse, trying to relay to the six helmsmen the distant trumpeted orders of the bridge. When the paddle-wheels finally turned, the population of the river lost their seven-years' disillusionment. 'Boats of every kind were launched,' said *The Times,* and 'thousands upon thousands crowded to the water's edge with an outburst of enthusiasm and delight. Even the wan inmates of the Seamen's Hospital crowded the ports to give one shout or a wave to the vessel, as she slid grandly past.'

The *Great Eastern* navigated the tricky point at Blackwall and released carrier pigeons to spread the news in the City. The shore features of Woolwich could hardly be distinguished for humans. Men in ship's shrouds bounced 'three times three' cheers against the banks as she came to anchor for the night in the river at Purfleet. Purfleet and Gravesend came out in boats to watch her. Little steamers ran round and round with brass bands playing 'Rule, Britannia!' and 'See the Conquering Hero Comes'. The Marquis of Stafford arrived panting from Scotland to get aboard for her next morning's progress to the Nore.

'The long-nursed pet of the shipbuilders' left for the Channel with a piper playing 'King of the Cannibal Islands' for the eighty men who walked her anchor capstans. They had the muscular aid of the Lords Stafford, Mountcharles, Alfred Paget and Vane Tempest. Fifteen merchant and navy captains beat time for the men who went down the iron sides 'like kittens on a tree' to adjust the anchors. She sailed in a mass caterwaul from the banks, 'which triumphant as may be her reception in the States is never likely to be surpassed', said the proud *Times*. The tugs cast off, and in ten minutes, 'she set at rest for ever all doubt as to her being the fastest [steam] vessel beyond compare in the world'.

The *Great Eastern* ran up twelve knots by the time the breakfast bugle blew. She skirted the treacherous Goodwin Sands on a typical windy September day in the Channel, into waves rolling high from Biscay, but 'their foaming surge seemed but sportive elements of joy, over which the new mistress of the ocean held her undisputed sway'. Rain and spray scudded through a burst of sunlight in a marine panorama of the *Great Eastern*, and pitching steamers, yachts and brigs come out under the leaden Channel sky to see her pass. The guests did not linger for after-dinner wine and toasts, but hurried on deck to enjoy the sensation unknown since Channel voyages began. The great ship moved on that unruly strait with a slight sway of chandeliers.

Off Hastings, 'there was throughout the whole vessel a sound of most awful import'. The forward funnel blew out of the ship, followed by the sibilants of escaping steam. The mirrors in the grand saloon, which the passengers had just left, 'were shattered into ten thousand fragments'. Captain Comstock ran out on the paddle-wheel guardwalk to look at the explosion hole in the side. The *Great Eastern* 'deviated a few yards, then her paddles wafted her lightly along'. The American saw that the hull was intact, despite the most 'terrific explosion a vessel has ever survived'. The scene was hidden in clouds of steam. Glass, ornamentation and bits of wood fell like hail. Captain Harrison ran from the bridge and yelled for six men to follow him. He went hand under hand down a line into the shattered saloon and searched it for survivors. There had been no one in the room when the explosion came, except Captain Harrison's little daughter. He found her behind a bulkhead which had preserved her from the blast. Harrison passed the child up through the broken lights and continued to search. He almost fell through the hole in the saloon deck. He saw below a red glare of open furnace doors, fed by the downdraught from the craters above. The furnaces were spewing flame and ashes. Captain Harrison yelled for the donkey pumps to pour sea water into the boiler-room fires.

The cry 'Man overboard!' was raised. People threw out lifebelts and wooden debris of the explosion. There was a man receding in the sea, a fireman who had escaped being boiled alive by diving down a coal-chute. He was drawn into the paddle-wheel and left broken in the wake. Crewmen went into the forward stokehole and brought out fifteen men. 'None who had ever seen blown-up men before could fail to know at a glance some had only two or three hours to live,' said an eyewitness. 'Three walked up to the deck with an indescribable expression in their faces resembling intense astonishment and a certain faltering gait like one that walks in his sleep. One man walked along and seemed unconscious that the flesh of his thighs was burnt to deep holes. He said quietly, "I am all right, there are others worse than me, so look after them".' He was the second of the five explosion victims to die. The oak stairways into the grand saloon were broadcast in splinters. Not a book on the shelves near the exploded funnel had been disturbed.

That evening the *Great Eastern* put in to Portland Bill. The captains declared no other ship could have survived such an explosion. The cause was steam building up in the funnel casing. The escape cock on the standpipe had been closed by some unknown person; so John Scott Russell testified at the inquest on the dead fireman. Three of the passengers blamed Russell, who had been standing on deck, issuing general orders to the engine-room. The inquest brought in a verdict of accidental death, but stated that 'sufficient caution was not used by the engineers'. Brunel, paralysed in his bed, was not told of the explosion and his partner's humiliation for four days. The news killed the Little Giant.

'Brunel was the right man for the nation, but unfortunately he was not the right man for the shareholders,' said an obituary in the *Morning Chronicle*. 'They must stoop who would gather gold, and Brunel could never stoop. The history of invention records no instance of grand novelties so boldly imagined and so successfully carried out by the same individual.' The British people thought back on the halcyon days of the little engineer, to the tunnel, to the broad gauge and the gold half-sovereign. *The Times* recalled Brunel's final visit to his last bridge, when the Little Giant was too ill to get out of bed: 'In the spring of 1859 the Great Saltash Bridge was approaching completion when one morning, a carriage truck was slowly drawn across it. On the truck was a couch, and on the couch lay the Great Engineer, whose name must for all time be coupled with the history of the Great Western Railway.' Brunel was buried at Kensal Green. His friends placed a window to him in Westminster Abbey and a marble bust on the Embankment below Temple Gardens.

The contest over the iron carcass rumbled on. 'The Kings were going mad,' *The Times* said. The directors held the contractors responsible for repairing the explosion damage. They finally decided to give Scott Russell £5,000 to repair the damage in three weeks, a rather punitive contract. The directors advertised her maiden voyage to New York for October 8.

The toppled funnel was purchased by the Weymouth Waterworks Company and buried in concrete at the bottom of the deep end of the Sutton Poyntz dam as a strainer shaft for the local water supply. It is still there.

There was a diversion in the intramural war on the *Great Eastern* in September when half the crew went on strike. The men refused to holystone decks on Sunday. The management insisted on a full-dress trial for mutiny. The ringleader got two months' hard labour, and the other thirty men two weeks in the quarry.

The ship was opened for sightseers during the repairs. The explosion damage was added inducement to the six thousand who bought half-crown tickets. The visitors contributed £120 for the families of the victims. There was a round of banquets on board, as the directors tried to keep up a brave front. But the sailing date passed—repairs were not finished. The passengers waited another ten days, then demanded their money back. The small shareholders revolted, and the directors were assailed with demands that they do something about making her pay.

By this time the directors were clinging to the only hope that had appeared—the sightseers. The big ship was losing her identity as a passenger vessel. The directors decided not to leave for America that year, on the grounds that winter would be a poor time to catch sightseeing crowds. They took the ship to Holyhead to mop up tourist half-crowns in the west. On the way an engine fitter named McGrogan had his hand torn off in the paddle-engine. At Holyhead they fired most of the crew but kept the *Great Eastern* band and the ship's stereo-photographer, who did a fine business picturing tourists. Many local chambers of commerce made representation for their ports to be selected as the home of the great ship, including the merchants of Southampton. The city was beginning to challenge Liverpool and Bristol as a steamer entrepôt, due to its excellent sheltered position and the unique double tide in the Solent which was the best for the new big ships. Bristol put forth its claims, reinforced by a large number of Great Ship stockholders who lived there. The directors chose Southampton and talked of sending her on a Mediterranean cruise from there. The Southampton Chamber of Commerce issued handbills, apprising the citizenry of the municipal triumph. Four days later the Society of Merchant Venturers of Bristol announced officially that the great ship would make their city her permanent port. They, too, had a written commitment from the Great Ship Company.

The addled directors decided to stand off the furious rival

ports by appointing a harbour committee to re-examine the entire question. When city deputations appeared before the committee its chairman piously reminded them that the *Great Eastern* was not 'an exhibition ship' to be taken from port to port. If that were the case, he said, 'we could have kept her moored in the Thames and netted £60,000'. While he was talking a paying crowd was tramping up and down above the grand saloon. Special trains were bringing people from the West Country. The meanest rural alehouse was charging London hotel rates for beds. Prince Albert came to Holyhead to inspect the ship, and the banquets rolled merrily on. Two hundred eminent guests attended a memorial dinner to Brunel in October.

Late in that month a tremendous storm struck Holyhead. Captain Harrison went out on deck to inspect the ship. His waterproof coat was torn to ribbons and he was tumbled along the deck. He fought his way into a hatchway, and realized that the *Great Eastern* had lost her mooring chains and was adrift at the mercy of the gale. The wind blew out the saloon skylights, and roared through the new decorations, letting a flood into the sumptuous room. Ships were going down all over the anchorage. The *Great Eastern* rolled and heaved towards the shore. Chief Paddle-Engineer Alexander McLennan started the paddle-wheels and through a night of masterful manœuvring, Captain Harrison kept her head into the gale. After eighteen hours the wind blew out. They had averted a crash, but the grand saloon was ruined again. In the storm the big screw steamer *Royal Charter* was wrecked on the rocks at near-by Anglesey with a loss of 446 lives and over £1,000,000 in gold. While the most significant aspect of the gale was that the *Great Eastern* had proved her storm-worthiness, the famous disaster was always called 'The *Royal Charter* Storm'.

After the *Royal Charter* Storm, the directors decided they had better seek the protection of Southampton water for the winter. A shareholder forced a company meeting, which was 'conducted in an uproar'. The financial statement was a sensation. The company was £36,000 in debt and the ship was mortgaged for £40,000 more. Her total cost had been £1,000,000. And the directors had a bank balance of £1,000. The shareholders yelled for them to resign. 'The New Year opened with gloomy prospects,' said *The Times*. Shares had depreciated by a half on the London exchange. The directors appealed to Mr. Gladstone, the Chancellor of the Exchequer, for a government subsidy. Mr. Gladstone demurred. A strange fact about the unprecedented undertaking was that the *Great Eastern* never had a government subsidy, the prior requirement of operating flag lines since 1843.

In January Captain Harrison went ashore in his gig with the ship's surgeon, seven crew members, and the nine-year-old son of Captain Lay, the chief purser. A squall came up suddenly. Captain Harrison, at the tiller, ordered down sail. The wet sail stuck. The wind hit it and capsized the boat. The boy, the coxswain, and the master of the great ship drowned.

The directors resigned. A new board was formed, which set out to recapitalize to the extent of £100,000 in £5 shares. The new men, led by Daniel Gooch, started out vigorously to undo the dissensions of the previous board, to restore public confidence and to complete the ship. Their first action was to sack John Scott Russell as consulting engineer. He had been thrice victimized by the colossus. He had lost his shipyard, his honour was under a cloud from the explosion, and now he was no longer allowed on the ship he had built.

Here was a third group of shareholders and the Wonder of the Seas had not yet carried a paying passenger.

CHAPTER FOUR

THE COMING MONSTER

Nor forget I to sing of the wonder, the ship as she swam up my
bay,
Well-shaped and stately the Great Eastern swam up my bay,
she was 600[1] feet long,
Her moving swiftly surrounded by myriads of small craft I
forget not to sing.
—WALT WHITMAN, *The Year of Meteors* (1859-60)

IN NEW YORK 'public expectation was on tiptoe' as the *Great
Eastern* lay in Southampton water in May of 1860, taking on
passengers for the maiden voyage. It was a portentous summer in New York. Bell, Breckenridge, Douglas, and Lincoln
had just been nominated for the Presidency. Captain John
Brown was restless in his grave. The city had reached a million population; Central Park and the Croton Reservoir at
Fifth Avenue and Forty-second Street were new. The first
Japanese to visit the United States were on their way.
What the *New York Herald* called 'the governing classes'—
the street boys and sporting element—were clamouring for
news by steamer of the first world's heavy-weight fight in-
volving a native pugilist, John C. Heenan, 'The Benicia
Boy', who was fighting Tom Sayers in London. Meteors were
being plentifully reported from rural parts and, although the
1858 Atlantic cable was dead, New Yorkers were reading late
'interestings' by another briefly lived medium, the Pony
Express. Not only was the British monster coming, but the
Chicago Zouaves, nonpareil of drill teams; and later the
Prince of Wales and Prince Napoleon. The *élite* shunned

---

[1] The ship was too big even for Whitman: he took nearly a hundred feet
off her length.

Newport and other resorts to stay in the baking city for the summer of spectacles.

Michael Murphy, a vaunted Sandy Hook pilot, who was known as Commodore Murphy, was quietly sent to Britain in the fast steamer *Teutonia*, to pilot the great ship into New York harbour. Eight cities were still vying to become the North American port of the *Great Eastern*: Montreal, Quebec, Portland (Maine), Boston, Philadelphia, Baltimore, Norfolk, and New York. When the word came back that a New York pilot had been seen on the bridge during the big ship's last trial, seven rival cities echoed with lamentations and charges of double-dealing, particularly Portland, which had built the £25,000 Victoria Pier especially to handle her. The Canadian Grand Trunk Railroad shared the cost of pier construction. Portland had been led on to the last minute by the company directors. The last traces of the Victoria Pier may be seen today at the foot of Fort Allen Park in Portland, and local people still hiss the name *Great Eastern*.

The Grand Trunk Railroad sued the Great Ship Company for leaving it with the white-elephant pier at Portland. (This was the railway on which Artemus Ward was once travelling when he summoned the conductor. 'Friend,' said Artemus, 'it is plain from the speed of this train that it could never catch a cow, but there is nothing to prevent a cow from catching up with us. I beseech you, therefore, to remove the cowcatcher from the locomotive and place it on the rear car to save us from disaster.') The Grand Trunk never collected. The *Scientific American* remarked,

> What in the name of Malthus and Cotton Mather would [the *Great Eastern*] do [in Portland]? Why, in two trips to Europe she would take away the whole population of that enterprising city, leaving its streets as deserted as Pompeii, and in six months she would denude the entire state of Maine of all its products and manufactures.

From Montreal the Portland *Eastern Argus* correspondent said, 'The indignation here is intense. Everybody denounces it as a shameful breach of faith.' New York spent only three thousand dollars to dredge a berth for her alongside a lumber wharf in the Hudson (otherwise known as the 'North' River).

The steamer *Niagara* arrived with news of June 2: the great ship was to sail on the ninth. Due to time consumed by the *Niagara* at sea, it meant that the ship was actually on her way. The papers announced the news to the waiting city. But the *Niagara* also brought John Yates, secretary of the Great Ship Company, who had been sent to New York to prepare the reception. He had a secret: the *Great Eastern* was not to sail until June 23. When Henry Raymond, editor of the *New York Times*, learned of this latest bit of confusion, he wrote in an editorial:

> The managers of the *Great Eastern* seem determined to play the public impatience to the last. It is quite doubtful whether she will come at all. The whole career of this gigantic ship seems to have been one gigantic blunder.

He added that she was probably not seaworthy.

At Southampton the ship was still unfinished, untidy, and in trouble. The Board of Trade enforced the new acts on passenger safety, which cost another twenty thousand pounds. Enough sightseers came aboard to pay for victualling the ship. She took aboard three hundred passengers, all she had beds for. When she did not sail as advertised, most of them got off and took a reliable Cunarder at Liverpool. At that point Lloyd's asked an unusually high insurance rate, which sent the directors into another money-raising dither. On June 25 a steamer brought a dispatch from the *New York Times'* special correspondent aboard the *Great Eastern*, the civil engineer, Alexander L. Holley,[1] who signed himself 'Tubal Cain'. It was written on June 12. Holley said he really believed the latest promise that she would sail on the sixteenth. Commodore Murphy had been very much im-

---

[1] Holley was a twenty-eight-year-old engineering journalist who had been reporting to the *New York Times* on European railway practices. Five years later he was to acquire rights to the Bessemer process and erect the first U.S. steel plant at Troy, N.Y. There is a bronze bust of him in Washington Square Park, New York.

pressed with the easy handling of the monster, said Holley. He added, 'I am distinctly informed by the company's office that no special facilities will be extended to the New York press'. It was a remark full of omens.

The same steamer mails brought a delirious dispatch from the *Herald*'s correspondent, datelined IN THE CONCERT HALL OF THE GREAT EASTERN STEAMSHIP OFF SOUTHAMPTON, June 10, 1860. His pen was apparently well inked in the wine vaults of the great ship. The *Herald* man jabbered away for a full column of hyphenated outcries and ended with a peroration to the New York hoodlums who were often sent to their work by the *Herald*: 'So get ready boys, the firecrackers. You burnt down City Hall in honour of the (1858) Telegraph. Why not fire the White House in honour of the *Great Eastern*!' His tone suited the mood of the city, 'million-footed Manhattan unpent', as Whitman described the current to-do over the Japanese Ambassadors.

The *Great Eastern*'s crew was suppressed by a tough boatswain's mate. The firemen complained so loudly of his beatings that the first officer had to pay him off. The mate sneaked back aboard to get some last licks at the stokers the day before the sailing. He was grappled by a big fireman. Kicking and gouging each other across the deck, the two men fell over the rail and landed thirty feet down on a scow; they continued the battle across the scow and into the Solent. The mate swam towards the ruined abbey on the bank, followed by the fireman. They were pulled out, half-drowned and still full of fight.

The great ship actually left Southampton on June 16, thereby confounding the company secretary who was in New York preparing for a sailing a week later. When 'the monster struck out for the New World,' said Holley, it was 'the final embarkation, the real trial trip, the first ocean voyage of a ship that has been the parent of more talk, speculation and wonder, and world-wide interest, than any craft since Noah's Ark'. A solitary tug saw them off, in a grey, squally morning. The *Times* man looked down at the melancholy faces on the tug and was reminded of a chromo of his youth, 'The Last Mourner', which depicted a drunkard's dog following his corpse to a pauper burial. Just east of The Needles, they passed a troopship that had been blown ashore the night before—'a decidedly cheerless sight,' Holley said.

There were only thirty-five paying passengers and eight company deadheads, but there were 418 crew members. The cargo consisted of five hundred gross of 'London Club' Sauce. Thirty passengers were Britons, eleven were Americans, and the rest of the family of nations was represented by two Russians, the Messrs. M. and J. Juravleff. There were three women, Mrs. Daniel Gooch, travelling with her husband, a company director; a Mrs. J. Stainthorpe, with husband, and an intriguing and unattached Miss Mary Ann Herbert. There were five British Army officers, four Royal Navy captains, the Rev. T. C. Southey and Professor P. Beresford. The five newspapermen aboard had to pay first-class fares of £25 each. The fourth estate was dominated by a dizzy New Yorker named George Wilkes, 'The gamecock of the press', publisher of the violent weekly, *Spirit of the Times*, and special *Great Eastern* correspondent for Horace Greeley's *Tribune*. (Historically Wilkes is noted as the man who claimed that Secretary Seward wrote Lincoln's Gettysburg Address.) Gamecock Wilkes had shepherded the Benicia Boy to London, and squawked so loudly after the fight, that both Sayers and the American were given championship belts. As an appropriate touch Wilkes's cabin-mate was a man who was carrying an English fighting-cock and three hens in wicker cages to a chicken fighter in California. Unlike Holley, Wilkes wasn't interested in how many revolutions per minute were made by the paddle-engine—he has left us the more interesting news that the *Great Eastern*'s crew consisted of peasants who had never been to sea, 'stokers who did not know how to spread coal', officers who had not been aboard on the trials, and a captain who had never crossed the Atlantic.

Captain John Vine Hall, selected to replace the drowned

Captain Harrison, was one of the many formidable Victorians entwined in the history of the great ship, men who recalled the universal Elizabethans. He was a professional astronomer, a musician, a respected civil engineer, the most experienced master mariner in the British East Indies traffic and the first to win a steamship master's licence from the British Board of Trade. In the white and gold parlour of his mahogany deckhouse quarters, Captain Vine Hall carried his own grand piano.

Two intimates of the late Little Giant were aboard. The chief paddle-engineer was Alexander McLennan, prototype of that obligatory figure in the British steamship epoch, the Scottish chief engineer. McLennan had shipped out on Brunel's *Great Western* in '38, and was for seven years chief engineer on the legendary *Great Britain*. The other friend was Daniel Gooch, who had been Brunel's locomotive superintendent on the broad-gauge railway. Gooch was a lean, silent man with wide-set blue eyes, now risen from his sooty beginnings to be a capitalist, the moving spirit of the third *Great Eastern* operating company and other bankruptcies to come.

The passengers were lost in the ship. They wandered through her like children discovering marvels. They stared at the four huge paddle-cylinders swinging on their trunnions. As in a dream they watched leviathan walking smoothly and puffing billows of smoke from her Quaker-grey funnels. The ship burned mixed Welsh and Lancashire bituminous, a slaggy coal that blistered the funnel casings which passed up through the saloons. The passengers had to abandon the main dining-saloon because of the heat.

In mid-passage the *Great Eastern* encountered a half-gale. She passed the emigrant ship, *Martha's Vineyard,* which rolled like a yacht. The wind grew. At its peak velocity an eighteen-degree roll was recorded on the oscillograph the journalists had brought along. Such an inclination in nineteenth-century seafaring was almost unnoticeable. To one of the Royal Navy captains aboard it was welcome evidence that she was seaworthy. 'Thank God, she rolls!' he declared. Only three persons reported seasick to Dr. Watson, the ship's chief surgeon (she carried three doctors). They were firemen overcome in the stifling boiler-rooms.

Most of the days were fair. Gamecock Wilkes had crossed the North Atlantic five times but he had never seen so much sail. Several times a day little ships closed in over the hills of the sea to look at her: the *Great Eastern* stood so much higher than any ship afloat that she could be spied from far away. Holley liked to take 'a lonely and contemplative walk, these fine summer evenings, around our acre of door-yard'. The spell-bound passengers discovered an irresistible resort, the guardwalk outside the paddle-boxes, at the extremes of the 120-foot width. 'The guardwalks will wellnigh hold all of us,' said Holley. 'Standing fifteen feet outside the vessel and watching her giant bulk gliding through the sea, which she scarcely seems to ripple, is a sight so decidedly indescribable that I would advise you not to be content until you witness it.' They stayed on the guardwalks for hours, staring along her sheer or sticking their noses through the vents of the paddle-box to watch the gigantic red wheel rolling over the waves.[1]

At night there were musicales in the grand saloon. The ship carried a six-piece band, led by Professor MacFarlane, a mighty artist on the cornet-à-pistons. He rendered solos, accompanied on the rosewood grand piano, and crew and passengers alike made vocal offerings. Captain Vine Hall joined the entertainment with concertos on the flute. Occasionally the harmonic evenings were marred by the music of the deck hands, blaring down through the open skylights. The crew had its own cornetist, who played a deafening rendition of 'Wait Till the Wagon Comes' on a dented in-

---

[1] Apparently the sails were not used on the first voyage: none of the reporters mentions them. With the exception of a trysail in '61 and sails raised on Monday, Tuesday, Wednesday and Saturday masts in '65, I found no mention of canvas in the *Great Eastern* data. Furled canvas is shown in photographs up to 1866, but after that the poles are bare and the yards are missing.

strument, to inspire the hauling of sail. The boatswain, who was seven feet tall, led the heaving deck hands in 'Adieu, My Johnny Boker', to which they roared innumerable responses, many unfit for the ladies' hearing.

They were Olympian days for those who sailed on the maiden voyage of the first ocean mammoth. No account of it—and there were inspired literary workers and diarists aboard—fails to mention divine sunsets, and storm effects, and the seraphic moods that came upon them as the *Great Eastern* strode homerically across the brine. She left a long triple wake, 'like two bridlepaths and a turnpike', and on the sixth night in the Gulf Stream, they stayed half the night at the taffrail, bewitched with the wakes receding phosphorescently into the dark. Holley said the ship ploughed 'a pathway as wide as the passage of the Israelites in the Red Sea'.

They did not dine on salt junk. The cattle pens on deck supplied fresh-killed mutton and fowl. At dinner the trumpet sounded 'The Roast Beef of Old England', and at supper, 'Polly, Put the Kettle On'. Champagne bubbled like the ship's wake. 'Enough wine to float her' was wagered on each day's mileage.

'Early risers got up appetite by walking nearly downtown and back,' said the *New York Times* correspondent. One of the Englishmen brought along nine-pins and set up an alley 'on a vacant lot somewhere'. This unknown fellow probably invented deck games. Daniel Gooch called him 'Skittles' and referred to Mary Ann Herbert as 'Miss Skittles'. In the balmy airs of the Gulf Stream the urge came upon them to have a quarter-mile foot race round the teak deck. Betting accounts were opened for an international match between a long-legged British officer, Captain Drummond, and Commodore Murphy, the short, thickset Sandy Hook pilot. Captain Drummond finished while Commodore Murphy was still rounding a bow capstan. 'Several vineyards changed hands,' said the *Times* man. They discovered the gymnastic possibilities of the rigging, and in the late afternoons the ladies were treated to the sight of the men hanging or stunting in the jungle of shrouds.

The crew was unusually well behaved. The log listed only two minor imbroglios among the black gang and the case of a fireman who was seized and put in irons for attempting to stab a mate. The joy of the trip had caught the engine crew: they were heard singing hilariously in the dark pits. In the number two and three cargo holds, the ship's carpenters worked all the way across building sightseers' stairs, installing ticket booths and a turnstile, a contraption that had not yet been seen in America.

The *New York Times* and the *Tribune* for June 27 carried an electrifying flash received at 1 a.m. from the telegrapher at Sandy Hook:

> A LARGE STEAMSHIP HAS STOPPED OUTSIDE THE BAR AND FROM PRESENT APPEARANCES I AM MOST SURE IT IS THE GREAT EASTERN AS SHE SHOWS A GREAT MANY LIGHTS—WILL REPORT OFTEN TO YOU.

The city leaped up from breakfast and made for the Battery. The telegrapher had the wrong ship. The populace swore a bit and went to work. The sunset telegraph from Sandy Hook read, 'NO SIGNS OF THE GREAT EASTERN YET'.

On the hot morning following, the Sandy Hook telegrapher saw six high masts rising from the sea and, lazily, a mastodonic black hull climbed into the broad sunlight. His signal was too late for the morning papers but the word flew from block to block. The city again rushed to the Battery.

Aboard the *Great Eastern* Michael Murphy took the bridge. There had been a debate among the harbour pilots themselves whether the great ship could get across the bar at Sandy Hook, where the depth was twenty-eight feet at high tide.[1] Murphy believed she could. He had piloted Train's Boston packet, the *Chariot of Fame,* across the bar with a lading of guano, drawing twenty-six feet, exactly the draught of the *Great Eastern*. He kept the big ship anchored broadside to await the noonday high tide. When news of

---

[1] The Ambrose Channel had not yet been dredged.

this delay was telegraphed to the city, thousands boarded
harbour craft, yachts, and ferries to go out to the ship, or to
take positions on Staten Island, Fort Hamilton, and Bayside
to see her come up the Narrows. It left enough people standing packed in the Battery to draw comparison with a Broadway omnibus in a sudden shower. The *Herald* rhapsodized,
'Her gigantic shadow is quivering in the waters, and before
another sun has set our Oriental friends will be almost forgotten'. The Japanese were still around, but in complete
eclipse.

By 10 a.m. the big ship was surrounded by hundreds of
little ones, full of enraptured New Yorkers. On board the
passengers met to present a memorial to Captain Hall for their
safe deliverance. He in turn told them that a plaque would
be installed in the grand saloon to carry for ever the names
of 'the select few, who were first to have practical faith in
the Great Ship'. John Yates hastily hired a steamer to carry
press and civic notables out to her. They got aboard for lunch.
Henry Raymond, who had just been saying the ship was a
hoax, responded eloquently to the toast, 'The American
Press!' It was the last fond note exchanged by the New York
papers and the great ship.

At 2 p.m. Commodore Murphy telegraphed to the engine-
room, 'Head slow with her paddles', and the monster made
for the questionable sand bar. She crossed it without a bump,
although watchers at the stern saw mud clouds boiling to the
surface. Murphy ordered the screw engaged and the *Great
Eastern* drew away from the escorts which swam below like
waterfowl. Gamecock Wilkes said, 'The boy who saw the
Bay of New York yesterday, witnessed a spectacle that he will
not be likely to forget, if he should outlive Methuselah'. As
she passed Fort Hamilton the garrison fired a twenty-one-gun
salute, which the great ship answered with a majority from
her four big brass Dahlgren guns. Harbour pieces joined in
the ovation to her march. In the upper bay she passed the
frigate U.S.S. *Niagara*, next largest vessel in the world. The
Niagara dipped her ensign but did not fire a salute. Augustus

Schell, collector of the port, came 'longside while she was under way. His boat was nearly drawn under the paddle-wheel, but he grabbed for a lower cargo port and was handed safely aboard. When the *Great Eastern* passed Castle Garden at the toe of Manhattan, thousands threw heads back and roared, then broke ranks and ran up West Street after her.

Daniel Gooch heard the immense and lucrative New York roar and saw people covering wharves, housetops, church steeples and 'every spot where a human being could stand', as the ship paraded up the North River to Forty-fifth Street. There Commodore Murphy turned her around in the stream, almost within her own length, by reversing one paddle-wheel, a sight that aroused screams of admiration from the banks. Then he took her slowly downstream to her berth, a lumber dock which extended from West Eleventh Street, past Bank and Bethune Streets to West Twelfth, a pierhead now occupied by Pennsylvania and Erie railway freight wharves.

The ship had never been berthed before, but had always been moored offshore. It was impossible to warp her hull along the wharf because the paddle-wheel structures extended fifteen feet from her sides. Commodore Murphy had the nerve to try touching with his port sponson. Below was a crowd jammed to the edge of the lumber wharf, and more panting arrivals were ploughing into it from behind. From the high deck lines were thrown down. The stevedores were lost in the mass. The crowd seized the mooring lines as she edged in.

The *Great Eastern* struck the wharf, which started to buckle. The crowd howled and fought to get out of the way. The paddle-box chewed five feet into the wharf before Murphy got the ship disengaged. No one was crushed. A dozen were slightly trampled. An eyewitness said, 'the *Great Eastern* tried to cut New York in two'. She was made fast without further damage.

The passengers came ashore and were nearly mobbed by admirers. The 'immortals' were caught there until dark be-

fore their baggage was got ashore. Daniel Gooch stayed
aboard, thinking about his new, strange problem. 'I was to
become a showman, as we expected to earn a very large sum
of money by exhibiting the ship. We therefore had to adver-
tise and organize our plans.' (Years later he remarked, 'I
cannot say, now that it is all over, that we were very clever
at our work'.) Fresh throngs continued to press their way
towards the ship through the moonlit night. The police were
kept busy stemming 'the light-fingered fraternity' which
found the *Great Eastern* heavenly. The targets milled around
with their faces up in the air, gazing at the dark cliff and
bumping into each other in their absorption. Occasionally a
head would look silently at them from the bulwarks. The
locals who had boarded her in the bay came off with the
report that the ship was unbelievably dirty, littered with
lumber and shavings, and with decks that had never been
holystoned. They had imparted this criticism to the company
directors, who received it stiffly.

In the morning carpenters were banging away as they erected
an extemporaneous fair along the access streets and on the
wharf. By noon booths were open to sell two-cent dippers
of '*Great Eastern* lemonade' from 'dark-looking' laundry-
tubs and buckets, '*Great Eastern* oysters', '*Great Eastern*
lager beer', and '*Great Eastern* lozenges', two cents a
paper. Hawkers arrived with weight-guessing scales and
carts of dust-covered fruit vocally advertised by Negro boys
as

> Sweet as sugar and cold as ice,
> Watery melons a penny a slice.

Before the first day was out there were 'an amazing number
of cabarets' built on Bank and Bethune, and a steamer fitted
with tables and awnings was moored under the big ship's
stern. A colossal flophouse was abuilding on Bank Street for
the expected farmers. It was called the Great Eastern Hotel.
The 'Great French Giant' was on exhibition and an 'Old
Adams' moored his floating menagerie near the ship and
cried his grizzly bears and fat girl.

The pilgrims came in an unending happy struggle, 'husbands and wives, brothers and sisters, all out in their prettiest attire', hurrying down the waterfront streets from omnibuses and horse cars which had been diverted from the West Side lines to the scene with newly-painted side banners, 'TO THE GREAT EASTERN'. The horse cars on the East Side ran nearly empty. Six thousand registrations above the daily norm were taken in the city's hotels, as out-of-towners arrived.

The stampede of the people threw up a choking cloud of dust, so pestilential that the ship's landward portholes were closed. Sightseers had to flip layers of dust from their glasses of lemonade. The City Street Commissioner pledged the ship operators that he would spread gravel over the area, but forgot. Gooch hired two sprinkling carts, which were unable to lay the dust. The ship was closed to sightseers for five days while the crew cleaned up and repainted, and the New York papers screamed for the show to open.

The city was in a state of mania when the July full moon came. Then New York went moon-mad. Two companies of city firemen answered an alarm at a blazing wine cellar on Worth Street, and entered the saloon above to sample the inflammable material. They fought each other with clubs, axes and trumpets, and continued on the street when it got too hot inside. By the time the building had burned to ashes, two dozen firemen were *hors de combat*. A *Great Eastern* hand named Thomas Leavitt was sent to examine the paddle-wheel and fell to his death. A drunken sailor skidded off the guard-walk and drowned. He could not be placed because his body did not come up and several members of the crew had already jumped ship. When the monster left, her paddle-wheel loosened the body from the mud and it floated to the surface.

Two sailors fell through an open hatch, and there was a mêlée in the boiler-rooms which added thirteen casualties, of whom one died. One of the aggressors, returning to the ship from gaol, attacked First Officer Henry Machin from the rear. Machin had to fight him and three others who joined cause. The directors became aware that, although the men were not allowed ashore, they were in possession of lashings of hard American whisky, and were wassailing in the boiler-rooms. (The crew called a drink 'a slap in the face'.) When fireman William Hicks killed a comrade named Thomas O'Brien with an engine-wrench (he was the twenty-second victim of the great ship), the New York Police Department put a six-man detail aboard to maintain order.

The *New York Times* felt that things were getting out of hand.

> Sensations and excitements are now multiplying so fast in New York that it is sincerely to be hoped that they will result in infusing a little of *nil admirari* spirit in the population. Grown men are just ridiculous when they clap their hands and cut capers for joy. This summer we have already had the Japanese, and are now in ecstasies over the *Great Eastern*, have the arrival of the Benicia Boy to look forward to next week, and are promised the Prince of Wales and Prince Napoleon. We must not and cannot get into hysterics over them all.

The Japanese Embassy quietly departed, viewing the *Great Eastern* with an 'inscrutable look' on their way across the river.

On the third of July the directors inserted a small advertisement in the amusement columns that the ship was to be opened that day at a dollar admission, 'bankable money only received'. The public was outraged at the dear admission charge. Barnum's Museum only charged twenty-five cents. Bennett's paper squawked, 'We are afraid our English friends do not correctly appreciate our community. It will not do to snub people when they go on board, and talk to them about the gentry.'

The ship wasn't ready, but the directors had to throw her open an the eve of Independence Day, the eighty-fifth birthday of the States. The customers traversed a gangplank through a cargo hatch to the new stairways. A patented counting machine clicked them off as they passed through the turnstile. They could stay aboard all day if they liked. Children under twelve were admitted at half-price. A turn-

C

stile-keeper noted that half the boys in America were giants eleven-and-a-half years old, and asked a New York newspaperman what fertility rite had taken place in the States in the spring of 1848. The journalist capped the joke. 'Why, they discovered gold in California,' he replied.

The directors, noting the American love of ardent spirit, had opened a large bar on board. An artist named Wood manned a booth where he sold seashells engraved with the ship's picture. A *Herald* reporter noticed an immobile group gathered under the open ironwork stairs to the wheelhouse. Ladies were climbing it, 'the wind making free with their crinolines' and 'knowing gentlemen on deck were studying as much anatomy as had thus found its way to view'. Fifteen hundred paid admissions were taken the first day, a figure that dismayed the directors. A half-million people had watched the ship come in. The papers continued to carp about the admission price and printed letters from indignant artisans who could not afford to see the 'wonder of this wondrous age'. Down on the wharf, proprietors of the 'liquor ranches' joined the peevish uproar. Not only was the British ship scaring away trade, it was running unfair competition with honest New York whisky merchants. Anglo-American amity was under heavy strain, and more so when the directors discovered that Americans were great chewers of tobacco. The ship was slippery with Burley juice. Gooch grimly ordered the main deck to be covered with sand.

On the Glorious Fourth only two thousand came aboard. The big ship was a calm island in an exploding city. In that time patriots celebrated the nativity of the republic by felling each other with private brass cannon, burning buildings, blinding each other with rockets, deafening themselves with firecrackers and knifing one another in fits of sublime passion. The unruly *Great Eastern* crew was overawed. At the end of the holiday it was brought to the attention of the directors that many portable fittings of the ship were missing. The crowd on the Fourth had consisted largely of brown-faced people in homespun. New Yorkers were mutinying against the dollar admission, but the farmers had come a long way to see the sight. They got their dollar's worth by pocketing souvenirs. Gooch posted sober crew members to protect property.

The purser came upon two visitors removing an oil painting from the grand saloon. He remonstrated with them. The guests struck him over the head with the picture and left him unconscious. A ship's quartermaster, James Darrell, was found dead in his berth. A verdict of death by alcoholism was returned by City Coroner O'Keefe. A rise of tide shoved the paddle-wheel against the wharf and broke bits off the thirteen-foot floats.

Among those who looked her over was the diarist, George Templeton Strong. 'The bulk of the ship impresses me less than that of the titanic engines,' he wrote.

> I dived into their depths by the help of certain slippery cobweb iron ladders. The huge cylinders and piston rods are awful to behold, even in repose. The big ship with all her apparatus of engines, telegraphs, corrected compasses and what not, is the incarnation of a good deal of thought, study and experiment by quite a number of generations. Such a result is not developed out of the coracle of our bare-legged, woad-stained ancestors, *tempore Julius Caesar*, by a single step.

Two wonders were combined for the price of one when the Chicago Zouaves came aboard and performed fancy drills on deck. The *Herald* said New York was 'glad to meet all visitors except country editors, who come here for a spree and very often get into the station house'. When the rural Bennetts got home, the *Herald* alleged, they told everyone New York was a wicked city.

People came from Chicago and Savannah and a special train brought a thousand from New Haven. A man came all the way from Janesville, Wisconsin, and asked to see Captain Hall. He presented a certificate made out by his pastor stating that he was totally blind. He begged the skipper to sign a statement that he had been aboard the *Great Eastern*. Another who had been unable to see the ship was Albert W.

Hicks, who was languishing in the Tombs during the civic dementia. He was the last man hanged for piracy in the United States. 'Pirate Hicks', as he was known in the headlines, had confessed to murdering his three companions on the oyster sloop *A. E. Johnson*. He added during interrogation that he had dispatched ninety-seven others in the California gold camps. The reporters felt that Pirate Hicks was piling it on a bit for a Philadelphia publisher who had got an option on his posthumous memoirs for fifteen hundred dollars, but there was no gainsaying that he was a villain worthy of that delirious season.

The Pirate was to be hanged on July 13 on Bedloe Island on gallows erected near the water to accommodate a huge crowd on boats. 'HO FOR THE EXECUTION!' read the advertisements for the 'beautiful and commodious' excursion steamer *Chicopee*. United States Marshal Rynders chartered the steamer *Red Jacket* to transport pirate Hicks, his marine guard and the marshal's numerous personal party, among whom were Pat Daly, Jordan the actor and Awful Gardner. The guests had to wait three hours for the pirate to be brought aboard. They were well in the marshal's buffet, as *Red Jacket* struck out for Bedloe. It was then that the pirate intimated his last wish. The boozy crowd loudly seconded it. The Marshal ordered the steamer up the North River, where it was nearly swamped by the starboard rail as the party gaped at the big ship. The marines redistributed *Red Jacket*'s burden and they turned downstream and hanged Pirate Hicks.

CHAPTER FIVE

LIONIZING HERSELF

AFTER a week the directors yielded to the sightseer mutiny
and lowered admission prices to fifty cents for adults and a
quarter for children. Thousands of children overran the giantess. Fortunately she had no rails, and her strong, oiled teak bulwarks tapered from a height of nine feet at the bow to five
at the stern. No children fell over the side. In four weeks the
Great Eastern sold 143,764 tickets. As the crowd thinned,
Niblo's Garden dropped the tableau, 'Arrival of the *Great
Eastern*'. The Benicia Boy himself turned up and George
Wilkes displayed the half-belt champion at a series of blow-
outs for the sporting element.

It was time for a *Great Eastern* excursion to cater for the
Americans who wanted to ride the great ship. In late July
Yates advertised a two-day cruise to Cape May for ten dollars, the passengers to buy their own meals aboard. P. T.
Barnum offered to take over the excursion, but the directors
preferred to keep all the profits for the company. Two thousand tickets were sold. Alexander Holley and Gamecock
Wilkes, the chroniclers of the maiden voyage, covered the
cruise. They had to buy tickets and went aboard in a grouchy
temper. They brought wicker hampers full of food and drink,
unwilling to pay the directors another cent. On the deck were
groups of New York merchants, capitalists, engineers, and
ship operators, eager to study the ship's performance. Among
them was the retired paper-manufacturer, Cyrus Field. He
had organized the unsuccessful 1857 and 1858 attempts to
lay an Atlantic telegraphic cable and was bent on raising
another cable expedition. Once, while the ship was building,

he had gone to Millwall, where Brunel swept his arm past the sky-filling hulk and said, 'Here's the ship to lay your cable, Mr. Field'.

Manhattan and Brooklyn poured out to see the *Great Eastern* pass the harbour, amidst flag-dressed shipping, wreathed in cannon smoke. One Henry Jones was killed by a misfired salute on the S. S. *Montgomery*. In the lower bay a catted bow anchor of the *Great Eastern* broke loose. She stopped for half an hour to haul in the big hook. The crew was all but shouldered away from the capstan by helpful passengers. Holley and Gamecock Wilkes exchanged knowing glances. The governing classes seemed to be well represented in the passenger complement, and every man jack of them bulged with a big brown bottle as a specific against the rigours of the bounding main off Jersey. Daniel Gooch wrote in his diary, 'It was a most extraordinary trip we had. The first night was no end of fun, and as the moon was very bright and the weather warm, it did go very well.' It is one of the most remarkable understatements to be found in English autobiography.

H. B. Dodsworth's military and cotillion bands played on the main deck as she steamed away. By the time the *Great Eastern* rounded Sandy Hook, the musicians were losing their *embouchures* and falling under the racks, in a combined seizure of alcohol and *mal de mer*. As a horn thudded from a failing grasp, it was taken up by an ardent passenger. Unidentifiable musical compositions drowned out the clank of the engines as she made the open water. In that grand hour on summer seas when the sun and moon are both in the sky, the trippers got out their dice and cards. Gaming circles formed on deck. Others chose pugilism as a vent for the uncontainable bliss of riding the *Great Eastern*. An observer counted four bouts going on simultaneously and saw men on the outskirts going through the preliminary insults and shoves to get on the card. The excursionists were having a whacking good time, each to his taste. The serious souls climbed ladders and took notes, impervious to deck riots and to a passenger who had an epileptic fit and fell from the wheelhouse.

A trumpet sounded 'The Roast Beef of Old England'. The descent to dinner reminded Gamecock Wilkes of 'the double-quick step charge of the Zouaves at the Academy of Music the other night'. The grand saloon had been transformed to a café, with extra seating for the crowd. Local waiters had been hired. They stood around in bewilderment, as passengers howled for provender. The waiters made no move. The superintending purser, young Henry Cox, was beset by passengers. He said there had been a bit of trouble; a pipe had burst in the provision room and flooded the food stores.

The waiters at length produced food from another storeroom. It consisted of desiccated fowl, maggoty beef, salt junk and biscuits as resilient as stones. The crowd choked the stuff down and bawled for ice water. Heretofore the company directors had not been acquainted with the American passion for ice water, which on that hot night took on the aspect of a crusade. Henry Cox had put aboard three tons of ice to cool the champagne. The wine steward was loath to surrender it. 'Tons of ice melted within the clasp of red tape', Holley lamented. Better-heeled passengers ordered Moet & Chandon to wash the biscuits down.

They climbed back on deck in a truculent mood. To deal with pickpockets, the New York Police Department had detailed to the cruise five plainclothes detectives under Sergeant Dickson. The cops were accompanied by narks, one of whom must have decided to become a double-agent. He pointed out the dicks to the governing classes. They dropped cards and a general chase ensued. The mob locked a detective in a sheep pen on deck, and put in a reporter to boot. A comedian climbed on top of the sheepfold and bawled, 'Here, gents, are some of the most extraordinary freaks of nature ever placed on exhibition. Feeding-time in fifteen minutes.' The crowd grabbed oars and boat hooks and tormented the captives through the bars.

The respectables turned in first. Gooch's diary said, 'But

as the passengers had no beds to go to, they lay about every-where'. He failed to add who was responsible for taking two thousand passengers on a two-night voyage when there were beds for three hundred. Those who got staterooms found that wives had been placed with wrong husbands, duplicate tickets had been sold for some berths, and the bedroom stewards were drunk and uninterested in the problem. Gooch and the company officials gave up their own state-rooms to furious passengers. The directors were as bewil-dered as the passengers and crew at the perversities of the ship. Holley reported cases of male passengers invading staterooms and throwing sleeping women into the com-panionways.

A number of thin, hair mattresses were dispensed on deck. Some sports grabbed two, one to use as a blanket. When the crowd saw a man with two mattresses, it stamped on him. As the supply ran out, the stewards demanded fifty cents apiece. A passenger who got up for a call of nature had his mattress stolen by a steward and was offered the hair pad for another fifty cents on his return. The only responsible crew member who could be found was a Scottish stewardess in charge of the ladies' saloon, who managed to bed down a few women and children.

The company managing director, Thomas Bold, had a painful case of neuralgia, which he was treating with snuff. Stewards told protesting passengers to look for a man with a blue ribbon who was always taking snuff. Bold had to hide. Aside from the miserable Henry Cox, the only name in the management known to the passengers was John H. Yates, who had signed the newspaper ads. 'Where is Yates?' the crowd roared. A muscular man from Philadelphia yelled, 'I'll smash his crooked head for him'. Yates prudently stayed incognito.

On deck the travellers settled down on mattresses, coils of rope and 'the soft side of a plank'. Dodsworth's musicians were still puffing at midnight and drunks were kicking up a lewd cotillion on the afterdeck. Gangs went round, awaken-

ing sleepers to ask, 'Did you have ten dollars worth of fun?'
If the answer was yes, they left. If the answer was no, they
grabbed up the man and took him along to 'take out the
balance'.

A rain of cinders from the five funnels poured over the deck
sleepers. There was a light shower and morning dew to help
cake the soot on people. 'In the morning they woke up very
cross,' said Gooch's diary, 'particularly the reporters to the
press, who thought they ought to have been supplied with
comfortable cabins.' He had slept on deck himself, and was
also a little cross.

When the passengers sought to remove their minstrel
make-ups, there was no hot water, but stewards could be
found who would supply ewer and basin for a dollar, and
face towels at 'one dollar clean, fifty cents dirty, and twenty-
five cents filthy'. The passengers' toilets 'would have disgraced a prison', said Holley. He expostulated, 'These were
the accommodations for gentlemen who are accustomed to
have an abundant supply of croton!'

When they went down to breakfast, there wasn't any, for
threats or bribes. The victuals had been exhausted the night
before. Stewards black-marketed coffee for up to a dollar a
cup. The reporters called an indignation meeting of passengers. Holley's remark described its tone: 'I cannot now be-
think me of a single means for annoying man, woman, or
child on a voyage of pleasure that these imperious gentlemen
left untried.'

The meeting was short and tart: each protestant wanted
to be the first ashore. The schedule called for an early-
morning arrival at Old Point Comfort, where the passengers
were to spend the day in that fashionable watering place.
The *Great Eastern* steamed through the morning without
raising land. Outrage took on a touch of alarm. Passengers
ran through the ship, looking for somebody who knew what
had happened. The directors had an embarrassed confession.
During the night the bridge officer had got off course and
taken the ship a hundred miles to sea.

c*

Lunch-time passed without food. In mid-afternoon the starving argonauts, croaking piteously for ice water, at last descried land. The *Great Eastern* moored in a long swell a mile off Old Point. Immediately little boats came out with seven thousand waiting sightseers who had come from North Carolina, Philadelphia, and Baltimore by special trains, had overflowed the hotels of Hampton, Norfolk, and Old Point, and had slept in thousands on the beach. Seventy choleric excursionists jumped on the boats and entrained for New York, via Philadelphia. A man was seen to leap forty feet from the *Great Eastern*'s paddle-box into the water. He reappeared and swam to the sponson ladder, dispelling the suspicion that he had chosen self-destruction as a reply to the *Great Eastern* directors. 'He was merely lionizing himself', was Wilkes's priceless remark. A thousand fans sneaked aboard free through an unattended cargo port.

Cyrus Field chartered a side-wheeler and seceded with his coterie. Others visited Old Point and investigated the splendours of the Hygeia Hotel, a spa which dispensed a healing flow of punches and juleps. Among the ship's sightseers were slaves brought by their masters. Gooch thought he had never seen such trust in 'the eyes of workmen', as that shafted by slaves to owners. It was refreshingly different from the looks of his crew. The crew, which had been in a subdued and wondering contemplation of the wild Americans, rose to the occasion. The gigantic boatswain gathered his men for a concert of shanties on the afterdeck. Anglophilic Southerners crowded in, and when there was a good audience, the boatswain led the chorus in a hit number from the popular London musical drama, *Uncle Tom's Cabin*. The concert broke up in disorders between artists and insulted customers.

The great ship, re-provisioned and well rewarded financially by Virginian hospitality, struck out for home. The dissidents were racing her back by steam cars. 'We did much better without them,' said Gooch. But there seemed to be more people aboard. At sea there appeared the grinning faces

of Philadelphians who had paid a half-dollar to stow away
to New York. The directors were not harassed on the way
home and were even tendered a vote of thanks by the guests.
There was a grace note at dinner: the passengers toasted the
memory of The Little Giant. 'But on the whole the trip was
not a success and did not pay us, and I was very glad it was
over,' Dan Gooch confided to his journal.

The great ship arrived at the New York lumber wharf in
a gale of abuse from the entrained refugees who had arrived
the night before. One opened his letter to the *New York Times*
with 'Fellow countrymen! Thank God I am home again.' He
signed it 'Indignant Victim'. The next letter was headed
'Another Explosion of Indignation', and a third was penned
by 'A Disgusted Individual'. The paper gave its front page
to the cruise, and began its General City News column on
page two with: 'The *Great Eastern* has returned to the city
and is advertised to start immediately for Annapolis Roads.
Don't go.'

The second excursion was planned at the importunity of
Baltimore merchants, now whetted by New York's dissatis-
faction. They wanted to sign up the great ship for their port.
A delegation from Philadelphia also waited on the bedevilled
directors with the argument that the Delaware River was
deep enough for the monster. The *Great Eastern* was de-
famed in New York. It did not matter that several passengers
wrote the papers saying the trip had not been so bad as all that.

The *New York Times* reporter assigned to the Chesapeake
excursion tried to beg off by saying the story was stale. Henry
Raymond replied that the *Great Eastern* would probably blow
up and it would not do for the paper to be caught without
coverage. At the wharf the *Times* man met two agitated citizens who had come fifteen hundred miles from St. Paul, Min-
nesota, to sightsee the great ship. They complained that the
ship's officers wouldn't admit them unless they paid the six-
dollar passage to Old Point. The reporter knew all about the
inflexibility of the ship's directors: he advised the Northwes-
terners to desist and go to Barnum's Museum.

The second American cruise drew only a hundred paying
passengers, mostly Southerners who had come to the city to
ride her home and step ashore to the adulation of kinsfolk.
The sailors took up the ponderous Trotman patent anchors,
so that they hung 'like jewels in a lady's ears', and the *Great
Eastern* walked into the river, unattended by harbour craft.
From Hoboken a Cunard liner saluted, but Yankee shipping
snubbed her. The *Times* reporter went below where he had
found that 'by purchasing a half-interest in a bedroom
steward you can always secure good attendance'. Gooch was
unaware of his presence (the reporter had to buy a ticket, of
course) and said 'none of the indignant press gentlemen'
was aboard. As a result, 'We had a very pleasant voyage',
the director added. At breakfast the journalist said he was
served 'a leg of the cock that crowed when Peter denied his
Master'. The great ship made Old Point and found ten thousand people waiting on shore. She stood there for two rich
days, then proceeded towards Annapolis. The directors had a
worth-while goal: in addition to sightseeing revenue, they
were going to load five thousand tons of Cumberland coal
presented by Baltimore capitalists and the Baltimore & Ohio
Railroad, as an engagement ring from the city.

Forty miles down the bay the *Great Eastern* was met by
the latest and fastest of Chesapeake steamers, *George Peabody*, carrying the Annapolis reception committee. The
Great Eastern was steaming at fifteen knots, faster than any
steamer had ever cruised before. Nobody aboard had the
sense to slow her down. She left *George Peabody* far behind.
The official party limped into Annapolis, belated and angry.
Great Eastern passengers who had paid eight dollars to
Annapolis were obliged to burrow into the ship's dark under-
world to find the gangplank of the ferry steamer tied up out
of sight under her stern. Crew members said they didn't
know how one got down there, and they probably didn't.
Crying directions to one another, the passengers wandered
into the iron vaults, like speleologists, and found an open
port, where stood a petty officer in Japanese pongee jacket,

who intoned, 'Take care of your 'eads, gentlemen! 'Eads, gentlemen, 'eads!' The crew were as fed up with the Americans as Americans were with them. The ship's officers were by now answering grouses with the outspoken wish that they could leave America soon. They were tired of running a 'visiting ship'. The *New York Times* reporter said, 'The responsibility for mismanagement was driven like a shuttlecock from officers to directors and back again'.

Excursion trains had brought thousands in dismal tropical heat to see the *Great Eastern* at Annapolis. At the end of the first day there was a stampede at the single exit port. People were swept off their feet and trodden under. The turnstile was closed on August 9, when President Buchanan came aboard with his cabinet for lunch. A singular discussion on the *Great Eastern's* American trade possibilities took place between Gooch and the Lame Duck President. The director asked the President's opinion whether the ship should be applied to carrying cotton from Savannah to the English mills. With the Civil War eight months away, the President 'thought well of the scheme', according to Gooch's diary. The two proposed a wonderful historical *if*. The big ship could have exported the entire Southern cotton crop. She was probably capable of overtaking, ramming and sinking any deep-water ship afloat, not excluding the ironclad U.S.S. *Monitor* built two years later. What would have happened to the Federal Navy's cotton blockade had the *Great Eastern* gone into Southern service?

When she returned to New York, the ship was met with indifference: the Prince of Wales was on his way there. She was as *passé* as the Japanese and the Benicia Boy. *Harper's Weekly* said:

> In a few days the *Great Eastern* will take her departure. She has certainly attracted a great deal of attention, more than any other ship that has ever anchored in the Bay of New York. At the same time it would not be correct to say she has been a success, or that we part from her with very much regret. [The managers were] grossly inefficient, the ship dirty, the officers

and crew discourteous and rude, and Americans who made
helpful suggestions were ignored and insulted.

The Americans were feeling their oats and getting into competition in the matter of size. The *Great Eastern* exacerbated
national vanities. She had a talent for starting fights. The
directors' catastrophic essay in catering was not unpleasing
to certain Americans, who did not want the British giantess
to be a success. The directors never understood that the free-
loading American journalist was a power in his own right,
and not a company clerk. There was also the ice water issue.
Perhaps it was the most serious of all.

The town had indeed turned on the ship. Captain Vine
Hall was served with a suit for infringement of a U.S. patent
on combined screw and propeller propulsion held by James
E. Smith of Greenpoint. Another local worthy threatened
to hail the monster into court for engaging in U.S. coastwise
commerce, contrary to her licence. These actions were never
pressed, but piled on other anxieties, they sent the skipper to
his bunk with nervous prostration.

Without salvo, escorts, or indeed a crowd on the wharf,
Brunel's 'great babe' slipped away for home two months after
she had sailed on her maiden voyage. She carried a hundred
passengers. The chief screw engineer informed the directors
that the propeller shaft was seriously worn away and might
not hold out for the return voyage. They couldn't hear. They
were studying their wounds. The *Great Eastern* had taken
£24,000 from visitors and excursionists, against a two-month
overhead of £14,400. However, when the profit was figured
against the company indebtedness and the £1,000 a day
interest on her investment, it was evident that the American
exhibition had been a disaster. They had expected to net
£140,000.

In the lower bay she was accosted by a steamer which had
on board a Manhattan victualler named Robert J. Williams.
He slapped down a £50 sheriff's attachment for provisions
furnished for the Cape May fiasco. Waiting at the foot of the
Jacob's ladder behind Williams was a threatening band of

plumbers, upholsterers and chandlers waving petty bills.
The directors made bond for Williams's claim and fended off
the others, but not before a citizen named Osborn scrambled
over the bulwarks with a detective, seeking fifty-five dollars
owed him by a crew member. Osborn whooped through the
iron labyrinth after his man. When he couldn't get the money,
he took it out in punches. The directors evacuated Osborn
and his aide and ran the ship for the sand bar. Commodore
Murphy navigated her across and was put off on the pilot
boat, *Washington No. 4*. Daniel Gooch passed a sigh of relief and made for Halifax.

That busy North Atlantic port, native city of the wily Sir
Samuel Cunard, was clamouring to see the great ship, and
Gooch was not loath to receive the Haligonians, who he felt
would certainly be better behaved than the Americans. But
at Halifax, 'We met a little sharp practice', said Gooch,
mournfully. The local lighthouse dues exacted of all ships
were based on tonnage. The *Great Eastern* was the biggest
flotsam that had ever fallen to the collector; he took £380
before she was allowed in the harbour. The directors went
ashore and asked the governor to rebate the tax, in view of
the fact that she 'had gone out of her way to please them'.
The governor declined. Gooch and company returned to the
ship and ordered all haste in extending the paddle-blades.
The empty monster rode so high that the blades had to be
adjusted to reach water for the homeward voyage. 'Let the
people see the ship in England,' Gooch muttered. The *Great
Eastern* departed next morning without boarding a single
sightseer.

It was an enjoyable passage. Captain Hall was unable to
regale the passengers on the flute, but the capable Henry
Machin navigated her home and left the entertaining to two
talented passengers, The Wizard Jacobs, Ventriloquist and
Improvisatore, and his brother, The Goblin Sprightly. In
mid-Atlantic the screw shaft gave out. The great ship hove
to for half a day, while temporary repair was made. Presumably this was accomplished with the use of her aftersails.

This test was impressive. The hulk rode the billows lightly while her engines were shut down. Despite the delay the great ship established an eastbound speed record—nine days, four hours.

She received a hearty welcome in Milford Haven, where a special train was drawn up to take the passengers to London. But nobody wanted to debouch, 'such was the comfort of the *Great Eastern*'. The directors were touched by this un-American sentiment. They held the train and allowed the passengers another night aboard. An entry in the log read, 'Seasickness has been annihilated'. Then the ship was floated over a grid on the beach, and as the tide receded, she was gently deposited dry.

The directors could not face the reality of her economic predicament. She had no dry dock, no shoreside organization, and no sister ships to provide scheduled service. She could not keep crews during her long layoffs, but resorted to crimps to man her with kidnapped farmers and unconscious seamen. She could not cross the Atlantic in winter, not only because it was the off season for outdoor exhibitions, but because she was too cold. The crew shivered and complained in her dank grottoes.

Running her on the North Atlantic had anulled Brunel's vision of the great ship plying around the earth for the riches of the Indies and the gold of New South Wales. It was not possible to think of economic logic if you were a director of that great presence, lying on the grid and eating money.

CHAPTER SIX

THE WAR EXCITEMENT

As THE Great Eastern rested her bones at Milford Haven, John Scott Russell, co-author of the dream of the Iron Age, re-entered her affairs. He was the red-headed son of a Glasgow clergyman, 'born to the manse', intended for the Presbyterian ministry. When he was twelve years old (in 1820) mettlesome boys spied new lights, not of the Knoxite battle against sin, but of steam engines pounding to drain the coal pits, to move the looms, to stroke the incredible journeys of steamboats on loch and stream. Science was Scott Russell's piety.

The thirteen-year-old entered ministerial training at the University of St. Andrew's. He transferred to Edinburgh University at fifteen, and at sixteen he graduated with a bachelor's degree in natural science from the University of Glasgow. He had chosen mechanical engineering, a call with the attraction that space travel has for boys now. Some will say the old dream was better.

Scott Russell went directly into a workshop, an ideal post-graduate course for a mechanical engineer. At nineteen, well tempered in his craft, he took up lecturing on science at Edinburgh. He addressed the largest classes in the University's history. The boy professor was that valuable Scottish type, an advanced theoretician with shop cinders under his nails.

Steam vessels were supplanting the horses that dragged coal, iron, and grain through the navigation canals. Scott Russell sat on a canal bank, studying the tugs. What were the laws of locomotion in this heavy liquid element? What sort of hull shape moved with the least resistance? He induced the directors of the Edinburgh-Glasgow canal to set aside a section for experiment on steamboat behaviour. He worked out a theory he called 'the wave-line principle' and shaped waxen model hulls that he pushed around in tanks. They were early inspirations for the *Great Eastern*, and of all the proud ships since.

In 1834 Scott Russell designed a steam carriage that ran without rails. He built six steam buses which carried passengers on schedule between Glasgow and Paisley, a distance of five miles. He did not live to see the internal combustion engine, but his road steamers give him claim to be the founder of the motor-bus transport.

The young Scottish engineer first attracted attention in 1835 when he expounded and demonstrated his wave-line theory to the British Association for the Advancement of Science. He was already managing Caird's Shipyard at Greenock, where he had built the first vessel by his theory, the *Wave*. Soon he was handing off ships by the dozen, including the original steam fleet of the West Indies Royal Mail Line. England demanded such talent. Scott Russell went to London, the port of the globe, where more ships were built then than on the Clyde, Bristol, and New York combined. He established an iron-foundry and shipyard at the Isle of Dogs, where he built H.M. frigate *Warrior*, an iron-armoured fighting ship, which ante-dated by a generation John Ericsson's U.S.S. *Monitor*.

Scott Russell in 1845 was elected secretary of the new Society of Arts, and found an unexpected accomplice in the Queen's husband. Prince Albert became patron of the Society. The Society of Arts was not an official royal organization, but a fellowship of foraging engineers, manufacturers, and idea men. From the guild came the 1851 Exhibition and the plunge of its members into the great ship scheme.

During the gestation of *Leviathan*, Scott Russell passed from his forty-sixth to his fiftieth year of age, the summit of his power. As the hide of the mammoth was rising, he launched a dozen little ships alongside; the coaster *Wave Queen*; the Channel packets, *Rouen, Baron Osy,* and *Lyons*; the mail steamer *Pacific* of the Sydney & Melbourne Line; and a distinguished pioneer in maritime history, the iron screw-ship *Baltic Trader*, the original steamer designed for cargo alone.

In 1853, before the bottom plates of the *Great Eastern* were laid, Scott Russell's works burned with a loss of £100,000. Two years later a fire broke out in a steam battery and was quenched with a loss of £120,000. In 1856, midway in the construction of the *Leviathan*, a third fire destroyed most of his machinery. It is not clear whether Scott Russell collected insurance, but the lost buildings and machines, whether or not indemnified, had to be replaced as he and the Little Giant continued to build the great ship. When she was at last aswim, the effort cost Scott Russell his shipyard, which was taken over by the Cumberland Iron Company.

The Great Ship directorate had hired Scott Russell as superintending engineer for a time, but they took his job away after the funnel explosion. However, Scott Russell was determined to make his presence felt once more, as the ship prepared for her second New York voyage. He was a creator turned litigant.

During the winter the ship had lain on the grid at Milford being fitted with a new propeller shaft of tough South American lignum vitae wood in a brass jacket. There were only twelve in her stand-by crew under Alexander McLennan. The directors discharged all others, including Captain Vine Hall and First Officer Machin. As she was swung off the grid in the spring tide, the hawser of a small sightseer's boat fouled in the screw. The boat was wound swiftly towards the huge blades. The sightseers jumped for their lives. Two were drowned in the fierce tide. Before the giantess could be moored she crashed into H.M. frigate *Blenheim*, removing her bowsprit, mainyard, and moorings. 'We afterwards had to pay £350,' mourned Daniel Gooch.

The *Great Eastern* was assigned her third skipper in the person of Captain Carnegie, R.N., a former member of the Board of Admiralty and a director of the company. He had been one of the immortals of the maiden voyage. At Annapolis the year before, the directors had promised the committee from Baltimore they would make that city her U.S. port, and had accepted five thousand tons of coal as a binder. Now war had come to the States and Baltimore was unsafe. Another city had been jilted. Thus the second voyage to America was to be to New York. It was advertised for May 1, 1861.

Captain Carnegie's command was the shortest in the ship's career. The first thing that happened to him was that the Sheriff of Pembrokeshire clambered aboard and slapped an attachment on the ship. A court had awarded John Scott Russell a judgment of £24,000 owed him on building costs and repair of the funnel explosion. The Professor had set his jaw against the capitalists. Then a special train arrived with a hundred passengers, who came aboard and started to eat their heads off. Carnegie warned them the ship might not be able to sail on time, but none asked for his money back. The directors pleaded with Scott Russell to let them sail and get some dollars; otherwise they could not pay him. The Professor was obdurate. Finally Scott Russell agreed to part payment. The money was taken out of the cash on hand for the voyage. To keep within the budget the directors fired six of the ten senior officers and a third of the crew. Captain Carnegie refused to sail short-handed. He resigned and was replaced at the last minute by Captain William Thompson.

Three hundred Welsh and German Mormons offered to let the *Great Eastern* carry them halfway to Zion at fifteen dollars a head in steerage, the pilgrims to bring their own food. Despite the fact that the ship was sailing with one-fortieth of passenger capacity, the management turned them down. They said Mormons had 'peculiar habits'.

The *New York Times* was the only paper which considered the second voyage worth covering and had appointed a

special correspondent, 'H.N.' He sharpened his finest quill
to meet the occasion. 'The great coquette, the sea, was in one
of her most dangerous and delicious moods,' he wrote. 'The
vast ship moved grandly across the main with a glory of foam
about her.' The passengers were 'in convivial high feather'.
There was no need for fiddles on the tables, until the fourth
day when the stewards fitted the guard-rails during a slight
roll. The wind freshened into a southwest gale. By the next
morning there was a near hurricane blowing.

The *Great Eastern* fell into the trough of the high waves
with a crash of crockery and restless activity of her iron
shrouds. Two heavy gaffs broke loose and swung from the
rigging, endangering the funnels. The undermanned deck-
crew secured the gaffs. A boatswain's mate broke his leg. The
storm was over in eight hours. The *Times* man remarked,
'The ship may never again encounter such a gale. If she ever
does she will meet it on fairer terms.'

Opportunistic New York pilot boats ranged far to sea to
catch the big prize. She arrived at Sandy Hook, nine days
thirteen hours and twenty minutes from Milford Haven. She
waited outside the bar overnight for the morning tide. The
next day, a Sunday, she went in and the passengers found
'H.N.'s chronicle of the voyage in the ink-fresh *New York
Times*, which had recently inaugurated Sabbath editions
'during the war excitement'. The Civil War was only a month
old. Most Northerners did not regard the organization of a
rump government, the seizure of Fort Sumter, and Lincoln's
proclamation calling for 75,000 soldiers as an actual war. It
was more damned arrogance from the South, which would be
put down by the volunteers, including New York's own glorious Fire Zouaves under the city's hero, young Colonel Elmer
Ephraim Ellsworth. Confederate leaders thought differently
and so did the directors of the *Great Eastern*. 'H.N.' had been
briefed on the way over on a fresh approach the directors
were to make to the Americans. His story in the *Times* said,
'I cannot state authoritatively that the direction of the *Great
Eastern* favours the chartering of the vessel for service of

war, but I am able to affirm that suitable propositions from the government *will be entertained.*' It seemed a wonderful idea: the thirsty dream of the shareholders to fob her off to a navy had begun in '58 and here was the biggest opportunity of all. The trial balloon did not get off the ground. Lincoln's cabinet did not even discuss the offer of the *Great Eastern.*

Nor did James Gordon Bennett give a hoot for the ship directors' new aspiration. The *Herald* said the crowds at the Battery 'went to witness the exercises and evolutions of the volunteer militia more than to see the ocean monster'. The publisher had just been converted from a loud Southern sympathizer to the biggest flag-waver in town, a transformation aided no little by a mob of patriots who had appeared under his sanctum howling for the *Herald* to put out an American flag. Horace Greeley's paper, which had something to do with mobilizing the auto-da-fé, claimed that Bennett had to send out for a flag and sneak it in the back door.

Instead of the British behemoth, 'Americans are now more concerned with the new steam gun, throwing five hundred balls a minute,' the *Herald* sneered. Bennett's steam gun was invisible, but while he was tacking bunting on his masthead, he was leaving no magic weapon on the copy hook. The *Herald* said, 'The English owners are justly proud of their vessel, which, by the way, they owe to us'. How Bennett's factual acrobats reached this attribution is one of the mysteries of journalistic flight. Advanced ship designers on either side of the Atlantic watched each other's work, and there was an interplay of influence between Brunel and Scott Russell and the genius of the Boston clippership, Donald McKay; but the *Great Eastern* was the beginning of an epoch in navigation, while McKay's clippers were the end refinement of the previous period.

The *Great Eastern*'s proprietors did not wish to stir up the bad blood of 1860 by inviting public inspection, nor was New York interested. People were all for the war excitement. Fierce Zouaves and society regiments were marching and countermarching in the streets. At night thousands of paraders turned Broadway into a 'sea of flickering torch-lights'. Troops were bivouacked at the Battery and had thrown up shacks in City Hall Park. The *New York Times* hinted to the police:

> The Park is used for drilling troops. At every movement they make, they are followed by a dense crowd of dirty urchins, of lounging loafers and idle lookers-on. Their steps are impeded, the officers are crowded—and the whole performance turned into a farce.

The street people, 'short boys', had found a bigger thrill than the *Great Eastern*. Bennett was noisily passing a paper hat for the benefit of the Old Revolutionary Soldier, Isaac Daniels, who told the *Herald* he could not have survived to the age of one hundred without his glass of toddy every day. Artemus Ward remarked, 'Because a man can drink a glass of liquor a day and live to be a hundred years old, my young readers must not infer that by drinking two glasses of liquor a day, a man can live to be two hundred.'

The ship was announced for sightseeing off Beach Street on the last days of her turn around. The *Herald* demanded that admission 'must be at a low figure'. It was set at twenty-five cents. Even then the going was hard. The British govern-ment made it harder. A steamer arrived with the text of the royal proclamation of neutrality in the American war, which was considered a tacit recognition of the Confederacy.

Grinnell & Minturn, freshly appointed as U.S. agents, an-nounced the departure of the *Great Eastern* on May 25, at $130 for first cabin and $75 for 'very superior accommoda-tions' in second. She competed for passengers with 'The World-Renowned Clipper Ship *Dreadnought*', an American Black Ball liner commanded by Captain Samuel Samuels, who often outraced the British steamers across the ocean tracks. Captain Samuels advertised an 'experienced' surgeon and music aboard, but did not mention how he beat the British smoke-boxes. He locked the passengers belowdecks, raised every thread of canvas, and deliberately hunted hurri-

canes to blow him rapidly across. Samuels's crews were usually
as seasick as the passengers.

The big ship loaded five thousand tons of barrelled wheat
and sailed for Liverpool with 194 passengers. New York had
no heart for running to see her go. It had been learned that
day that Colonel Elmer Ellsworth was killed in the first sortie
of the Fire Zouaves.

The ship returned to England to find Whitehall taking
steps about the American situation. The government was
planning a large show of the flag for the benefit of the
Yankees—and the Irish Fenians in the States, who were
talking of raids into Canada. The War Office had indeed
taken a decision to charter the *Great Eastern* to carry an
unprecedented number of reinforcements for the Canadian
garrison. The shareholders rejoiced. At last Her Majesty's
ministers had seen the ship's value as a war vessel and her
financial troubles were over. The ship was closed to visitors
while artisans from the Birkenhead Iron Works made her
ready as a troopship.

A new skipper was borrowed for the single voyage, from
the Liverpool, New York and Philadelphia Steamship Company, thirty-year-old Captain James Kennedy, who had an
impressive record in steam. He had never navigated a ship
up the St. Lawrence to Quebec City, but the *Great Eastern*
did not scare him. 'I'll handle her in just the same way as
an ordinary vessel,' he declared. Captain Kennedy boarded
2,144 officers and men of the Royal Artillery, the Thirtieth
Regiment, the Sixtieth Rifles, and components of three more
rifle regiments. They were accompanied by 473 women and
children and 122 horses. The mounts were stabled on deck
with the ship's livestock, while the soldiers were confined to
the cargo holds. With his crew of four hundred, Kennedy
was entrusted with over three thousand lives, not counting
horses—twice as many people as had ever sailed in a ship.
Not until the troop voyages of the First World War, over half
a century later, were as many persons carried on a vessel.

Captain Kennedy, however, found himself one hundred

short in the crew. He did what was usually done in those times: he sent for the crimps. The press gang raided the boarding-houses and dives of Liverpool and filled the shortage. Military bands blew on deck as the *Great Eastern* glided down the Mersey in view of the customary masses on shore.

At sea on the first morning there was a mutiny by the impressed seamen. The affair received no publicity from Captain Kennedy or the military commander, Colonel J. T. Mauleversee at the time, but years later, when he was a famous commodore of the Inman Line, Kennedy would tell the story at the captain's table. All hands were ordered out to scrub down. The 'hard' cases obtained by the crimps refused to scrub. Kennedy borrowed a company of soldiers from the colonel and the men were brought on deck at bayonet point. To emphasize his wish, Captain Kennedy sent the mutineers into the yards, at the urging of bayonets. He kept them aloft all day in the smoke of five funnels, which was heavy enough to turn the sails black. After that there were no disciplinary incidents on the crossing.

At sea there was great fun in the holds as five female stowaways were liberated to the arms of their warriors. Two babies were born on the passage. In the last days of the voyage people were still discovering friends they had not known to be aboard. A sailor named James Pollard was killed in a fall, and a benefit was held for his widow, in the 'Atlantic Theatre, by permission of Neptune'. A young officer delivered Hamlet's soliloquy, another recited 'The Death of Nelson', and there were two ambitious production numbers, a treble hornpipe by the 'corps de ballet' and a turn by the '*Great Eastern* Minstrels'. The widow received £52 and a £20 pledge by the Great Ship Company.

Captain Kennedy goaded the mighty ship as though the Fenian were scaling the Citadel at Quebec. On July 2 he encountered a dense fog, but did not reduce speed. He logged 320 miles in the first twenty-four hours of fog. For two days the lookouts called out icebergs, which suddenly materialized from the pearly gloom. The impetuous Kennedy dodged them without slackening speed. The only casualties were two horses which took fatal chills from passing too close to icebergs.

The fog grew even thicker off Cape Race. There the bow lookout saw emerging from nowhere a huge and dreadful figurehead, the famous Arab chieftain of the Cunard liner *Arabia*. His scimitar was held ready for the clash. The *Great Eastern* missed the red-stacker 'by the length of the bowsprit she did not carry'. There were 3,400 people on the two ships: the *Great Eastern* narrowly missed a disaster that might have set the record for that ship-wrecking age. Hothead Kennedy slowed down off Cape Pine light, where many ships were bellowing in the fog. He had made the world's record crossing of eight days and six hours.

'*Le Great Eastern est à l'ancre dans le port de Québec!*' caroled the *Journal de Québec*.

> *C'est une grande fait. Il y est dans toute sa majesté, dans ses proportions gigantesques, flottant et se mouvant à l'aise dans le fleuve, sous les murs du Gibraltar américain.*

Canada forgot the bitter betrayal of the Grand Trunk Railroad in 1860. The Mayor of Quebec and the councillors rushed on board and handed Captain Kennedy a hundred pounds. The Sixtieth Rifles unpacked the silver claret jug that had been trustingly engraved in Liverpool with a tribute to Kennedy for a safe crossing. The reverberations swelled to Upper Canada, where Captain Smyth of Toronto advertised a nine-day excursion in his 'superior upper cabin steamer *Bowmanville*' to take folks to see the great ship. Several enterprising Lake Ontario skippers turned a pretty penny on cruises to Quebec.

It took Quebec ferries two days to empty the *Great Eastern* of her men, women, children and horses. Lumber schooners lay about, begging for hands, but none of the big ship's crew jumped. The mutineers had become transformed by Kennedy's heavy hand, or the flattering welcome of Canada. Colonel Mauleversee sent fulsome praise of the ship to her directors.

Young Kennedy was the lion of the hour. He gave out interviews praising the fine anchorage at Quebec, which he declared was superior to any port at which the *Great Eastern* had called. He had handled her in but one other port, Liverpool, but it was not the moment for quibbling. The people of Quebec threw out their chests and predicted they had the future American Liverpool. She made for home early in August with 356 passengers and Godspeed from the Montreal paper, *La Minerve*, which said she would return '*bientôt à Québec avec huit à 10,000 hommes de troupes*'. It was a prediction with a true Brunel ring. The *Great Eastern* never returned to Quebec. When she got home the War Office ended the charter and demolished the day-dreams of the stockholders.

CHAPTER SEVEN

ROCKED IN THE CRADLE

THE *Great Eastern* plied the North Atlantic in the first generation of steamships, when men still marvelled at them. Professor Longfellow's toast was: 'Steamships! The pillar of fire by night and the pillar of cloud by day, that guide the wanderer over the sea.' Dr. Emerson put it less poetically, when he said, 'There are many advantages in sea-voyaging, but security is not one of them'.

In the year of the great ship's launching the immigrant ship *Austria* caught fire in mid-Atlantic when the crew was ordered to fumigate the steerage with boiling tar. Of the 538 people aboard, there were 46 survivors. The S.S. *Atlantic* ran out of coal off Halifax in 1873 and foundered on the rocks, drowning 560 persons. Early operators raced for the Blue Riband, overheating and exploding the boilers and crashing icebergs and each other. Before the Civil War the U.S. Congress tried to fight British steamers with dollars. Congress endowed a packet operator, E. K. Collins of the Dramatic Line, with four magnificent wooden steamers. The Collins liner *Arctic* collided with the French steamer *Vesta* in a Grand Banks fog in 1854, drowning 322 passengers, including Mr. Collins's wife and two children. The surviving lifeboat held fourteen passengers and thirty-four crew members, a ratio which did not reflect credit on U.S. seamanship. The Collins sister ship, *Pacific*, left Liverpool two years later with 159 aboard and is not reported. The passenger who fought his way into a boat sometimes only prolonged the agony. The S.S. *William Browne* encountered an iceberg in 1841 and lowered one crowded boat. The crew threw out sixteen passengers to lighten it

The fate of the coaster *Royal Tar* is one of Edward Rowe Snow's picturesque researches. She steamed out of St. John, New Brunswick, for Maine in 1836, carrying a circus and two side shows, Dexter's Locomotive Museum and Burgess's Collection of Serpents and Birds. Off Fox Island, Maine, the *Royal Tar* caught fire. Resourceful passengers ripped up deck planking and lashed together a raft. When they were aboard it in the water, an elephant jumped on top of them. A passenger named H. H. Fuller descended a line over the smoking stern and tied the rope around his neck for support in the water. Several swimmers grabbed him. Fuller narrowly escaped being hanged. He transferred the bight to his ankle. A woman seized his other leg. He was spread-eagled thus for hours until rescue came. He was luckier than another passenger who dragged his trunk on deck, removed five hundred silver dollars and put them in his money-belt. He threw the trunk over the side and dived in after it. The trunk floated.

The *bon voyage* party originated as a premonitory wake. The passenger's loved ones would gather for a tearful good-bye and a morbid inspection of the coffin-like cabin. There was no fun in ocean voyaging. Only such gadflies as preachers, authors, diplomats, entertainers, and commercial agents voluntarily crossed the sea. The emigrant masses were not tourists: they were driven by desperate courage and heavenly hope. When and if a ship arrived safely, it was the custom for the passengers to vote the skipper a silver plate as a life-saving medal.

Not the least of the *Great Eastern*'s appeal lay in her safety features. She had proved herself against the ocean's whims and man's errors in the *Royal Charter* Storm and the funnel explosions. Perhaps her sailors were unruly at times, but the passengers saw no prospect of sharing a lifeboat with them. The record number of four hundred paying passengers who boarded the *Great Eastern* at Liverpool on September 10, 1861 had only the usual worries. 'We found on board the ship the greatest disorder and worst possible arrangements. All the passengers complained,' said one. 'Very portly directors with red geraniums in their buttonholes and shining, benignant after-dinner faces, had been inspecting the great ship and said all was very well. I was glad when these gentlemen left, for I had not the slightest confidence in their judgment about sea matters.' One of the satisfied directors was Daniel Gooch. He went ashore and entrained for Worcester to talk with the current board chairman, Colonel Baker, 'about her bright future'.

It was the big ship's second sailing from Liverpool; 300,000 people cheered from the Merseyside, guns boomed and bands played. The *Great Eastern* had a new commander, the Cunard captain, James Walker, appointed only ten days before sailing. Mark Twain once said, 'The Cunard people would not take Noah himself until they had worked him up through all the lower grades and tried him ten years. It takes them about ten to fifteen years to manufacture a captain and when they have him manufactured to suit at last, they have full confidence in him.'

The passenger list included many Americans, among them Benjamin F. Angle and Montgomery Gibbs of New York, the Rev. D. V. McLean of Easton, Pennsylvania, and a Massachusetts civil engineer named Hamilton E. Towle. Among the Yankees was an apprehensive youth who had a secret weighing on his mind. He was a Union Army Lieutenant in mufti, who had been sent to Britain by Lafayette C. Baker, head of the Federal Secret Service, which was then part of the army. The young officer's mission was to travel back and forth on British vessels, informing on Confederate agents who were slipping into the North via blockade runner from Savannah to United Kingdom ports, and thence by steamer to New York or Boston.

The agent was hardly the ancestor of an FBI man. His espionage technique consisted of sidling up to conversational groups and cupping his hand behind his ear. The engine roar of the big ship was tough on eavesdroppers. At first the passengers scowled at him, then they started to laugh, guessing his occupation. Some British leg-pullers, including a Liverpool ship operator named William B. Forwood, improvised lurid anti-Union talk for his benefit and were delighted to see him slipping away to write in a large notebook.

The big ship walked down St. George's Channel on a sunny afternoon. The passengers sang and danced on deck. They overtook the swift packet *Underwriter* of the American Black Ball Line. She was under full topsails, beating into a head sea that threw spray over her bows. The *Great Eastern* was steady as a church. Forwood noted 'feelings of immense superiority' among the passengers. On the second evening they passed Fastnet Light, the last landfall in the United Kingdom and went into the ocean in a freshening wind that veered from south-east to north-west. The next morning they awoke to a grey, squally day, with the wind rising and blowing almost due northerly.

The monster steamed on, swaying slightly, but not uncomfortably. On the Quebec voyage just before, she had rolled only nine degrees in a forty-mile-an-hour gale. Brunel had calculated that her heaviest roll could not last more than six seconds. The wind rose to small hurricane strength, but it seemed a freak local storm that would soon pass. At noon tremendous seas were crashing on the starboard beam, and at four o'clock the log entry was 'heavy gale'. The *Great Eastern* was three hundred miles west of Ireland.

A Liverpool merchant named George Oakwood kept an hourly diary of the events that ensued. 'She begins to roll very heavily and ship many seas,' he wrote that afternoon. 'I now begin to understand the true meaning of a gale in the Atlantic. The Captain looks anxious, but the passengers have faith in the big ship. None but experienced persons can walk about.' Another passenger named Percy de Corwin said, 'The waves were as high as Primrose Hill. Even the oldest sailors could not get their sea legs.'

The wind threw the *Great Eastern* into steep port rolls, plunging the gigantic paddle wheel under the waves, so that the guard-walk disappeared for long moments. The ship heeled under a great sea that swept down fore and aft. When the paddle-box tilted up again Captain Walker heard a scraping noise above the engines and the crash of water. He scrambled sixty feet uphill and downhill on the see-sawing bridge and was carried under to his neck as the guard-walk plunged again. As the wheel climbed free, he looked through the sponson vents and saw that the girders were bent and the thirteen-foot oak floats were splintering. The wheel was scraping against the side plates.

The skipper fought back to his post and rang to stop the paddle-engine, for fear the broken wheel would hole her side. When the stroke of the massive engine ceased, he heard strange noises in the paddle-engine room. A junior engineer climbed up and reported that several rolls of heavy leaden plates had broken loose and were tumbling from side to side, battering at the inner longitudinal bulkheads. Scott Russell's strong interior framing prevented the berserk plates from striking the outer hull.

Two large tanks of fish oil, poorly secured between decks, tore loose and fell through a hatch to the engine-deck with a thunderous impact. They split open and spread hundreds of gallons of oil, the stench of which permeated the ship. During the coming days of the ordeal the smell of fish oil was so compounded with storm terror that the survivors could never again smell the stuff without feeling the agony of the *Great Eastern.*

The paddle-engine oilers and firemen left their useless posts. Without paddle power, the propeller alone could not keep the ship on her heading. The hurricane was coming harder. The *Great Eastern* fell broadside into the trough of alpine waves. An extraordinary sea drove upon them, swelled over the weather side and crashed. When the lee bulwarks climbed out of the water, there was no longer a port paddle-wheel. It was stripped clean to the boss.

As the ship rolled, the port lifeboats pounded into the sea. The forward longboat on that side tore away from one of its davit falls and, swinging in crazy arcs from the other, struck the deck and bulwarks. A barefooted sailor and a boy scrambled into the boat to secure it. They clung to the thwarts as it swung out on a twisting flight, but the wind had a merciful moment. The boat swung back and shook the sailors out on the deck instead of into the sea. The remaining fall parted and the longboat sailed away upright, seemingly as dry as a chip.

More boats came loose, several on the starboard side.

A boat just forward of the remaining paddle-wheel went on the rampage, endangering the wheel. Captain Walker attempted a complicated manœuvre to save the paddles. He ordered the boatswain, 'Cut away number five boat!' and simultaneously instructed the remaining paddle and screw to be reversed in order to clear the boat as it fell. It did not hit the wheel. One by one the sailors cut away the flailing, splintering lifeboats, until the *Great Eastern*'s davits were empty.

Captain Walker decided to use all his power to bring the ship into the wind, to escape the awful valley and meet the waves head on. She was now rolling to forty-five degrees. First Officer Henry Machin put eight men with relieving tackle on the helm in preparation for the effort to bring her head up. Before they could apply the engines, the starboard paddle-wheel was smashed and carried away in a single sweep of water.

The Captain ordered the screw released, but the *Great Eastern* would not turn out of the trough. In the stern wheel-house, Machin heard fearful sounds from the rudder and screw assembly. He went down a ladder to the auxiliary tiller room in the counter, or overhang, where the rudder-post entered the ship and was engaged by the steering-chains. The post was a cast-iron column eleven inches thick, set in a waterproof stuffing box and a wooden collar containing a ring of cannon balls that served as bearings.

Half-way down Machin stopped and held on. Below him he saw that the steering-chains and rudder-stock were a

D

dismantled, sliding tangle of wreckage. The vast rudder-post was shorn off two feet above the cannon balls. It whirled out of control; which meant that below the rudder was flapping freely in the water. When the counter lifted out of the sea, Machin heard the big oaken rudder smashing against the still-revolving screw. He could not see what was happening, but the revolutions of the torn stump showed that the rudder was swinging more than two hundred degrees, and at each end of the arc he heard it smash. It was being chewed up by the turning blades of the thirty-six ton propeller. The first officer ran headlong to the bridge, where Captain Walker ordered the screw stopped. The ship fell silent, except for the donkey engines labouring at the pumps. The *Great Eastern* had lost all mechanical means of propulsion.

Captain Walker gathered his officers out of earshot of several anxious passengers who were still clinging on deck, and summarized her predicament. He enjoined the officers not to speak to the passengers. To maintain appearances he ordered eight-men watches kept on the useless helm. There was one chance left to bring the vessel into the wind. Captain Walker ordered a trysail hoisted. As the donkey-engines set the canvas, it ripped, parted from the halyard and streamed away in ribbons.

Towards evening the wind changed to southwest. The silent ship wallowed before the wind towards Ireland at three knots. There were no steam tugs afloat that could have taken her in tow in such a storm, even if help could have been summoned. The ship had been blown out of the Great Circle steamer tracks. Forwood, Oakwood, and the American engineer, Towle, questioned the officers but could get no clear explanations of the situation. They pieced together some knowledge from listening to officers yelling to each other in the storm. Now the gale was shoving them over to starboard, as though trying to hold the bulwarks under.

Oakwood went below to the grand saloon. The rosewood grand piano was rambling back and forth, crashing the buffets with a twang of strings. It cast off its legs, hurled its lid away and rent itself to splinters. 'Chairs are frantically chasing those who but a few moments before have been their fair occupants,' he wrote in his journal. Velvet sofas, footstools and chairs marched to and fro, scouring up the rug and ripping down the red silk portières. 'The stewards are capturing various articles of furniture and binding them down as they would so many wild beasts,' said Oakwood. The saloon stove went adrift and headed for the pier glass on the funnel-casing. Oakwood and two stewards bounded into the stampede of furniture to intercept the stove. Men and stove crashed the mirror together. 'It falls into a thousand pieces and inflicts injury upon many,' the Liverpool passenger wrote. 'I am perhaps the greatest sufferer. I have my head cut, my little finger dislocated and a tooth knocked out.' Oakwood returned to the deck, when an officer, in an unguarded moment, blurted to him that Captain Walker considered the ship unmanageable. Oakwood went below and wrote, 'May the Great Ruler of the Waves have mercy upon us this night'.

De Corwin's spirited diary of the storm said, 'The *Great Eastern* is a most determined cradle. The oldest man has not been rocked in all his life as much as we are.' He decided 'to die comfortable', and went to bed with his arm lashed to a stanchion. He heard frantic noises from the first dining-saloon. He untied and staggered to it.

> I saw the most curious sight I ever saw. Tables and chairs were dancing a hornpipe, the stove joined most heartedly in the fun, and the dancers seemed determined to break down all the nicely turned mahogany columns and banisters, which snapped like glass. It is a noise as if rocks were shifted to and fro by an angry surf.

That first day the ship's surgeon, Dr. Watson, treated twenty-seven major fracture cases, including a woman with a broken arm, and the ship's baker with a triple fracture of the leg. The surgeon had no time for a large assortment of black eyes, broken noses and contusions. Many of the cabin ports had been smashed and the staterooms were soaked.

The passengers huddled in corners of the saloons. The women knitted and led the children in hymns.

Another active passenger was the Rev. David V. McLean, D.D., former president of Lafayette College in Easton, Pennsylvania, who was homeward bound after preaching for several years in London. He went to the aid of two women in the wreck of the grand saloon and was thrown heavily on his arm and hip. 'I expected many of the ladies and children would be instantly killed,' he said.

The storm was still at hurricane force on the second morning. Captain Walker tried to curb the *Great Eastern*'s appalling gyrations by an old sailor's trick. A four-ton spar was heavily weighted with iron and thrown overboard on a thick hawser to serve as a sea anchor. It seemed to reduce her motions. The *Great Eastern* rolled ahead of the wind at four knots an hour. The spar was torn away and the ship returned to her rolls.

'Only with danger of life could people cross one of the saloons,' said de Corwin. 'The gentlemen were more frightened than the ladies, who behaved without exception as men ought to. But there were plenty of old women among the men.' Waves climbed over the deck, and by now the skylights were broken. Water fell in by the ton and drained away to the bilges where the pumps were barely equal to the deluge. An unusual wave uprooted the cattle pen on deck and hurled two cows into the ladies' saloon. The cows bawled and one tried to rise on a broken foreleg. An Irish sailor entered with a long knife and yelled, 'I'm going to kill the cow to save her life'. De Corwin, who saw it, burst into laughter, 'notwithstanding the roaring of the sea'. The animals were killed, hoisted out and thrown into the ocean.

A swan, liberated from one of the demolished deck pens, found itself in the grand saloon, where it ran desperately on the sliding debris to get up take-off speed. But Brunel's grand saloon was too small. The bird crashed the bulkheads several times and fell broken and dead.

No one had eaten for twenty-four hours. Cooks and

stewards attempted to feed the passengers. A cook was
thrown against a stove, and suffered grave internal injuries.
In a lull in the storm they got the food to the dining-saloon.
Oakwood relates:

> The rocking movement comes on again with renewed force.
> The passengers catch hold of the tables for support. The tables
> are not fastened, for whoever supposed the big ship would be
> so rampant? Tables give way and the scene of the grand saloon
> is enacted again. Stewards rush to the rescue, but in two
> minutes every piece of crockery on the table is smashed, knives
> and forks fly about in reckless confusion, and the scene closes
> by a general accumulation of tables, chairs, crockery, passen-
> gers and stewards in the middle of the saloon.

From below they heard an echoing tumult of shifting
cargo and the thump of water rocking in the holds. Ponderous anchor-chains in the bow chain-locker thundered back
and forth until the links were brightly polished. Then the
chains broke through the single thickness of hull plating that
began six feet above the waterline. Cables hung festooned
from the hole, beating at the double hull below. There was
no means to make them fast. The chains attacked tirelessly
but the hull plates held.

A group of male passengers had, by the end of the second
day, gathered an idea of the *Great Eastern*'s true plight. They
called a meeting of thirty men to wait on the captain and
protect the passengers' interests. The master had not slept for
forty-eight hours. He and Machin had spent every measure
of seamanship, without effect. The skipper agreed to meet a
passenger committee, composed of the Americans, Angle,
Gibbs, and the Rev. D. V. McLean; the Englishmen, Forwood,
Oakwood, Cecil Mortimer, and Cornelius Walford of London; and James Phalen of Paris. Oakwood was elected chairman. By virtue of his office Captain Walker permitted him
to inspect the entire ship. The passengers had deduced many
things wrong, but the inspection revealed a lot worse. Cargo,
gear and stores were loose in the compartments. Tallow casks
and crates were battering themselves to pieces. Oakwood was
a Liverpool shippinng man and he saw that the managers of

the *Great Eastern* had simply put things aboard as in a store-house. Nothing had been made fast properly. His inspection showed no discernible sprung plates. The hull was sound. But the water she took through the open ports and skylights was rising in the holds and some of the pumping machinery was probably going to be submerged soon.

The *Great Eastern* slumped out of control during a second night of storm. The rudder continued to smash into the idle screw, chewing more oak with each impact. Hamilton E. Towle went to the rudder-room and inspected the revolving post. He drew a plan for controlling the rudder and showed the sketch to Henry Machin. Apparently Machin took the scheme to the captain. Several passenger accounts have it that way, but for one reason or another, Captain Walker did not act on the engineer's idea. Towle had the impression that the ship's officers were at the end of their resources, and were simply waiting for the storm to blow out, before attempting anything more. But still he thought he had a good idea.

Towle was a thirty-eight-year-old Harvard man, who prac-tised civil engineering in Exeter, Massachusetts. He was returning home after building immigrant docks for the Austro-Hungarian government at Fiume, the port through which the Hapsburgs were planning to export their restless peasants for an imperial head tax and a per capita fee from the contract steamship lines. (The peasants ruined the scheme by travelling across Germany to Hamburg to take ships for the New World.)

That night Captain Walker summoned the passenger com-mittee. The haggard master said, 'Gentlemen, I have a mutiny on my hands'. He said the black gang had broken into the liquor stores and refused to take commands. The com-mittee volunteered to patrol the passenger decks to protect the women. Captain Walker armed the posse. They put on kerchief armbands and went forth into the weather.

There was little to this mutiny. The firemen were fed up with dodging flying oil tanks, and standing under waterfalls thick with coal dust. They crawled forward through the communication alleyway and broached the wine-locker, where they lay sprawled within reach of the nearest unbroken bottles of cognac and vintage champagne. They were enjoying final comforts before they departed this world. The black gang had no intention of going topside where the vigilantes were tumbling around in the spray. The anæsthetized mutineers had also attacked the food cargo and were eating, which no one else was.

Another attempt was made to feed the passengers, this time without tables. The cooks managed to heat a stew, despite being flung against the hot stoves. Barrels of smashed crockery were rolled into the saloon. The stew was served out on the largest shards a passenger could find in the barrel. Casks of sea-biscuits were lashed to the bulkheads and people helped themselves. The deck patrolmen let the 'mutiny' rage while they ate.

The passengers were wet to the skin and their cabin wardrobes were soaked. The committee asked the purser to open the hold baggage to get dry clothing. Oakwood went to the baggage-room. He said:

> The scene defies all description. Water has got in to float even the larger articles. The rocking of the ship has set the whole mass in motion. Friction has reduced portmanteaus, hatboxes, dressing cases, and all the personal chattels of four hundred passengers into a mass of pulp. Here are the spangles of the dress of an actress, and the sleeves of an officer's coat, the rim of a hat and the leg of a dress boot. I see men feeling cautiously with their bare feet for jewels and money in which this desolation is said to be rich. How they will identify their own and resist the temptation of taking that which is not theirs is beyond my philosophy.

Water scaled the sides and flashed like grapeshot across the deck on the third day of the tossing. No one had yet been killed. The *Great Eastern* was standing up to a fury that could have destroyed another ship in her plight. The passengers were learning to live with terror. They no longer petitioned the gates of eternity with every roll. There were sad jokes and high-strung laughter as the castaways on the

iron island surveyed their plight. Captain Walker burned
blue lights and fired distress rockets in the stormlight as the
third night fell.

Then the brig *Magnet* of Novia Scotia sailed into the desolate orbit of the *Great Eastern*. Shouts brought the passengers
on deck. The cocky little Bluenose drew in very close, looking about the size of one of the lost lifeboats. Captain Walker
trumpeted, 'Will you stand by?' and the master of the
Magnet shouted back, 'I'll stand by you'. A male passenger
climbed the bulwarks and yelled down, 'I'll pay a hundred
pounds a day, if you'll stand by!' Another passenger raised
the bid, 'I'll buy your ship and cargo!' Henry Machin hauled
venturesome capitalists from the rail. The tiny ship circumnavigated the iron walls and the *Great Eastern*'s population
limped around the bulwarks to peer at the little pink faces
below in the wide, grey sea. The brig brought a hope of life.
Actually she could do little, if the big ship were going down.
The *Magnet* had room for a handful of her 832 souls. The
two-master hung around for several hours, and then left by
mutual consent and at full speed.

The Novia Scotian was eager to make Liverpool and file a
claim for demurrage, a payment for delaying goods in transit.
Later the Bluenose skipper collected from the Great Ship
Company for inconveniencing his cargo of salt cod.

In the loneliness after the lights of the brig had vanished,
Towle took his plan for saving the *Great Eastern* to the passenger committeemen. They insisted that Captain Walker
hear him. Towle showed sketches for getting control of the
rudder. Captain Walker agreed to put the engine department
at Towle's disposal. The captain himself went to the tiller-
room with Towle's party. They found that Robinson, the
chief paddle-engineer, had already tried an unfortunate
plan. The rudder-post had broken off partly within a huge
iron nut. Robinson had tried to remove the nut to attach an
emergency tiller in its place. He had backed the nut off an
inch and a quarter, where he could force it no farther. Towle
saw that the rudder was hanging almost entirely on the

weakened nut and might literally fall out of the ship at any minute. Robinson had the nerve to fight Towle's plan. There in the tiller-room the captain reflected on the opposing schemes. Brittain, the chief screw-engineer, backed Towle. Irving Grinnell, a passenger, waded into the argument, supporting Towle, and convinced the master. Grinnell was a partner in the New York steamship agency, Grinnell & Minturn, which represented the big ship in the States.

Before Towle could put his scheme in operation he had to turn the nut back home. Not only did he have to turn the nut, but somehow lift the berserk weight of the rudder while doing so. It was the supreme test of the strength of the forgings and the men. The ship carried a big wrench to fit the nut, but human power was incapable of turning it back. Towle asked the men to sling the wrench from the overhead beams and lash its handle firmly. Then when the sea swung the post violently to port, he slipped the wrench on the nut. At the end of the starboard swing, he disengaged the wrench. The rudder itself provided the power to turn the nut back to its seat, in many repetitions of this tactic. It took three hours.

Towle ordered fifteen fathoms of chain cable, composed of sixty-pound links of two-and-a-half-inch iron bars. The men advanced on the whirling stump to lasso it with chain, and were thrown heavily by the deep heeling of the ship. The chain smashed fingers and toes. But they continued the fight into the night. Towards morning they had succeeded in carrying the chain three times around the post and had lashed it firmly. Towle's plan depended on the fortunate proximity of two heavy mooring bitts situated forward of the post, forming a triangle with it. He carried the big chains around the bitts and secured them by tackles to the port and starboard frame of the ship. Then two lighter chains were carried down from the wheelhouse and shackled to the two ponderous reins Towle had placed on the rudder. The chains were tightened and the rudder became motionless. Towle informed Robinson that the ship could now be navigated on her screw.

D*

The chief engineer turned to the master and said that Towle's jury rig would not work. Robinson demanded that Towle's apparatus be left as it stood while he saved the ship by a plan of his own. Captain Walker assented. Robinson's notion was to get steering chains on the rudder from the *outside*!

A boy held a lantern on a boat hook out over the pitching stern of the *Great Eastern*, while a man was sent down in a boatswain's chair. The volunteer had a light line, with which to follow Robinson's instructions to get a purchase on the trailing edge of the rudder, where a notch had been chewed out by the banging against the screw. Once the line had been settled in the notch, a chain would be sent through, and after it heavy cable. The cable was to be passed up to the after-port and starboard capstans. By turning the capstans the ship could be steered. Such was the Robinson plan.

The boatswain's chair disappeared and the sailors heard the occupant curse as he was hammered against the transom and then swung out on a long ride over the hissing sea. They continued to pay out the boatswain's chair. The wretched sailor twirled and swung into the propeller cage, sank under the waves, and was jerked out and swung again. He tried to get a straddle grip on the rudder and succeeded only in driving splinters into his thighs. A succession of glum heroes were sent down in Mr. Robinson's chair all day Sunday.

The storm abated this day. The *Great Eastern* drifted south-west. Three divine services were held, beginning with that of Mr. Patton, a New York clergyman, and going on to prayers by the Rev. David McLean. The latter, in his capacity as member of the passenger committee, begged off the evening reading by an English colleague. McLean was busy. Chief Engineer Robinson's scheme had utterly failed and his face could not be saved. The passenger committee was in a rage. It escorted Hamilton E. Towle to a showdown with the skipper. Captain Walker sent out orders to man the helm and admit steam to the screw engine. He would test Towle's jury-rigging steering system.

The screw-engine turned at 5 p.m. Sunday, after seventy-five hours of helplessness. The helmsmen tried the wheel. The rudder responded and did not shift. The position was 280 miles west of Cape Clear, Ireland. The screw pushed her up to eight knots and the great ship set a course for Ireland. Nobody seemed disappointed at not continuing to New York. The emergency steering system worked beautifully.

After a night of sleep the delivered people were roused to the main deck by joyous hails. It was the Cunarder *Persia*, 'The ship for which we all longed,' said de Corwin. The red-stacker was the next largest ship in the world, one-third the bulk of the *Great Eastern*. She had left Liverpool four days after them and was carrying important letters and business drafts to them in New York. Captain Walker raised a sign-board, 'HAVE LOST RUDDER COME AROUND LEE SIDE'. The *Persia*, Captain Judkins commanding, came around as requested but did not seem to understand why the monster was steaming east. Captain Walker showed a sign, 'CANNOT STOP MACHINE'. Judkins paddled completely around the *Great Eastern*, saw the bare bosses of her paddle-wheels, and made all steam for New York. He was carrying the Royal Mails and there was a penalty for delaying them.

That afternoon the Great Ship Company office in Cannon Street, London, received a telegram from an Irish corres-pondent, which stated that the *Great Eastern* had been sighted off the Old Head of Kinsale, on a course for Cóbh, then known as Queenstown. London couldn't make head or tail of the message: the ship was due in New York in three days. In Worcester Gooch and Colonel Baker had just fin-ished dinner and were seated before a comfortable fire, talk-ing of coming prosperity, when a servant handed them the relayed message. The baffled directors went to bed. 'I was not long asleep,' said Gooch, 'when poor Baker walked into my room with a fresh telegram. I will never forget his ap-pearance as he stood at the foot of my bed, wrapped in a white flannel dressing-gown, and one of the old-fashioned nightcaps on his head, a lamp in one hand and the telegram in the other.' It was a wire Captain Walker had dropped to a pilot boat off Queenstown: 'HAVING LOST BOTH PADDLES AND RUDDER HEAD IN A TERRIFFIC GALE I HAVE BEEN COMPELLED TO PUT BACK.' It was enough to tell Gooch and Baker that the *Great Eastern* had swallowed another fortune.

The *Great Eastern*'s ordeal was not over. As she limped into the harbour, a new wind arose, and Towle's rudder tackle began to shift. The Cork harbourmaster sent a boat to tell Walker he could not enter while only partly under control, lest the *Great Eastern* smash up the anchorage. Walker put to sea again. The passengers had seen land, however. They broke into wild thanksgiving. The band played in the ruined grand saloon and the survivors galloped and sang. They embraced each other and strangers kissed, roaring at each other's black eyes and puffed noses. The wine locker yielded its last unbroken bottles. One lady's nerves were unequal to salvation. She collapsed on the dance floor. When they brought her to, she got up and danced again. She fainted three times, but was still whooping it up at 2 a.m.

At dawn the more seriously injured were taken off by lighter. The ship hung off Cork for three days before H.M.S. *Advice* sighted the distress flag raised eight days before in the ocean. The *Advice* passed a tow cable and dragged the Great Eastern into the harbour. The thing dreaded for all the miraculous days occurred that morning, when a quartermaster was struck on the head by the backspin of the helm and killed instantly.

The anchors were lowered. The great ship settled unwillingly into her moorings. She struck the American bark, *Samuel Maxley*, stoving the stern, wiping off the davits and removing an anchor and chain. The passengers went ashore at last, with unanimous resolutions thanking God, Captain Walker, Hamilton E. Towle, and the master of the *Magnet*; denouncing the directors, and demanding a full investigation by the Board of Trade. They were going to sue for personal injuries and their lost baggage, which was delivered ashore in buckets.

Captain Walker had, according to a letter Dr. McLean wrote to the Easton *Express*,

> behaved with great courage and coolness *after the disaster*, and laboured most incessantly night and day to save his ship and passengers: yet it is my deliberate conviction that he is greatly to blame, and that his conduct before the disaster was reckless. He took the ship only a few days before she sailed, a stranger to her: he ought to have known how she was provided for sea, as to ballast and in other respect, and if not suitably provided, should have had the defects remedied, or refused to have taken command of her. There is every reason to believe he went to sea under instructions, and himself determined to make the shortest possible passage. The new steamer, *New York*,[1] was to sail the day after we did and it was presumed she intended to try her speed. The *Persia* was to sail four days after us, and it was known she had put on coal of an extra quality, determined to do her best. Under these circumstances and feeling that if he made a very short passage, his own reputation and that of his ship would be made, there was every temptation.

Dr. McLean's analysis was accidentally underlined in the very next item in the Easton paper, entitled 'The Business of the Country'. It said, 'The exports from Liverpool to this country in August 1860 were $8,350,000: those for August this year were but $2,250,000, or $6,100,000 less!' Small wonder the *New York*, *Persia*, and *Great Eastern* were trying to make names for themselves.

The great ship went to Milford Haven to be swung upon the grid and have her parts renewed. There Captain Walker discharged his officers and men. He wrote a certificate for Second Officer John McAllister which got him a berth as first officer of the new mail steamer *Anglo-Saxon*. She was lost on her maiden voyage in a Cape Race fog with over half her 446 lives, including John McAllister's.

[1] North German Lloyd.

CHAPTER EIGHT

CAPTAIN PATON

DANIEL GOOCH and Colonel Baker showed up at Queenstown with all the cash they could raise to settle spot claims for storm loss and injury, rather than test the hurts of the passengers in court. The survivors were either paid off immediately or given tickets from Liverpool to New York on the fast screw steamer, *Norwegian*, of the Allan Line. (A few months later the *Norwegian* was lost, but after the *Great Eastern* passengers had been landed in the States.)

William B. Forwood arrived at New York Quarantine, and watched the revenue cutter come 'longside with various inspectors, including the United States Marshal. Forwood was summoned to a cabin, where Marshal Rynders greeted the Liverpool merchant with the news that he was under arrest as a Confederate agent. Forwood was speechless, while his brain reeled back for a reason. Then he remembered the Union spy of the storm voyage. The silly young man had kept his mind on business through hell and high water. Forwood chuckled and attempted to set the marshal straight on the joke. The law had no sense of humour. He bundled Forwood off to the Tombs, while the other *Great Eastern* survivors watched in fascination. It took Forwood twelve hours to talk himself out of the charge. When Cornelius Walford arrived in Boston, the United States Secret Service was waiting for him, too.

The big ship was fitted with strong, new paddle-wheels, six feet less in diameter. The steering tackle was replaced by one that allowed emergency control from two lower stations. The repair cost £60,000 and 'cleared away much more than our profits,' Gooch said. The ship had won universal tributes for her victory over the storm, however, and hope still throbbed in the breasts of the directors. They planned a busy year for 1862.

As she was floated on the spring tides, trade observers did not give her much of a chance to pay. It was a hard time in England. The stoppage of Southern cotton left mass unemployment in the English mills. The Union blockade was drawn tight. In the previous year a record for Southern cotton imports had been reached—41,000 tons. The *Great Eastern* could have exported the entire crop in five or six voyages. But Britain had no American cotton in 1862.

Startling changes had come to the North Atlantic tracks as well. During the fifties the American merchant marine persisted in its romantic obsession with wooden clippers, a dream loomed in bright threads as the clippers raced around the Horn to the goldfields of California. The money was in speed. There was no thought of schedules and economical capacity. Britain launched fleets of side-wheelers, sturdy plodders which laid an avenue of smoke across the ocean. Samuel Cunard's vision of 'an ocean railway' had come true. Confederate raiders suddenly exiled the clippers from the sea. They lay rotting in South Street, Gloucester, and Boston, as idle as blockaded Southern merchantmen. The American seaman sang the blues:

> O, the times are hard and the wages low,
>   Leave her, Johnny, leave her;
> I'll pack my bag and go below:
>   It's time for us to leave her.

The sailors went to the army, the factory and the farm. A million and a half acres of virgin land were settled during the war. More than seven hundred U.S. ships went over to the British register. British net ocean tonnage increased by 80 per cent during the American Civil War. America turned its march inland to the cadence of steam hammers, the song of pouring iron, reaper clatter, drumbeats of rails

growing west, and the hen-cluck of telegraph keys. Base-
ball was a sensation: in 1862 Brooklyn played New York
on a November Monday in Hoboken and drew twelve thousand people. They came despite a postponement announcement. New York emerged victorious, thanks to the stout work
of its battery, McKeever and Cohen.

> I am for those who believe in loose delights,
>   I share the midnight orgies of young men,
> I dance with the dancers and drink
>   with the drinkers,

Walt Whitman sang. In Virginia City, the tubercular
humorist, Artemus Ward, received a telegram from the
manager of the San Francisco Opera House, 'WHAT WILL YOU
TAKE FOR TEN NIGHTS IN SAN FRANCISCO'. Ward replied,
'BRANDY AND WATER'. The bucks of San Francisco took him
into the vault of the U.S. Mint where they gathered in a
clapping circle and sang 'Skip Light, Lou', while Artemus
did a step dance on a pavement of gold. Altogether it was too
busy a time to think about the sea.

The Union carelessly, even gratefully, surrendered world
trade to the British steamer. 'Steam is almost an Englishman',
said Emerson. The steamer brought the emigrant to Castle
Garden, ticketed to a relative or a mill. Many a man went
from the steerage to a rifle company. The two-step of the
Union was out of hearing of the Parrott guns, the screech of
Minié balls and the crump of land mines. Mail order em-
balmers followed the armies; spirit mediums flourished and
practical Christians bought Bibles guaranteed to stop bullets.

The American war meant a drastic change for England,
too. It ruined British agricultural self-sufficiency. Professor
G. M. Trevelyan calls it a 'collapse'. Machine-harvested
wheat from the virgin prairies, where you dropped a seed
and wheat jumped at you, was cheaper than the corn of
the English shires, even at a carriage of £5 a ton across
the ocean. British cornlands went to pasture. The *Great
Eastern* had struck the first blow at British agricultural
sufficiency in 1861 when she loaded five thousand tons of

prairie wheat for Liverpool, the largest cargo a ship had ever carried.

Her directors did not, however, grasp the importance of such a trade, even when they had £ 25,000 in pocket for a single wheat lading. They saw no profit in emigrants either, despite the fact that 800,000 went to the U.S. in the war years. When one assesses the lavish reasons why the *Great Eastern* failed, the incredible refusal to carry emigrants counts as much as any other. The owners did not send the ship to the emigrant staging areas in Cork or Hamburg, where they might have beaten the competition to a frazzle. With £ 20,000 in westbound humans and a like amount in eastbound wheat, the great ship might have paid. The directors were obsessed with first-class passenger fares between Liverpool and New York.

Competing lines took to the North Atlantic in the sixties, and harassed the Great Ship Company with price wars, scheduled passages and fleets of ships. By '62 Cunard had a dozen capital steamers on the Atlantic shuttle. The powerful Inman Line was in operation. Germany, the first European power to adopt the English formula of government-subsidized flag lines, had entered the trade with the formidable Hamburg-America and Norddeutscher Lloyd Lines. Louis Napoleon was planning to give France a flag line with such subsidies that a French steamer could circumnavigate the globe empty and return a profit. The Anchor, Guion, and National Lines were coming, and the Canadian government-backed Allan Line was doing its best, despite the loss of five of its liners during the early sixties. They were all after the emigrant. He was not only creating the capital organizations but, in a sense, designing the ships. Third-class space was becoming larger, and urbane touches, such as water closets and washrooms, were being installed in the steerage.

The lonely monster carried on. She attracted only 107 passengers for her first voyage after the storm. She had been debarnacled and her strong new paddles sped her across at unprecedented speed. She also had a new captain, Walter

Paton. He was a thirty-seven-year-old Leith man, who had been schooled as deck officer on the first Cunarder, the *Britannia*. The short, personable Paton was a master of the new mystery of steamships, which required the popularity and seamanship of the sailing skipper, plus techniques they never needed. Paton knew paddle-engines, screw-engines, and high-speed navigation, and an art which is now called labour relations. He dealt with a four hundred-hand crew, itself twice as large as the total crew and passenger complement of a sailing packet. He was in charge of a plant built fifty years before its time.

The paddle-engine weighed 836 tons and drew steam from four boilers containing 160 tons of water. On her trials the *Great Eastern* made eight knots on her paddles only. William McFee, the distinguished marine writer, remembers studying the model of Scott Russell's engine in the Science Museum, South Kensington, as a boy:

> The average person has probably never seen an engine with oscillating cylinders, that is, without a connecting-rod—the piston rod connecting directly to the crank. The *Great Eastern* had four cylinders working on two cranks and were situated under the cranks in an inverted 'V'. It was what is now called in automobiles a 'V-Job'.

James Watt's screw-engine was direct-acting with four cylinders, seven feet in diameter with a four-foot stroke, paired on either side of the crankshaft. On the engine tests in 1859 the screw alone pushed the ship up to nine knots, using six boilers with a 270-ton capacity. The screw-shaft was 150 feet long and weighed 60 tons. There was a single cast-iron propeller, weighing 36 tons, 24 feet in diameter— the largest a ship has carried. Each of the four turbiston bronze screws of the *Queen Elizabeth* weighs 32 tons and is 18 feet in diameter: the *Queen Mary*'s propeller, of which the ship has four, is slightly larger than that of her sister, but does not exceed Scott Russell's.

However, the great ship was woefully underpowered for her size. Her total 'indicated' or potential horsepower,

11,000, probably never exceeded 5,000 H.P. in performance. A remarkable comparison is furnished by the American Export liner *Independence* (1951), almost a century after the *Great Eastern*, and uncannily like the old ship in length, moulded beam, dead tonnage, draught, displacement, cargo capacity and cruising radius. The *Independence*, a steel ship running on oil-burning steam turbines, develops seven times the cruising horsepower of the *Great Eastern* on half her fuel load, and makes twice the speed. The key contrast is in boiler pressure: 25 lb. per square inch in the nineteenth-century wonder and 620 in the *Independence*. Brunel and Scott Russell built a capital ocean liner before there was power and technology to run one.

Together with the new captain, she had a new port agent, Charles W. Whitney, an enterprising type who answered the first telegram from Sandy Hook by chartering a tug and taking the port surveyor, Secret Service men and health officer to meet her at the bar. Whitney was able to file her clearance papers at Bowling Green within ten days of her departure from Milford Haven, a startling new record.

The *Great Eastern* anchored in the stream between Canal Street and Hoboken. Whitney advertised first-class return passage from £19 to £27. The directors had abolished second class, by combining first and second, while retaining the same fares. It sounded better. Third-cabin tickets were £6 to £10. The papers said she would take on sightseers, adding for those who remembered the maiden visit, 'Captain Paton's mates and other subordinates are all different from those who first came over on the ship. The only one of prominence still retained is Chief Engineer McLennan.' The release failed to add that the company directors were the same, although not present in New York this time.

By a noteworthy coincidence her arrival day, May 17, witnessed a heart-warming ceremony at which the Life-Saving Benevolent Association of New York honoured Hamilton E. Towle 'for his ingenious contrivance of a steering machine, which he fitted to the steamship *Great Eastern* under circumstances of great peril, and subsequently of complete success in saving numerous passengers and that great ship.' Towle thanked the Life-Savers for a gold medal and said it was indeed fitting that the award had been given during the first *Great Eastern* call since the storm. Hamilton E. Towle had a wasp in his bonnet.

The ship was thrown open on the last days of the turn-around to crowds averaging three thousand a day. However, the press gave more space to Rarey the Horse-Tamer, who was appearing at Cooper Union. J. S. Rarey was an Ohio farmer who, at a time when horses were worked by beating, had discovered that kindness and an appreciation of the equine psyche got better work out of them. He had electrified London in '58 by taming vicious horses and even a zebra. On the Cooper Union stage the farmer stood before packed houses and won the complete obedience of the most desperate horses New York could offer.

The horse-tamer suited the humane mood of a city reduced from its pre-war swagger by the blood on the battlefields. People did not laugh, but nodded solemnly when they read such a news item as, 'Solomon Sturgess, the well-known Chicago steamboat man and capitalist, has become insane, largely owing to the deep and intense interest he manifested in the overthrow of the rebellion'. People didn't have nervous breakdowns and schizophrenia at that time. If the spirit mediums and phrenologists couldn't help you, you went crazy.

The *Great Eastern* sold four hundred first-class passages and three hundred steerage billets and was loading three thousand tons of cargo when Hamilton E. Towle manifested himself two days before sailing. The United States Marshal sued the ship for £20,000, upon Towle's claim of salvage money. The suit was well grounded in maritime law. The salvage was freshly publicized by the Life-Saving memorial, and Towle struck at the critical moment. Charles Whitney had about £25,000 in the till for the passage. Towle hadn't saved the ship with thought of a reward, but he was smarting under the complete absence of thanks from the Great Ship Company and certain strange reports of the storm published in the British press, which credited the salvation of the *Great Eastern* to Chief Engineer Robinson, whose weird scheme had failed and delayed the use of Towle's steering rig.

As agent, Whitney would have to return passage money and pay demurrage on cargo if the ship did not sail on schedule. He went into judicial chambers with Towle's attorneys and agreed to settle for £2,000, not at all a punishing award compared with the ship's usual disaster bills. Whitney was discharged for his pains. Towle had no spite towards the British—he lived his last years in England and died here in 1881.

Whitney had got up special advertising lures for the *Great Eastern*. He crowed her unique advantages to the family trade: the expansible cabins kept the family together and there were special group rates. One who welcomed this pitch was a Latin paterfamilias whose party headed the passenger list on the outbound voyage. It read: 'Don Juan Yzidoro Moncado, Mariano Moncado, Antonio Moncado, Feodora Moncado, Manuelo Moncado, Conception Moncado, Guadalupe Moncado, Doloreiro Moncado, Yzabel Moncado, Ramiro Moncado, Rebecchine Moncado, Francisco Moncado, Ma de Jesus Moncado, Feodora Moncado and three servants.' One would have liked to have seen the Moncados, the younger presumably held in arms by the servants, as they put their faces to the sponson vents, and watched the big wheel thrashing across the deep.

Wartime life on board ship was sensitive to American issues. War came to the great ship on this crossing. The purser refused to trim the grand saloon with the Stars and Stripes for a ship's ball. Angry patriots battered on Captain Paton's caboose and demanded satisfaction. Paton was a man of summary finesse. He sent a boy to the flag locker for the two biggest British and American colours aboard. He personally climbed a ladder in the saloon and nailed the flags to the ceiling. In Liverpool he discharged the purser and saw that the news was sent to the New York papers.

The company held a meeting at London Tavern, Liverpool, and invited the new skipper to report. Before Paton came on, Director Barber tossed some figures into the air and caught as many as he could: the company was £1,200 in the hole in general and the last voyage had lost only £320. The ship was now in 'a perfect state' and would clean up plenty if the shareholders would only get up some working capital, say £4,000. There were to be four more voyages that year, well into the autumn, because vast numbers of Americans were coming to the latest reprise of the Great Exhibition. A Member of Parliament named Jackson arose and 'strongly advised the directors to continue' with the autumn programme. He said he would put in a thousand pounds to start the collection. It was the end of the collection. After a lengthy silence, the directors put Captain Paton on. He said the ship had made eleven and a half knots against the wind, there had been no seasickness, and a veteran traveller had been able to write all the way across. 'He said he could not do so in Cunard boats owing to vibration,' said Paton, 'but he felt none on the *Great Eastern.*' The skipper added that, among the ten steamers he had commanded, he had 'never known so good a seaboat.' Paton concluded with a revealing glimpse of steamship operating economics: 'Every day the passengers were at meals. It is very different providing passengers with dinner every day, instead of having a large number of sick as in other ships.' The crowd thawed. They subscribed the full £4,000 then and there.

When Paton next arrived in New York on July 11 the *New York Times* remarked,

> The voyage was much enhanced by the gentlemanly and patriotic Capt. Walter Paton, who is becoming a great favourite with the American travelling public. He assisted in celebrating the Fourth of July on board his vessel.

Paton, like so many British masters, had become an honorary American. Among the 376 passengers were His Excellency J. J. Roberts, the President of Liberia, and Annie Fish of the New York shipowning clan founded by Preserved Fish.

The *Great Eastern* was heavily laden. Rather than risk the shifting channel at Sandy Hook, Paton took her in Long Island Sound and moored off Throg's Neck. The passengers were ferried to lower Manhattan and the cargo was sent by lighter to Pier 37 in the North River.

There was no American salute for the hopeful ship's fourth arrival. The dead roll of the Seven Days' Battle filled the front pages. People were shocked at the revelation of the federal debt, £100,000,000. Lincoln was needling the pusillanimous supreme commander, General 'Little Mac' McClellan, and had asked the country for 300,000 more men. Crowds of young slackers gathered around the Relief Association on Broadway to watch the arrival of lousy, wounded, tattered, barefooted, and dying soldiers.

While the lighters were unloading the *Great Eastern*, the city held a mass recruiting rally in Union Square, with six speakers' stands. Mrs. Lincoln came up from Washington for it. She brought Tad Lincoln along. One can imagine what the spoiled, bright child demanded of his mother's escort, Colonels Sweeney, Howe, and McLeod Murphy.

Mrs. Lincoln, Tad, and the colonels embarked on the revenue steamer *Winant* to visit the *Great Eastern* at Throg's Neck. Captain Paton received them with jovial courtesies. The ship's band played them aboard with 'Hail Columbia'. Tad saw the paddle-wheels. Perhaps he had read the steamship propaganda: 'Fancy the pair rolling down Fifth Avenue at twenty miles an hour, filling up the roadway and overtopping the houses!' Paton conducted them through the caves of leviathan and the visit went long past schedule. Back on deck the crew gave a 'grand impromptu' entertainment. When the visitors left, the band played 'Yankee Doodle', the crew cheered three times three and threw their caps, and the guns fired twenty-one mighty rounds in a presidential salute. The *New York Times* said, 'Mrs. Lincoln and her friends expressed themselves highly gratified with the pleasant excursion'.

Quite a number of outbound *Great Eastern* passengers were fellows escaping the draft call. There were two hundred cabin passengers and over three hundred in steerage for the eastbound voyage in late July. They were ferried from the Battery to Throg's Neck by the *Red Jacket*, the steamer that had taken Pirate Hicks for his assignation. The ferry also stopped at West Tenth Street for 'uptown passengers'. A huge cargo of 'breadstuffs and provisions' already had been put into the *Great Eastern*: sacked wheat and barrelled flour, amounting to eight thousand tons, a new record ship's lading. She ran swiftly home with her highest gross, £45,000, to the beaming Daniel Gooch. She was the talk of the steamship business, with her ten-day crossings, her fabulous earnings and the popularity of Captain Walter Paton, who knew how to run a ship and attract passengers. Rival shipowners shook their heads when they thought of what she was going to do if she ever filled her projected four thousand berths. It would be something like what Brunel had been talking about when he dreamed the ship—a £200,000 return trip!

She took only ten days to turn around in Liverpool, before sailing on August 17 with 1,530 passengers for New York. From 107 passengers in May to fourteen times as many two voyages later was an increase that made for happy shareholders. Furthermore, she carried so much merchandise that she drew thirty feet. It was finished manufactures and products, of high value and potent profit. American merchants awaited it with special advertisements for goods rushed by the famous *Great Eastern*.

On the passage Paton encountered a gale that renewed old fears. The great ship rolled heavily and shipped green seas. The chief officer and a sailor suffered broken legs. Paton never relaxed his hand. He stayed on the bridge and drove the monster full speed ahead, never admitting the weakness of the engines for a vessel of that size. By this time the indicated horsepower of the *Great Eastern* was being approached by much smaller steamers. (In 1859 William J. Macquorn Rankine, the Scottish steam theorist, had already blueprinted engines of vaster power.) Paton had what he had and he drove them on. In the caboose was his bride, four months pregnant.

The storm fell astern and Paton arrived at Montauk Point, Long Island, on a calm moonlit midnight, ten days from the Mersey. It was August 27, 1862. The Captain would not risk Sandy Hook with his deep draught. He would go in again by the Sound and moor in Flushing Bay. He slowed his paddles, applied the idling engine to the screw, and dallied in sight of the Montauk Light to await the Sound pilot. Two miles northwest lay the Endeavour Shoals which rose to within nineteen feet of the surface. The pilot would know how to pass the *Great Eastern* through the tricky channel between the Shoals and False Point. At 1.30 a.m. the pilot came aboard and rang for paddle and propeller power. The ship picked up speed and wended its way through a channel in which the navy hydrographic soundings showed a depth pattern (in feet) of 49, 47, 35, 40, 49, 47, 47, 36. Then she would be home free in the deeper waters of the Sound. At 2 a.m. the men on the bridge heard a dull rumble and the ship heeled a few degrees to port. The *Great Eastern* continued on her way. The pilot said she could have touched a shifting sand shoal. Captain Paton sent an officer to survey the bilge. He reported no leaks. The ship made Flushing and moored in the dawn. The passengers had been sound asleep during the curious tilt off Montauk. Unaware of any incident, they were disembarked on ferries for Manhattan. The ship's officers told reporters about the funny jolt.

The *Great Eastern* was listing to starboard. Paton hired a diver named Peter Falcon to go down and look at the ship's bottom.

CHAPTER NINE

THE GREAT EASTERN ROCK

As PETER FALCON brought his diving gear to Flushing Bay to have a look at the bottom of the *Great Eastern*, James Gordon Bennett was suddenly smitten with the ship. Last year the New York *Herald* had sneered at her, now the giantess was Bennett's girl again. The *Herald* announced that the Harlem Railroad would run five excursion trains a day from Fourth Avenue and Twenty-sixth Street, Manhattan, to Port Morris, where ferries would carry people to the *Great Eastern* at fifty cents a head for the whole outing. No other paper mentioned the excursions.

The publisher's flag-waving act had not gone over with the 'governing classes' and he needed a circulation stunt. Here was the *Great Eastern* again, the philosopher's stone of the ballyhoo boys. Gardiner Howland of the ship's new port agency, Howland & Aspinwall, had made the deal with Bennett in the hope of raising money during the turnaround.

Walter Paton, however, couldn't use Bennett's untamed readers on a distressed ship listing heavily to starboard. He requested Howland to call off the short-boy invasion. The embarrassed agent advertised, 'Circumstances of a peculiar nature having arisen, the agency has decided not to admit visitors during her present stay in port'. Bennett was furious. He dispatched a scouting party of reporters to intimidate Paton and expose the perfidy of Albion. The skirmishers naturally got what the boss was after. 'Injuries very slight,' they reported. 'Her bottom has been thoroughly inspected by divers. There is nothing to prevent her return to Europe. The excoriation of the outer hull sheathing is eight to ten inches

at the widest part.' It was a notification to people who knew
how to read the *Herald* that the *Great Eastern* was in a lot
of trouble.

Peter Falcon was equipped with the first closed diving-
dress, which had been invented twenty-five years before in
England by Augustus Siebe. It was practically the finished
model of the present-day salvage diver's outfit: a flexible
watertight suit, heavily weighted boots and a brass helmet,
into which compressed air is pumped through a pipe with a
non-return valve. Falcon's air was forced down to him by
two men on a hand pump. He was working at a depth of
twenty-seven feet, where water pressure is almost twice that
of the atmosphere. It took days of hard pumping and moving
the tender to permit the diver to survey the huge expanse of
hull. Falcon surfaced from his last dive and drew a picture.
He announced to Paton that the *Great Eastern* had a rip
along her flat bottom, near the turning of the starboard bilge
keel. The hole was eighty-three feet long and nine feet wide.

The *Great Eastern* had a gash in her bottom as large as the
hull of many a ship in Flushing Bay. No other vessel could
have survived the crash, and yet the inner hull of Brunel and
Scott Russell was not admitting water. When soundings were
made off Montauk a rock needle was found that towered
within twenty-four feet of the surface. The *Great Eastern*
had made a contribution to American geography. It was
called the Great Eastern Rock and is still carried under that
name on mariners' charts. The rock reached up far enough
to pierce the inner hull, but the breaking resistance of the
outer plates and the strength of the transverse braces between the hulls had carried the inner shell over the Great
Eastern Rock without damage.

Here was the great ship serenely floating in the bay, but
it looked like her finish. There was no dry dock in the world
large enough to take her. The nearest extreme tides which
would allow her to be beached dry were hundreds of miles
away at Passamaquoddy, Maine, and the Bay of Fundy. But,
even if Paton were to risk a voyage north, the ship could not

be repaired on the beach. The hole was in a flat bottom. With the exception of Brunel's *Great Britain*, the monster was the only flat-bottomed ocean ship in the world. Other vessels had rounded bottoms with pronounced keels. If one were stove below the waterline and could make land, the ship was careened on the beach to give access for repair. The *Great Eastern* could not be careened. She was still the heaviest man-made object. Paton well remembered the three awful months it had taken Brunel to move her down inclined ways. With these heavy thoughts, he told his wife, Jane Eliza, 'It looks as if we will be here a bit, my dear'. She had come along impulsively for a bracing sea voyage, before settling down at home to have her baby.

The *Great Eastern*'s sailing advertisement was removed from the papers. In its stead was run:

> The *Great Eastern* having touched the ground on her late passage from Liverpool, it has been considered advisable to make a thorough examination of her bottom before sending her to sea; her departure will, therefore, be delayed beyond her previously advertised date of sailing. Holders of return tickets will have them renewed or the money returned as they may desire. Due notice will be given of the ship's departure.

The notice ran for sixty-three straight days, through a harsh episode of American history, the rout of Pope at Second Bull run, Stonewall Jackson's bag at Harper's Ferry, and one day at Antietam when 23,000 men fell. Their lives won something: the British and French governments were about to recognize the Confederacy, but drew back in fascination at the bloody intensity of the first modern war. While the advertisement ran, Lincoln issued his feeler of the Emancipation Proclamation, J. E. B. Stuart raided Chambersburg, and a United States Army general officer was cashiered for dereliction of duty.

The managers of the great ship saw these events as a convenient screen for the troubled leviathan. They were embarrassed over what everybody else would have considered an epic: the vessel had survived the rock. Instead of arousing admiration by revealing the facts, the cryptic advertisement was repeated every day and a chance for American sympathy lost.

The crew and most of his officers begged Captain Paton to sail her to Milford Haven. They pointed out that the inner hull was as strong as any bottom afloat, and it was not leaking. The skipper was tempted, but he refused to sail her home in the gales of autumn with a heavy list and a pronounced drag. He told the crew the ship would remain in Flushing while every expedient was examined. They cursed and grumbled at imprisonment on an idle ship in Yankeeland.

Although the public was not told of the dilemma, the engineering fraternity buzzed with it. The *Great Eastern* had a magnetism for brilliant men as strong as her attraction for disaster. One day in September Gardiner Howland received a caller, a tall, handsome, blue-eyed man who walked carefully and kept a cautious hand in front of him. He was a consulting engineer named Edward S. Renwick, who had lost most of his eyesight while labouring in Washington as a patent examiner. The agent received him with deference. Renwick came of a distinguished New York family. His father, Professor James Renwick of Columbia University, wrote the first American text-books on physics and geology. His brother James was the leading U.S. architect, now at work building St. Patrick's Cathedral, after his notable success with its opposite number, Grace Church. The architect had also designed Vassar College, the Smithsonian Institution in Washington and the Croton Aqueduct. One of the near-blind man's uncles was Captain Charles Wilkes, U.S.N., who had almost provoked war with Britain in the *Trent* affair the year before. Edward Renwick, however, hadn't much to recommend him. He had failed as an iron-master in Wilkes-Barre, and had several unsuccessful inventions to his name, including a self-binding reaper. He had sued Cyrus McCormick, who had the money and luck behind his reaper, to a legal draw, but got no royalties.

The visitor told Howland he had a plan for repairing the hull of the *Great Eastern* just as she lay in Flushing Bay. The situation was so desperate that the port agent disobeyed his impulse to shuffle papers, clear his throat and say, 'Good day, sir'. The groping man said he and his older brother Henry would offer to repair the ship under water on salve and pay: if they did not succeed the Great Ship Company paid nothing. He introduced Henry, a large man with one eye blinded in the Wyossing Iron Works. Henry was a former steamboat inspector, and co-author with his father, the professor, of lives of John Jay and Alexander Hamilton. Howland looked at the two big men with the sight of slightly more than one eye between them, and took them out to the ship to meet Captain Paton. It was a clan meeting: the Renwicks were transplanted Scots—their grandmother had been the beautiful Jean Jeffrey of Lochmaben, to whom Robert Burns addressed three poems. The mariner from Leith saw merit in the salvage scheme. He told Howland he would endorse it to the company. Nothing was being risked but time, and Captain Paton had much of that. There was no hope for the *Great Eastern* but the dim-sighted brothers.

The forty-year-old Edward Renwick was newly wed to Alice Brevoort, a lively young woman who demanded to see the *Great Eastern*. Her husband took her aboard and introduced Jane Eliza Paton. The two brides hit it off immediately and Jane Eliza asked Alice Brevoort to share the great ship while the husbands were tinkering down below. Both girls were pregnant with their firstborn. So the crystal palace of the sea became a bridal cottage and Alice and Jane Eliza crocheted and poured tea in the reaches of a saloon that beat Mrs. John Jacob Astor's. They had more servants than Queen Victoria. The men, meanwhile, prepared to deal with the incision in the ship's bottom, twenty-seven feet under water.

The problem is pictured in a manuscript by Edward Renwick, which was discovered by Mrs. Sturges Turner, his granddaughter-in-law, in a barn in Washington, Connecticut, in 1953.

The whole space between the two skins at one side of the ship, three feet in breadth and 680 feet in length, became filled with water, and the vessel came into Flushing Bay with a heavy list to starboard. The first thing to be ascertained was the form of the exterior of the ship. This was done by making templates of the inner skin, and when these were laid down on the moulding floor, and the breadth of the space between the two skins, three feet, was added to the curved lines of the templates, the form of the exterior was determined.

The engineer hired a yacht moulding floor to dummy up the complex curved area of the bilge. Although a mere preliminary of his repair scheme, it was a job comparable to that of laying down a large yacht.

Renwick had 'decided to do the work by means of a caisson', or what would now be called a cofferdam, a semi-cylinder of heavy wood, 102 feet long, and 16 feet wide, with its gunwales curved to suit the form of the hull. He proposed to sink this shell, fit it over the long hole and pump it dry, so the repairmen could descend through dry shafts and patch the hull. In effect, Renwick sought to clamp a fair-sized ship to the bottom of another—under water.

Cofferdams were not an original idea with Renwick, but none had ever approached the scale and complexity of the *Great Eastern*'s poultice, which was itself a vessel of about sixty tons capacity. It had to be built in a shipyard, launched like a ship and towed to Flushing Bay. There it was heavily ballasted and lowered by derrick on lighters. Peter Falcon dived to see that it was accurately fitted over the hole and then stout chains were carried around the *Great Eastern* and the cofferdam, and tightened to fasten it to the ship. Renwick provided for a watertight seal by fitting the coffer-dam gunwales with Brussels carpets. He was also going to make water pressure work for him. As the cofferdam was pumped out, external water pressure 'would crowd it firmly against the ship' and Falcon would go down and feed sea-weed along the joint of the carpets to make a hermetic seal.

Renwick used a powerful centrifugal pump to suck the tremendous volume of water from the hull compartments and the caisson. Falcon surfaced and said the pumps were drawing in all the weed he could gather. The ship's officers joked about the possibility that the skeleton of the ghostly riveter would be siphoned from his tomb in the double hull and poured out in bone fragments by the flashing centrifugal pump. As it showered the bay, the great ship's sides arose and her list was disappearing. Edward Renwick was not pleased with the rate of flow. The nozzle streamed heavily, but the water level was not sinking fast enough in the coffer-dam shafts. He stopped the pump and strained his eyes into one of the chutes. The water level climbed steadily and maddeningly towards him. The heal had failed. The chutes filled to the surface.

The next day he unloosed and brought up the cofferdam by hard effort and floated it. It was structurally sound and and undamaged, a perfect, mocking negative mould of John Scott Russell's iron adaption of Hogarth's line of beauty. From among the engineers, workmen, and onlookers in Edward Renwick's blurred world came derisive conversation, little laughs and now-look-here-old-man advice. Renwick must have felt like Brunel and Scott Russell. He asked for a gang of carpenters the next morning.

He instructed the carpenters to hollow out the gunwales on the cofferdam, along the entire adhesive joint, 235 feet around the caisson's edges. Into the groove he laid a heavy fire-hose and padded it with the carpeting. When the coffer-dam was again chained fast to the bottom, Renwick pumped water into the hose and inflated it until the cables round the ship and caisson squeaked. He set the whirling pump going to drain the submerged structure. The pump roared for a day and a night and then coughed dry. There was no water visible from the mouths of the chutes. The submarine passages were evidently dry.

The riveters showed no alacrity to descend those two black shafts to the keel of the ship. Renwick's first scheme had failed and none of them wanted to test the next. He and Captain Paton argued that the cofferdam was demonstrably

Science Museum

Here is the Wonder of the Waves under full power of paddlewheels, propeller and sail

One of the five Currier and Ives lithographs of the great ship. She was one of the most popular print subjects of the century

The Great Eastern, ready for launching in 1857 at the Isle of Dogs. On the right, wearing a top hat, is John Scott Russell, her builder.

The Little Giant, Isambard Kingdom Brunel, creator of the great iron ship, poses for a stereophotographer against the 60-lb. links of the launching drum cables.

The broadside launching from the river bank. Brunel stands on the high platform to supervise the first disastrous slide, October, 1857.

C. C. Bennet

Daniel Gooch, locomotive engineer, whom the ship made a great capitalist, if not a successful showman.

Scott Russell, an apprentice named Wakefield, Brunel and Lord Derby watching the great ship prepare for her maiden voyage. Brunel collapsed with a stroke a few hours after this photograph was taken.

The *Great Eastern* in the Thames, during the eighteen months which it took to fit her out for her ocean adventures.

The grand saloon sketched by a passenger, C. F. Hayward, during the storm of September, 1861. The

ie grand saloon, photographed at Quebec in 1861. The lady stands
r the skylight well. On the right is the funnel casing covered with
mirrors and arabesques.

Jimmy Paton, born aboard the *Great Eastern*, in his mother's arms, 1863.

Walter Paton, master mariner. He tamed the *Great Eastern*.

Edward Renwick, the engineer who repaired the *Great Eastern* under water.

Captain John Vine Hall, who had a nervous breakdown after the maiden voyage.

New York, 1860. 'The boy who saw the Bay yesterday witnessed a spectacle that he will not be likely to forget, if he should outlive Methuselah,' said Gamecock Wilkes.

Mariners' Museum

The monster at the lumber wharf in the North River, New York. In the foreground are some of the booths and side-shows which sprang up during her stay.

A stage-coach from the Western Hotel brings sightseers to view the great ship on her maiden visit to New York in 1860.

Sich a getting up stairs

Harper's Weekly

Nobody knew the way round the great ship, visitor or barefoot crew. There were 143,000 paid admissions in New York.

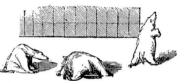

The Urbanity of its Officers has been frequently mentioned : but

having seen Old Adams' Bears previously we were disappointed.

Harper's Weekly

The *Great Eastern's* officers were unpopular in New York. Old Adams' bears were being shown at the street fair near the ship.

Harper's Weekly

Visitors were allowed to stay on board all day for a dollar.

A proper regulation

Harper's Weekly

Sightseers covered the deck with tobacco juice, took everything loose as souvenirs, and played in the rigging.

In the Spring of 1865, the *Great Eastern* takes a length of the Atlantic cable aboard from a Royal Navy hulk at Sheerness.

Lowering the mark buoy after the cable was lost in mid-Atlantic. At the bow pick-up wheel the grapnel has been rigged for an attempt to recover the cable.

Telegraph Construction & Maintenance Co.

'Oxford Street', the port promenade deck of the *Great Eastern*, during night cable-laying in 1866. Cablemen on watch at the cable trough, right.

Jules Verne takes his ease in
rocking chair aboard the *Great*
Eastern on the French charter
voyage, 1867.

Belle Halpin

Captain Robert Halpin, who laid
26,000 miles of deep sea cable.

Mrs. C. M. Hindle

George Beckwith, the engineer,
who served in the ship from
1860 to 1886.

Visitors aboard the whitewashed *Great Eastern* in Bombay. In the foreground is Captain Halpin's dog, Harold.

A few of the half million who visited the great showboat
at Liverpool in 1886.

A last glimpse of the *Great Eastern*, a floating advertisement
hoarding, off Liverpool in the Summer of 1886.

safe. The men clung to their dread of being smothered in water down there in the dark. Walter Paton said, 'Falcon and I will go down and show you'. The diver, in the tassel-cap of his profession, followed the master of the *Great Eastern* down the ladder of the stern chute. The workers crowded around the pit mouth listening for the diminishing voices. They watched Peter Falcon's tassel disappear round the curve into the cofferdam. Sounds from below ceased. The explorers were gone a minute, and two minutes. People retreated from the fringe and spoke nervously to Edward Renwick and another minute passed. And another. They heard a shout. Off in the sunlight at the mouth of the bow chute the captain and the diver waved and yelled. They had walked through the undersea tunnel and their clothes were dry.

The Great Eastern Rock had nicely turned the torn plates inward so that the drillers had a smooth surface to make rivet holes. Obtaining repair plates was another matter. Scott Russell's seven-eighth-inch plating was almost unknown in the States. Furthermore, Renwick was told there was a war on. It required full rolling-mill capacity and new plants to beat the secession. The United States Navy was armouring. The vogue had been introduced that spring when the U.S.S. *Monitor* had fought a draw with the Confederate States' ship *Virginia* in Hampton Roads. (The latter was a prize, ex-U.S.S. *Merrimac*. The *Virginia* was burned by the rebels before she saw another engagement. The *Monitor* never fought again and foundered under tow off Cape Hatteras while Renwick was replating the *Great Eastern*.) Militarily, Hampton Roads had resulted in the *status quo ante*, but the fight gave Northern propagandists and iron salesmen a sorely needed victory. The 'decisive naval battle' resulted in prosperity for Northern iron-mills. However, the war was decided by the deaths of 600,000 infantrymen.

The Renwick brothers found a mill which rolled five-eighth-inch charcoal boiler plate. It was not thick enough, but they said it would do, and ordered four hundred plates.

E

'It will take at least a year,' said the iron-master. The brothers were iron-masters, too. They inspected the mill and showed the supplier how to make their plates in three months' time, without interrupting his war orders.

'The iron plates were taken into the caisson,' says Edward's manuscript, 'and riveted to the ship with hot rivets.' The plates arrived on a ration. They were lowered through the chutes into the underwater tunnel and the old hammer-clangour of the Isle of Dogs arose from Flushing Bay. When the day's plates were expended, the men came up and knocked off work, sometimes as early as noon. Then Peter Falcon would dive to survey the cofferdam. One day he was lowered, and the tenders were pumping vigorously, when Falcon sent up four sharp tugs on his air pipe, the emergency signal to haul him up. The tenders removed his helmet and the diver's face was white. 'The ghost is hammering inside the hull!' he said.

Captain Paton was shocked. The old superstition of the entombed riveter was current among simple people, but he did not expect the fearless Falcon to believe such nonsense. 'I heard the basher,' Falcon insisted. 'He is hammering on the inside.' The workmen gathered around with sagging faces. The Renwicks sent them home on the ferry.

The next morning the riveters refused to go down. Edward Renwick was faced with a strike over a ghost. He asked the men to act like grownups, but they refused to enter the chutes. The engineer ordered several men down. They stood firm. One explained that they had absolute proof there was a ghost in the hull cells. From their ranks came a curious individual in a stovepipe hat—Professor Thomas, by profession a spirit medium. He told the engineer that the spectral basher was present inside the ship 'both in body and spirit'. Today this sort of industrial psychology would get the practitioner transferred to some less sensitive line of endeavour, but the riveters closed ranks round the luckless medium. Walter Paton intervened. He leaped to the platform around the chute and vanished down the shaft. He returned and said nothing. He drew Edward Renwick aside and said in a low voice, 'I heard it. Something is pounding on the hull.' The engineers and skipper inspected the entire bilge of the great ship. There was no one hammering on the inside, but they heard a distinct sound of banging on plate, apparently coming from below the waterline. Paton got into a skiff and had himself rowed around the ship, checking the cofferdam tackle. A few feet under water he saw a heavy swivel hitting the ship's side as she oscillated in the swell.

Paton showed it to the men, made the swivel fast, and sent the spirit medium packing. The men went down the shafts and the hammers of the mortal bashers rang again. The work was completed at the end of December.

The *Great Eastern* was loading three thousand tons of wheat and provisioning for twelve hundred passengers on New Year's Day, when the President issued the Emancipation Proclamation, that all slaves in areas in rebellion were 'then, thenceforward, and for ever free'. The ship sailed five days later.

The *Great Eastern*'s emancipation was less spectacular. She departed with an edgy crew and a tired and anxious master. The Renwick bill was £70,000, and Paton would have to face a board of inquiry on the accident when he got home. And Jane Eliza was about to give birth. The captain ran full steam, bucking strong easterly winds and January seas with his heavily laden ship. A passenger, Edward Parbridge of Monmouthshire, died a natural death at sea, and on the tenth day, when Captain Paton should have been in Liverpool, but was still struggling off Cape Clear, nature replaced his deceased passenger with a braw baby boy, born to Jane Eliza.

The *Great Eastern* babe, Jimmy Paton, turned out to be a mettlesome fellow. His mother died when he was ten, and with his father at sea, Jimmy shipped out on the bark *Craigmullen* at the age of thirteen. He sailed to the Pacific and saw many a parlous sight. In San Francisco the lad was watching a saloon poker game, when one of the gamblers assassinated his neighbour with a knife. The players eased the body into a corner and called for draw cards. When his half-brother was drowned off the Horn, Jimmy's aunts grounded him. He set up a tinsmith's business in Bootle, consisting of himself and a stack of impressive letterheads. His biggest account was with a company owned by an uncle, who, when he discovered the identity of the president and board of directors of his supplier, said, 'James, I never do business with relatives, and especially when they are minors'. He closed the account and Jimmy's business ended.

The boy got a job as the Clan Line's port agent, responsible for stores, repairs, coals, captains, doctors, and crew procurement. The latter duty he fulfilled by searching the pubs of Liverpool and fishing out drunken sailors, 'being strong and useful with my fists', he said later. Again he went into business for himself with a paint-cleaning compound he invented in a copper cauldron in his landlady's back parlour. 'At that time,' he recounted, 'the sailors used a paint cleaner known as soogee-moogee caustic potash, which used to make their fingernails drop off.' When the sailors discovered that Jimmy's stuff not only cleaned but allowed them to retain their nails, he was solidly in business. It was the beginning of the large contemporary firm, Paton, Calvert & Company, Ltd., of Liverpool, which manufactures polish, packaging and lithographed metal articles. The *Great Eastern*'s formidable infant went on to be Lord Mayor of Southport and a knight, owner of a town house in London and a patron of the opera. At the end of this book he reappears as the avenger of the *Great Eastern*'s honour in her pitiable final days.

CHAPTER TEN

THE RAFFLE

HOME from the Great Eastern Rock collision, Paton moored the ship in Sloyne Pool and awaited the inquiry. The directors convened aboard two weeks later, 'kindly assisted by Lloyd's agent at Liverpool, Mr. H. E. Chapman'. He was present merely in the capacity of guest quizmaster. The insurance company had already refused to entertain a claim for damage. Daniel Gooch could not sue the United States for failure in geography. The company was £70,000 deeper in debt.

Paton testified and was given a letter:

Having fully investigated all circumstances, the directors have arrived at the conclusion that no blame whatsoever attaches to you or any of your officers, but the accident is solely attributable to the ship striking on a sunken rock in the fairway channel, which is not laid down in the charts.

There remained the question whether the Renwick plates were sound and this was going to cost a lot more money. The company asked the Liverpool Dock Board for the loan of a beach, upon which a four-hundred-foot grid could be built to support the *Great Eastern* while a tunnel was dug under her appendectomy. The board said there was no space available.

The company leased private frontage on the New Ferry shore, south of Birkenhead. Board of Trade inspectors burrowed under the wounded bilge and passed the Renwick job as seaworthy, without need of further repair. While the ship lay there the Prince of Wales got married and the Queen decreed a national holiday. Thousands hastened to Liverpool to see the *Great Eastern*. In New York, Cyrus Field was still plugging away on his grand obsession, the Atlantic telegraph. He had lost two ocean cables and although the Civil War delayed a new attempt, he was building up propaganda for it. That spring the New York Chamber of Commerce held an extraordinary meeting to 'further and bring to completion the great Atlantic Telegraph Enterprise'.

On the first of July of the dread year of '63, Paton left for New York with 650 passengers and an enormous load of tea. While the ship was at sea the Battle of Gettysburg was fought. The *Great Eastern* arrived in New York as the Fifth Column replied to Gettysburg with the Draft Riots. The short boys had a genuine issue—'the rich man's war and the poor man's battle', the monstrous system by which a draftee with three hundred dollars could buy a man to fight for him. Abetted by the governor of the state and a line-up of newspapers, the 'governing classes' ran amok in a defenceless city. Manhattan saw more destruction and killing than any given battle of the American Revolution. Sixty thousand drunks sacked the town. They burnt fifty buildings, including the Coloured Orphan Asylum and two Protestant churches. Property loss amounted to £1,000,000, of which the city treasury later indemnified one-quarter. The inspired mob killed at least four hundred people (highest report: one thousand), including police, soldiers on leave, and scores of their special prey, Negro freemen, of which the ritual victim was a nine-year-old girl clubbed to death in the orphan home. All business closed except for the city's five thousand beer tunnels, barrel houses, gin palaces, and sawdust *Élysées*. After three days two hundred combat men from the Army of the Potomac detrained with fixed bayonets and sent the rats back to their holes.

The *Great Eastern* made one more return trip to New York that summer. Back in Liverpool, the season's loss was established as £20,000. Competing steamer lines were subsidized for the most part and could stand the continuing fare-cutting war, but the big lone ship could not. In the autumn, the

directors told the shareholders to raise more money or face
collapse of the enterprise.

The 1864 company meeting in the Albion Hotel in Manchester opened with long faces. A representative of the creditors took the floor, a Mr. Davey of Liverpool. He had a rabbit
up each sleeve. Davey beamed on the sufferers and said, 'You
are doubtless aware of the Frankfurt-am-Main scheme for
selling the *Great Eastern*'. The crowd nodded. The subject
had been widely talked about. The company chairman inter-
jected to ask whether the people behind the Frankfurt
scheme were reliable. Davey said, 'Mr. Fabricus, the proposed trustee from Frankfurt, and Mr. Stoess, the Frankfurt
consul to Liverpool, are waiting outside. Information may be
had direct.' The shareholders clamoured to meet the miracle
men.

What was proposed was to raffle off the *Great Eastern* in
a colossal lottery. Herr Fabricus would organize it, under the
tolerant laws of Frankfurt, and sell tickets all over Europe.
The Germans, and the French as well, had long itched to
take over the ship that the English didn't know how to man-
age. The company meeting, worthy of Dickens, ended with
the solemn appointment of a committee to fend off the sheriff,
while Herr Fabricus organized his game of chance.

Unfortunately Fabricus was quickly pushed off the paddle-
box. The Liverpool *Albion* warned against 'circulars of certain firms in Frankfurt, which style themselves "bankers"'
and 'extensively circulate in this country by post, recom-
mending subscriptions to the periodical lottery'. A committee
of Frankfurt bankers sent word that they 'were very much
annoyed that the concocters of the *Great Eastern* lottery had
chosen this town as their headquarters'. Who knows? Perhaps anyone who drew the lucky bean could have run the
ship as well as its directors.

The third company gave up the ship. She was offered at
auction in the cotton-room of the Liverpool Exchange by
order of the mortgagees, in January, 1864. The disused
cotton-room was an ironical port of call for the vessel that

might have been bringing the absent cotton to Britain. To the rostrum came the jovial auctioneer, none other than the Hon. Joseph Cunard. The Cunard Line had let the calf have all the rope. The large crowd applauded the auctioneer. He announced the conditions of sale. 'Ten per cent of the purchase is to be deposited with bids and the remainder within fourteen days. Otherwise the deposit is forfeited and the vessel sold by private or public sale. The loss, if any, to be made good by the defaulter.' The mortgagees reserved the right to withdraw the ship, if the bid did not exceed £100,000.

Cunard banged his gavel and asked for an opener. A long pause ensued. The auctioneer tried to warm up the crowd. 'The biddings, gentlemen, must be at the rate of one thousand pounds a bid. A nod or a wink shall be worth a thousand pounds and very cheap at the money.' (Laughter.) 'What do I hear to open?'

A clear voice in the back of the room said, 'Fifty thousand'. Cunard said, 'Do I hear fifty-one thousand pounds?' Nobody spoke, winked or nodded. The ushers could not locate the original bidder. Cunard joked and cajoled for fifteen minutes and there was no bid. The crowd had come to see the auction, not to bid. 'To save the time of the gentlemen present,' he said, 'I shall put in the owner's bid, the most disagreeable bid an auctioneer can put, I need not remind you.' Silence. Cunard withdrew the ship, and announced, 'The *Great Eastern* will be offered at a peremptory sale without any reserve', in three weeks' time.

Daniel Gooch talked with Cyrus Field and found two other *Great Eastern* directors who would join him on a bid of £80,000. The second auction opened with a bid of £20,000. Gooch restrained the company secretary, John H. Yates, who was bidding for him and waited several minutes. No one raised. Gooch signalled Yates to put in £25,000. Cunard knocked the ship down to him for that amount. Gooch wrote the good news to Cyrus Field at the Palace Hotel in London. Field replied, 'I received a telegram from Liverpool previously announcing the sale of the ship, price, etc. I shall be truly glad to have the *Great Eastern* used in laying the Atlantic cable.' The day had arrived, when the mission jokingly discussed by Cyrus Field and I. K. Brunel in 1857 was about to be realized.

There was still the matter of the shareholders. They were called to a meeting in October at London Tavern in Liverpool, and the directors all but wept for the people with the pretty share certificates. The directors did not hold back any bad news. Discovering the Great Eastern Rock had cost £70,000, a marine chandler named Parry who had been suing since 1860, had exacted a second mortgage on the ship of £7,000. Desperate fare-cutting by competitors had swallowed another £20,000. The first mortgage amounted to £40,000. £1,200 had been paid for petty repairs and services and the working account showed an excess of disbursements over receipts of £19,000. If this did not weaken their will to hold on, there was the regrettable matter of the ship *Jane*. Coming up St. George's Channel on her last voyage home, the *Great Eastern* had smacked into the *Jane* in such an effective manner as 'to induce the crew to abandon her and seek refuge on the *Great Eastern*'. The owners of the *Jane* had applied for an Admiralty warrant to seize the big ship.

The meeting closed with an ultimatum from the chairman, William Barber: unless the shareholders put up £24,000 immediately, and found 'a further sum' for outfit, repair, and maintenance, it would mean 'total sacrifice of the property of ordinary shareholders'. The ordinary shareholders replied with an angry rump meeting in Manchester. A Mr. W. Hawes was elected chairman. He did not reciprocate the directors' sympathy for the downtrodden shareholders. Hawes said the management had caused all the *Great Eastern*'s troubles: Gooch, Barber, and company had made their greatest error in putting her on the Atlantic instead of the Indian or Australian run for which she was designed; that the losses had been grossly exaggerated; and that Barber's report had been deliberately designed to cause despondency

E*

among the shareholders. 'The cry about selling the ship is a bugbear,' said Hawes. He predicted that the main creditors would not foreclose if the management pulled itself together and went into the Oriental trade. Hawes's talk swept the disgruntled shareholders—they passed his motion that the ship should be placed on the Australian service immediately, where she would net £40,000 a year. The rebellious Hawes concluded by hinting they should vote out the present directors: 'It is a significant fact that it is the large bondholders who want to buy her, men who have hitherto been the principal management.'

The power over the investment lay with the management. Gooch's charter with Cyrus Field was all set. The creditors foreclosed; the ship. was bankrupted, and shorn of its army of one-pound stockholders; the title to the *Great Eastern* reverted to Gooch and his two partners.

One of the partners was thirty-two-year-old Thomas Brassey, who had put up most of the £100,000 pooled for the auction. Brassey did not lack money. His father was the biggest international railway contractor of the century. In the year 1850, the Brassey Company employed 75,000 men on four continents at contracts totalling £28,000,000.

Young Brassey later received a peerage and became Civil Lord and Secretary of the Admiralty. Under his regime, he reformed the Royal Navy and swept away serf-like conditions in the yards.

CHAPTER ELEVEN

ELEPHANT SPINNING A COBWEB

THE most famous war correspondent of the nineteenth century was Sir William Howard Russell of *The Times*, a high-flown Irishman whom Abraham Lincoln called 'Bull Run' Russell. He invented the profession. No journalistic trouble-seeker of our day can match Bull Run's collection of wars, beginning with the Danish struggle for independence from Germany in 1849. When he was thirty-three he took over the Crimean War. His reports of the maltreatment of the sick and wounded almost unhorsed the Imperial General Staff, but it held on and Lord Aberdeen's cabinet fell instead. Russell's agitation led I. K. Brunel to build the Renkioi Hospital and inspired a nurse named Florence Nightingale to go out there and organize medical care.

Russell's dispatches from the Sepoy Rebellion in 1857 almost drove the *Great Eastern* launching from the papers. He covered the U.S. Civil War from both sides, the Franco-Prussian War in 1870 and several of the recurrent campaigns in Africa and Egypt.

Russell was a cultured Dubliner with grand airs. When he arrived in Washington, soon after Lincoln's inauguration, he was invited to the first formal cabinet dinner and was introduced by the President as 'the Ambassador of the London *Times*'. His dispatches on the First Battle of Bull Run led many Britons to believe the North was doomed, and consequently Russell was refused further accreditization to McClellan's armies.

In 1865 Russell was between wars. He found a peacetime epic worthy of his pen. He chose to accompany the *Great*

139

Eastern on an attempt to lay a telegraphic cable on the bottom of the sea 2,300 miles from Ireland to Newfoundland. The big ship was going to spin 'a thread of thought between two continents'.

I. K. Brunel had been interested in the Atlantic telegraph from its first conception by Frederick N. Gisborne, an English engineer, who had gone to New York in 1854 and induced Cyrus Field to form a cable company. Brunel was soon writing Field voluble memoranda on cable-laying. British capitalists were as ready as British engineers to throw in their lot with Field on the Atlantic cable. The British bought 229 of the £1,000 par value shares in the company. Only eighty-eight shares were sold in the U.S.—all to Field himself.

Field's first attempt to lay the cable in 1857 employed Her Majesty's Man-of-War *Agamemnon* and the U.S. warship *Niagara*, which met in mid-Atlantic to share out the cable east and west. The inferior wire broke off both ships when only two hundred miles were down. The next year the *Agamemnon* and the *Niagara* started from opposite shores to meet in mid-ocean. The cable broke six times, but sufficient wire was carried to replace the lost lengths. When it was announced that words could be transmitted from America to Europe in two minutes the world marvelled at the portent. Four hundred messages flashed back and forth in the first three weeks. Then the signals mysteriously died.

Cyrus Field's company had lost £500,000. The quiet Yankee capitalist, however, was made of the same obdurate stuff as his late friend Brunel, the volatile engineer. By 1864, Field was ready to move again, and now the *Great Eastern* was available. She had betrayed three corporations which had tried to make her pay as a transatlantic liner. Her total bankruptcy score was around a million pounds. The *Great Eastern* was twice the financial flop that Field was. The resolute entrepreneur decided to put two failures together and make a success.

Daniel Gooch offered his white elephant free of charge if

she failed to lay the cable. If she succeeded, he wanted
£50,000 in cable stock. Cyrus Field was overwhelmed by
the sporting offer and arranged to have Gooch and Thomas
Brassey, co-owner of the ship, elected to the board of the
Telegraph Construction Company. Cunard furloughed Captain James Anderson, the redoubtable skipper of the *China*,
to command the cable ship. He and Field struck up a solid
friendship which had much to do with the eventual triumph
of the ocean telegraph.

In May, 1865, the *Great Eastern* lay at Sheerness taking
wire from two navy hulks which had brought it down from
London. The cable was coiled in three gigantic tanks that
had replaced saloons, cabins, and holds. The fourth funnel
and two of the ten boilers were also removed to stow wire.
The Prince of Wales came aboard and was invited to make a
statement. He said, 'I WISH SUCCESS TO THE ATLANTIC CABLE'.
A telegrapher tapped it on his key and the impulses went
round and round 1,395 nautical miles and came out in two
seconds for the royal visitor to hear.

In July the vessel headed for the west coast of Ireland,
where the European end of the cable was to emerge from the
sea at Foilhummerum Bay on Valentia Island. It was County
Kerry that was to be honoured, and Irish folk were eager to
see the great ship. Yachts came round from Cork and fishermen paddled into the bay in canvas coracles. Country people
perched on the rock escarpment under the mouldering Crom-
wellian fort and boiled mighty pots of potatoes over turf fires.
There were whisky tents and sharpers and tinkers come to
tell fortunes, spin wheels of chance, trick the peasants with
peas and shells, and deal the game of spoil five. Fiddlers and
pipers played planxties and jigs in the fresh blue air. Shoe-
less children and women in bright shawls gathered under
the green flag of Erin, the Fitzgeraldine banner of the Knight
of Kerry, the Stars and Stripes, and the Union Jack. Indeed,
there was even a pure white temperance flag rippling over
the convivial scene.

The Knight of Kerry made the principal oration to a crowd

that had lost its eyes to the sea. They strained for the sight of the darling ship that was to string the telegraph to their relatives in America. They saw steamer smoke rising, but it was only that of the cable-layer's escorts, Her Majesty's Ships *Sphinx* and *Terrible*. The knight's speech was lost in babble when the news spread that the *Great Eastern* could not come near shallow Foilhummerum Bay, but was standing in Bantry Bay handing the cable end to the small steamer *Caroline*. The *Caroline* appeared and passed the cable to shore over a bridge of twenty-five local yawls. The Knight of Kerry lost most of his audience to the whisky tents. He ended with a Victorian *non sequitur*, 'I call upon you to give three cheers for Sir Robert Peel'. The son of the inventor of the hated English police was present to take a bow. Sir Robert delivered an address. To an intimate group of the knight's tenants he ended with an appeal to give three hearty cheers for the Queen, the President, and the Knight of Kerry.

Russell told how the cable voyage began:

> The bight of the cable was slipped from the *Caroline* at 7.15 p.m., and the *Great Eastern* stood slowly on her course N.W. ¼W. Then the *Terrible* and the *Sphinx*, which had ranged up alongside, and sent their crews into the shrouds and up to the tops to give her a parting cheer, delivered their friendly broadsides with vigour, and received a similar greeting. Their colours were hauled down, and as the sun set a broad stream of golden light was thrown across the smooth billows towards their bows as if to indicate and illumine the path marked out by the hand of Heaven. The brake was eased, and as the *Great Eastern* moved ahead the machinery of the paying-out apparatus began to work, drums rolled, wheels whirled, and out spun the black line of the cable, and dropped in a graceful curve into the sea over the stern wheel. The cable came up with ease from the after tank, and was payed out with the utmost regularity from the apparatus. The system of signals to and from the ship was at once in play between the electricians on board and those at Foilhummerum.

The cable-ship sent regular reports announcing its progress and the London press replied with news dispatches which were posted on deck. The voyagers cheered a report that their shipmate, Daniel Gooch, had been elected Conservative Member of Parliament for Cricklade. He had been absent during the polls and had in fact not made a campaign speech. Gooch sat in four Parliaments and never said a word. He was the ideal party man.

Aboard the *Great Eastern* was published the first ship's newspaper, *The Atlantic Telegraph*. It was not the publicity handout that passes as a newspaper on present-day liners. *The Atlantic Telegraph* was written by the community on board, ánd edited by an impish fellow named O'Neill. Bull Run Russell's artist-in-attendance, Robert Dudley, drew shipboard incidents on the lithographic stone. One inspired contributor wrote:

> The *Great Eastern* speeds nobly on her mission of towing Great Britain and Ireland to America. In less than ten days it is expected that a splice will be affected between the two countries and long, long may it last.

The brain centre of the expedition was a caboose under the forward flying bridge, the testing room with blackout curtains on its doors. Within, electricians sat on constant watch in the dark over wires which led down to the end of the ocean cable coiled in the tank. They continually sent Morse code letters to Ireland in a prearranged set of twenty-nine possible messages, and the Valentia operators had thirty-five confusing ways to reply. On both ends, however, the electricians minded one small thing, a pinpoint of light in the dark, which showed if the cable was alive. The speck was reflected on a graduated index by a tiny mirror attached to a magnet at the end of the conducting wires. It was the key test instrument, Professor William Thomson's astatic mirror galvanometer, the talisman of ocean telegraphy. It read the ohm resistance of the cable in little jiggling flickers. If the dot bounced off the index it meant a fault in the wrapping allowing the current to escape to the sea, or a cable break. If that happened the watch electrician ducked through the curtain and struck a bronze alarm gong hanging outside the door.

The ship would stop and the electric theorists would get to work with the problem. They had formulas for tracing a fault in the submerged wire. The ohms of resistance had been measured in each cable length before it was stowed. They could send a return current into the trailing cable and compute the distance to the fault by equating ohms, and temperature of water on the floor. Depth temperature was a pure guess on the basis of surfacing water samples. The deep-sounding bathythermograph had not yet been invented. If the gong rang, the ship would have to pick up cable until it brought up the fault.

During the first night, eight-four miles out the light leaped off into the dark and the gong rang. Anderson stopped the ship. Five electrical experts scribbled away at formulae. They predicted that the fault was twenty-two miles, nine, sixty, ten, and forty-two miles astern. Gooch wrote in his diary, 'If our difficulty is known in London it will have very important effect on Atlantic cable shares'. To bring it in was a hard and perilous job. The cable could not be reeled back over the stern. There was no deck engine to haul it in and the ship could not reverse paddles for fear the rising line should foul the propeller. The cable had to be shackled with a retaining iron rope from a yard-arm and cut and carried down the side to a bow pick-up wheel, motivated by a steam windlass. Then the *Great Eastern* would have to be delicately turned about towards Ireland to draw in cable at one mile an hour. She laid cable at six knots.

The sailors sprang upon the yards, bulwarks, boats and guard-walk to pass the severed end on its shackle outboard along the seven-hundred-foot length of deck that they called 'Oxford Street'. It was a dangerous game of cat's cradles, boatswain's chairs, stays, dipping yards, davits, and agile men. They took the telegraph wire to the bow wheel, passed the end through the dynamometer, the sheaves of the brakes, and around the steam drum. The ship bent daintily to the pickup task. Russell said, 'She put one in mind of an elephant taking up a straw in its proboscis'.

All night they rewound cable, which was covered with grey ooze, the microscopic skeletons of millenniums of dead animals on the floor. When ten miles were recovered they came upon the fault. A two-inch sliver of copper wire was driven through the tarred manila wrapping, permitting the electrical current to escape into the water. 'Flagrant evidence of mischief', thought Russell. They cut out the recovered section, passed the end to the paying-out wheel and spliced into the tank cable. They telegraphed to the operators who had been anxiously waiting on a dead wire in Ireland for twelve hours, and the *Great Eastern* resumed her progress. She laid only half a mile before the line went dead again. Captain Anderson stopped the ship. 'Even the gentle equanimity and confidence of Mr. Field were shaken in that supreme hour,' said Russell. They prepared to cut cable and return to the dreary process of reeling it in. Suddenly the galvanometer light flickered on and transmission was clear. The ship made steam again, sixteen hundred miles from Newfoundland.

A small gale came up. 'The *Great Eastern* was steady as a Thames steamer,' said Russell, although, 'the *Terrible* thumped through a heavy sea, and buried her bows in foam.' The escort *Sphinx*, which was making soundings for the cable-layer, fell out of sight, leaving the *Terrible* alone to carry out the swift, destroyer-like reconnaissances which warned passing ships away from the path and wake of the plodding giantess. The cable fell on the long slope of a submarine valley nearly three miles deep.

The process became routine and the men planned shooting in Newfoundland and travels in the States. Russell said they

stretched their legs lustily along the decks, or penetrated with easy curiosity into the recesses of the leviathan. None of them found the hiding-place of the ghost on board the *Great Eastern*, which is believed to be the disembodied essence of a poor plate-riveter, who disappeared in some aperture of the nascent ship, never to be seen of mortal eye again. He is heard at all hours, with ghostly hammer, tap-tap-tapping on the iron walls of his prison, even through the clangour of donkey-engines and the crash of matter. Every hour on board increased our regard for the *Great Eastern*'s qualities, except her capacity for making noise and producing smoke.

Two lazy days passed as the cable uncurled smoothly from the tank, ran along a trough through the brakes and dynamo-meter and over the wheel into the Atlantic. Miles below the black line crossed the valley and climbed the so-called 'Telegraph Ridge', the charting of which by the crippled hydrographer, Lieutenant Matthew Maury, U.S.N., had made Atlantic cable-laying feasible.

At noon on the eighth day, the light jumped off the index and the testing-room reported, 'Dead earth'. The current was entirely leaking into the sea. Again they shackled and cut the cable and the end, shackled to a retaining line, splashed into the water. As the ship idled, gangs of cable-men scrambled forward, passing the retaining line to the bow. The bow wheel brought the end of the cable aboard and they reeled it in during a still, foggy night. On deck blacksmiths worked with open forges beating out repairs for a damaged capstan. Bull Run Russell described the night of anxiety.

Out in the midst of the Atlantic, anvils rang and sparks flew. As the blaze shot up, ruddy, mellow and strong, and flung arms of light aloft and along the glistening decks, and then died into a red centre, masts spars, and ropes were for an instant touched with a golden gleaming, and strange figures and faces were called out from the darkness—vanished—glinted out again—rushed suddenly into foreground of bright pictures, which faded soon away—flickered—went out—as they were called to life by its warm breath, or were buried in the outer darkness. Outside us all was obscurity: but now and then vast shadows, which moved across the arc of lighted fogbank, were projected far away by the flare; and one might well pardon the passing mariner whose bark drifted him in the night across the track of the great ship, if, crossing himself and praying with shuddering lips, he fancied he beheld a phantom ship freighted with an evil crew, and ever after told how he had seen the workshops of the inferno floating on the bosom of the ocean.

Along 'Oxford Street' the cable-men stood searching for the fault by feeling the cold, slimy wire with their hands as it passed. Field remarked, 'I have often known cables to stop working for two hours, no one knows why, and then begin again. Most likely it's some mistake on shore.' Captain Anderson and First Officer Robert Halpin stayed on the bridge and paddle-boxes for twenty-six hours, deftly manœuvring the great ship to avoid straining the cable.

The recovered section was cut out, and the skein spliced to tank cable. The signals carried to Ireland at a perfect electrical impulse of a billion and a half British Association units. The next day the officials gathered beside the testing-room to hold an autopsy on the dead cable. Robert Dudley sketched the coroner's jury standing in Sunday sunlight, a fine group of stags in corduroys, shooting-jackets, billycock hats, and white yachting-caps, watching the chief electrician, C. W. de Sauty, examine the offending cable which was fed to him by a jack tar in whites. Above them slouched an officer on the bridge and the cinders of the *Great Eastern* rose in clouds from the funnels.

The cable was stripped to the core. 'An exclamation literally of horror escaped our lips!' said Russell. Driven right through the centre of the coil was a piece of iron wire,

> bright as if cut with nippers at one end and broken off short at the other. No man who saw it could doubt that the wire had been driven in by a skilful hand. Was it not likely that the former fault had been caused in a similar manner? It was curious that the former fault occurred when the same gang of men were at work in the tank. It was known there were enemies to the manufacturers of the cable; whispers went about that one of the cablemen had expressed gratification when the first fault occurred.

Bull Run's ocean adventure had been full of weary interludes of back-tracking and picking-up. He had not been able to run the cable-ship the way he shook cabinets and instructed generals in strategy. Perhaps the 'exclamation literally of horror' escaped only from Bull Run's avid pen. Sabotage! There were Irishmen in the cable-tanks. A skulking

Fenian might have seen it as his duty to obstruct the English cable.

Samuel Canning, chief engineer of the Telegraph Construction & Maintenance Company, showed the bow cable-men the suspected wire. They said that 'it must have been done on purpose by someone in the tanks'. Bull Run heard mutterings about lynch law.

The suspected tank-crew was transferred to deck duty and Captain Anderson posted watches consisting of officials and drones over the new tankmen. A number of young gentle-men, the sort who pay to accompany expeditions, had been whiling away their time in the grand saloon, playing the piano and whist, and drinking wine while the cable-men worked. The captain was relieved to find something for them to do. It was not their idea of adventure. 'I have to go on watch tonight in that wretched tank', said one, 'to stand for two hours in a tank of cable covered with tar, and, like a girl on a skipping-rope, jump over the cable as it runs out, or sit on the edge of an iron bar with legs upraised.'

The *Great Eastern* crossed the halfway mark. At dawn on August 2, Bull Run was awakened by an odd sensation. He looked out of his porthole and saw that the ship was paddling backward. He ran to the testing-room. His sabotage theory was exploded. When the new mishap occurred, Cyrus Field himself was on watch in the cable tank, wrapped in his Inverness cape and wearing his specs and a deerstalker cap. Field heard a grating noise. A tankman yelled, 'There goes a piece of wire!' pointing up to the cable passing out through a canvas funnelling apparatus nicknamed the 'crinoline'. Field yelled up to the deck watch, but the alarm did not reach the brakeman in time to check the fault before it slid into the sea. The accident fanned sparks from a corporate friction aboard the *Great Eastern*.

There were two parties of technicians aboard. The first belonged to the Telegraph Construction & Maintenance Company of London, led by Samuel Canning, who was top boss of the cable-layers, and his chief electrician, C. W. de

Sauty. The managing director of this company, Richard Glass, was also aboard. Cyrus Field had leased them the contract for laying and maintaining the cable in return for most of the actual capital laid out for the third expedition. They had manufactured the cable, chartered the *Great Eastern* and completely controlled the laying.

The second group was led by Field and his electrical superintendent, Cromwell F. Varley, representing the Atlantic Telegraph Company. Professor William Thomson of Glasgow University was their scientific adviser. Professor Thomson was the greatest physicist of the era. He is better known by his later title, Lord Kelvin, which he was given after fifty-one years in the chair of natural philosophy at Glasgow. Thomson lives in physics as the formulator of the second law of dynamics. He established today's standards of electrical measurement. He revolutionized the mariner's compass and was the foremost theoretician of submarine telegraphy. The cable was designed on his principles, and his invention, the mirror galvanometer, was essential to laying it. He was an expert of far greater calibre than de Sauty, but the latter could overrule him aboard the cable ship. De Sauty was uneasy, however, because when they reached Newfoundland, the contract gave Field, Varley, and Thomson the right to refuse the job as sub-standard.

Now here was the cable dead again and the experts at odds. Professor Thomson, who was a shy, almost diffident man, opined that in this case the fault might work itself out. He explained: 'When the current is sent through a wire from one pole it produces an electro-chemical reaction on the wire, and at the place of an injury, it leads to a deposit of a salt of copper in the breach, and impedes the escape of electricity; and when the opposite current is returned, the deposit is reduced and hydrogen gas formed, a globule of which may rest in the chink, and by its non-conducting power, restore the insulation of the cable for a time.'

The professor thought the cable could transmit four words a minute, enough for 'an amply remunerative return'. De

Sauty more or less agreed, but Canning would not take a chance of Cyrus Field's refusing the job in Newfoundland. Canning ordered the cable to be picked up to find the fault. Then a tankman showed up with a small piece of wire he had grabbed off the cable as it uncoiled. It was similar to the piece of wire which had started the sabotage rumours. This discovery made them think that the cable was suicidal. Bull Run pulled in his horns.

Now they were trailing 1,186 miles of cable. The cable was cut, and dropped, secured by its grapple and iron rope. Although the wire was partially alive, de Sauty neglected to telegraph Ireland about the new accident before the cut was made. The severed cable was carried back successfully to the pickup gear in the bow. There was a slight starboard wind which chafed the inreeling cable against the rims of the *Great Eastern's* stem hawseholes. The stress shown on the dynamometer was heavy, but not near the breaking-point. Suddenly there was a jerk, caused perhaps by the ship, or by the shackle fastened to the cable. Russell said, 'The cable parted, flew through the stoppers, and with one bound leaped over intervening space and flashed into the sea. The cable gone! gone for ever down in that fearful depth! There around us lay the placid Atlantic, smiling in the sun, and not a dimple to show where lay so many hopes buried.'

Samuel Canning was a man of purpose. He had supervised the two lost cables of the fifties, and would not surrender his third effort. He decided to grapple. There were men aboard who had fished up Mediterranean cables from depths of seven hundred fathoms, but the Atlantic telegraph was lost miles down. No one knew the depth. The *Sphinx*, carrying their only depth-sounding gear, had not been seen for six days. Canning broke out a small five-hook grapnel on five miles of wire rope. Captain Anderson steamed fourteen miles into the wind and shut down both paddle- and screw-engines. First Officer Robert Halpin rapped out orders to the boat-swain, who relayed them in a stentorian voice to the sailors.

On this unique occasion, the *Great Eastern* went under sail, and sail alone. They shook out canvas on Monday and Saturday masts and spread the vast square-sails on Tuesday and Wednesday. As the biggest sailing-ship the world will ever see, the *Great Eastern* glided towards Telegraph Ridge. In a heavy silence, they let the grapnel line over the bow pickup-wheel. The small squeals of the machinery were the only sound on the water.

After several hours the dynamometer showed a lessening strain on the line, perhaps indicating that the grapnel had touched bottom. They calculated it was three miles down. None could hope that they would recover a cable at this depth. Some said the grapnel would foul a rock and rip loose. If, by a miracle, it did hook fast, it would probably tear the cable in two, said others. The cable consisted of seven copper wires twisted in soft rubber, then wrapped with eight thicknesses of rubber compound, and covered by ten charcoal-iron wires spun in tarred manila yarn. The whole was a little over an inch thick. As Captain Anderson put it, 'Cable? Thread!' The *Great Eastern* slowly and silently drifted towards the unmarked patch of ocean under which lay a million pound investment and the long endeavours of Cyrus Field and his men.

All evening and night the *Great Eastern* worked slowly towards Telegraph Ridge. At 6 a.m. the bow turned slightly and the dynamometer registered a heavy strain on the grappling line. 'We've caught it! We've caught it!' the yell went around. The pull was steady. They had hooked something on the bottom, but was it the cable? Canning ordered the grapnel to be hauled in. The grapnel wire was not a continuous line, but one pieced together of twenty-five lengths of a hundred fathoms each, joined by shackles and swivels. In the first two hours the cablemen brought in four of these joints. The wire snapped once, but the brakeman caught it before it flickered into the sea. Two cablemen were severely lacerated in the face by the parting line. By early afternoon they had brought in about two-fifths of its length, when a swivel pin gave way and the line, grapnel and cable fell to the sea floor.

Fog enveloped the ship as they marked the spot with a big red buoy topped by a black ball and a red flag. They moored the buoy with a mushroom anchor and three miles of the cable itself. Canning ordered the cable men to rig a second grapnel. Whistling and firing the cannons to warn off the *Terrible* in the fog, the *Great Eastern* steamed away to attempt another blind grope on the bottom. The rope-makers improvised depth-sounding tackle with all the spare manila they could find aboard and hove it over. They believed the sinker to have reached bottom two and three-quarter miles down, but, as they hauled in, the line broke and another tangle of thread settled on the bottom.

All that day and night the great ship drifted in 'a grey and polished surface of cloud'. In the eerie quiet, shoals of big grampuses and porpoises larked round the high iron flanks. The wind was not right for the course of drift, so Canning held the grapnel. The fog persisted through the fourth day. No sun or stars were visible with which to fix their position. Russell was bored. He lay on a sofa in the ladies' saloon, musing on the questionable charm of the assignment he had picked. 'You were really on the bosom of the Atlantic', he wrote, 'not a bulkhead creaking, not a lamp moving, or a glass jiggling. The *Great Eastern* is a wonder!' Some of the officials proposed that they steam to Newfoundland and commandeer warships to grapple for the cable. Others wanted to go to England and get proper fishing-gear. There was a peep of sun on the fifth day and the wind was right for drifting under headsails. Canning lowered the second grapnel.

Again they struck something and began reeling in. As the stress continued they knew they had hooked the cable again. By midnight they had recovered three hundred fathoms of iron rope. A beautiful moon brightened this hopeful night, and the line came aboard at a rate promising that they would see the cable before nightfall of the next day. They had hauled a mile of grappling line aboard at 8 p.m., when a swivel parted exactly as had the previous one. 'The rope flew around the capstan, over the drum, through the stops,' said Russell. 'The end of the rope flourished its iron fist in the air, and struck out right and left with it, as though it were animated by a desire to destroy those who might arrest its progress. It passed through the line of cablemen with an impatient sweep, dashed at one man's head, was only baulked by his sudden stoop, and menacing from side to side the men at the bow, splashed overboard.' The *Great Eastern* signalled the news to the *Terrible* and the escort replied, 'Very sorry'. There was left on board nineteen hundred fathoms of wire rope and five hundred fathoms of manila hawser, and the indomitable Canning. He ordered another try.

The wind rose in the afternoon and by nightfall there was a half-gale blowing. The sea ran high and the great ship rolled uneasily. On the seventh morning they lost the buoy. All day the cable-ship and her escort hunted the buoy in the stormy gloom. On the rainswept deck smiths hammered out new shackles and swivels. The ropemakers went over the three miles of wire and manila line. Captain Anderson miraculously found the red buoy in late afternoon.

The eighth day was clear and sunny, and the third grapnel was let down in the morning. The *Great Eastern* glided over the cable without making contact. Canning brought up the grapnel and found that it had tangled with its own chain so that it could not have picked up the cable.

The twisted and mutilated line was repaired overnight and pieced together with 1,600 fathoms of wire rope, 220 fathoms of hemp and 510 fathoms of manila. The ropemakers said a third of the line was 'suspicious'. Nevertheless Canning ordered it to be sent down on the ninth morning. In the afternoon the dynamometer registered a strain that meant contact with the cable. They reeled in the fourth grappling line. The young gentlemen could not bear the suspense. They went below to the grand saloon and listened to the piano. 'None liked to go forward, where every jar of the machinery, every shackle that passed the drum, every clank, made their hearts leap into their mouths,' said Russell.

In the evening Russell heard a whistle from the bridge, and agitated cries from the bow. Their last grappling line had parted into the sea. The watch officer methodically entered in the log: 'Latitude 51° 24′ Longitude 38° 59′; end of cable down North 50 West 1¾ mile.' The heroic venture had been lost. The *Great Eastern* set her course home into the rising sun. The lantern of the *Terrible* flashed, 'Farewell!' and the signalmen replied from the paddle-box of the *Great Eastern*, 'Good-bye. Thank you.'

The ship's newspaper maintained its saucy spirit in the hour of defeat. It referred to the lost cable as 'the sea serpent', upon which their 'bait was useless'. It announced that the next day Captain Anderson would hold an auction of the *Great Eastern*, the good-will of the Atlantic Telegraph Company, and Bull Run Russell's free pass on the Cunard Line from America back to Britain. Cyrus Field, who carried the deepest wound, laughed dryly at the jokes. He was busy with Professor Thomson, Glass, and Canning drawing up the prospectus for the third Atlantic Telegraph Company.

The operators in Ireland had watched a dead line for ten days. A superstitious chorus of 'I told you so' arose in Britain. Many were willing to believe that the *Great Eastern* had sunk. While the defeated ship was steaming home, the anti-Brunel camp explained that the *Great Eastern* had never been strong enough, that she had probably fagged in the middle, or had hogged, which is that unfortunate situation when a ship's stern and bow fall away. As she approached Crookhaven, on the sixteenth day of silence, an enterprising news agent met them in his boat and yelled, 'We thought you went down'. The cable-men gave him the complete story to telegraph to the newspapers while the ship continued around to the Nore. The safe return of the cable-ship set off public rejoicing. The cable-men told everyone of the admirable performance of the *Great Eastern*. In the hour of her

deepest failure, the big ship was a heroine. And Cyrus Field
was the hero. He had eclipsed biblical Job, who had endured
only seven years of misery. Field had survived eight years
of knockouts, and still had some time to go.

By the spring of '66 Field, Gooch and Glass had reorgan-
ized the cable company at a capitalization of $3,000,000,
and loaded a new cable on the *Great Eastern*. Bull Run
Russell did not go with them this time. He was diverted by
the Seven Weeks' War. As the *Great Eastern* passed the Nore
the guardship band played, 'Good-bye Sweetheart, Good-
bye'. Daniel Gooch was stirred at the sight of a little Cork
steam-tug, which assisted them in Bantry Bay. The tug bore
the name, *Brunel*.

The *Great Eastern's* second cable-voyage embarked an
even larger group of young gentlemen. Their adventurous
illusions were promptly shattered when Samuel Canning
placed them on watch in the cable-tanks. He ordered them
to wear fantastic canvas dresses which covered their elegant
persons from head to foot, hooked up the back and had no
pockets. The company had so designed the gowns to fore-
stall attempts to carry sabotage tools. The *Great Eastern*
departed amidst the cries of its deck passengers, ten bullocks,
a milch cow, a hundred sheep, twenty pigs and five hundred
fowl. The 1866 cable whirred smoothly into the ocean.

On July 22 the Foilhummerum operator relayed to London:

FIELD TO GLASS: THE GREAT EASTERN HAS PASSED THE PLACE
WHERE THE CABLE WAS LOST LAST YEAR AND ALL IS GOING WELL.

The next day:

FIELD TO GLASS: PLEASE OBTAIN THE LATEST NEWS FROM EGYPT
CHINA INDIA AND DISTANT PLACES FOR US TO FORWARD TO THE
UNITED STATES ON OUR ARRIVAL AT HEARTS CONTENT.

The following day, a Tuesday:

FIELD TO GLASS: WE ARE WITHIN FOUR HUNDRED MILES OF
HEARTS CONTENT AND EXPECT TO BE THERE ON FRIDAY WHEN
SHALL THE ATLANTIC CABLE BE OPEN FOR PUBLIC BUSINESS.

The reply came:

GLASS TO FIELD : I SEE NO REASON WHY IT SHOULD NOT BE OPEN
SATURDAY.

On Thursday, July 26, 1866, they carried the cable ashore
to the Hearts Content relay station from which lines already
ran to Canada. Veteran cable-men carried high the end of
the black wire that ran under the wide sea to Europe. They
capered round it like Druids. Gooch said, 'One man actually
put the end in his mouth and sucked it'. The next day they
made the final splice. The Queen sent greetings to President
Johnson. Wall Street read the closing quotations from the
City, the Bourse and the Brussels grain market. Europe
learned that the State of Tennessee had been readmitted to
the Union. The mighty measures of *The Times* leader on
the completion of the Atlantic telegraph were cabled in
full and posted on the ship. Canning and Professor Thomson joined the revel of the crew and a giggle of local girls,
invited aboard to help celebrate. The dancing kept Daniel
Gooch awake. He imparted his new-found joy to his diary,
'Yesterday we had fifty messages, paying us, I suppose not
less than twelve hundred pounds'. The rate was 5s. a word.

FIELD TO MRS. FIELD NEWBURG NEW YORK: WE LEAVE IN ABOUT
A WEEK TO RECOVER THE CABLE OF LAST YEAR.

The *Great Eastern* returned to the red buoy with the black
ball under which lay the 1865 cable. They grappled three
times and brought it up. Field said, 'One of the most interesting scenes I have ever witnessed was the moment when,
after the cable had been recovered, it was brought to the
electrician's room to see whether it was alive or dead. Never
shall I forget that eventful moment when, in answer to our
question to Valentia, in an instant came back those memor-
able letters, O.K. I left the room, went to my cabin and locked
the door. I could no longer retain my tears.' They buoyed
off the '65 telegraph and ran for Britain for cable to string
on to Newfoundland.

CANNING TO GLASS : I HAVE MUCH PLEASURE IN SPEAKING TO
YOU THROUGH THE EIGHTEEN SIXTY FIVE CABLE JUST GOING TO
MAKE SPLICE.

The *Great Eastern* steamed home from Newfoundland a happy ship. The cable-men pitched quoits and got up theatricals. The Bishop of Newfoundland, who was a passenger, laughed so hard he broke up the actors. He had not seen a play in forty years.

The victorious ship launched six baronets, whom Victoria dubbed Captain Sir James Anderson, Professor Sir William Thomson, Sir Richard Glass, Sir Samuel Canning, Sir Curtis Lampson (a company director), and Sir Daniel Gooch. There was no title for John Scott Russell, nor any posthumous honour for Isambard Kingdom Brunel.

CHAPTER TWELVE

LE GRAND ORIENTAL

CHARLES LOUIS NAPOLEON BONAPARTE was the name of the scheming mountebank who ruled France from 1848 to 1871. A nephew of the original Napoleon, this histrionic type started out as a 'liberal' with a grab bag of theories varying from socialism to his own divine right. He passed his youth in exile, and served six years in the fortress at Ham for a hare-brained attempt at a *coup d'état* in 1840. He escaped, resumed his plotting from Britain, and became President of the French Republic in a controlled election after the defeat of the 1848 rising. He proclaimed himself Emperor Napoleon III four years later, to avert embarrassment of a one-term presidential law. Then he gaoled and exiled his Republican friends.

His travesty of an empire included bits from his uncle's script and features of the old Roman promotion, cheap bread and holidays, with a modern overlay of press-agentry, big war talk and plenty of loot for the boys in the back room. As was inevitable, this inflated personality and the *Great Eastern* came together in 1867, when Louis Napoleon produced a fête that surpassed New York's delirious summer of 1860. First, the imperial showman dreamed up the circus, then he leaped up one night from an inventive doze crying, '*Le Grand Oriental!*' He was planning a Universal Exhibition to knock the previous ones into a row of camp meetings. And the *Great Eastern* was just the carry-all to speed myriads of rich Americans to Paris. Napoleon III saw millions in it.

The *Great Eastern*'s owners harkened to the hullabaloo from Paris, and lost no time in baiting the impetuous monarch. An alarming story reached France that Napoleon was about to lose to a rival sublimity of immense wealth and insatiable yearning for the monster ship. The directors had long made a speciality of rumours, and this one was a beauty. His Transcendent Highness, Sultan Abdul-Aziz of Turkey wanted the *Great Eastern* as a harem. His grand vizier, Ali Pasha, was said to be hastening to London to buy the ship and start installing pillows. The scenario was ready-made for an emperor who considered himself the biggest potentate in Christendom. He sent emissaries pelting to London to beat the grand vizier. Louis Napoleon had picked out his most deserving intimates to grow rich from the big ship, and he had them so heated up that they capitalized for two million francs, which was then worth £80,000, and formed the *Société des Affréteurs du Great Eastern* (Company of *Great Eastern* Charterers). Toasts were rapturous when word came that Napoleon's emissaries had wrested the precious ship from the clutch of Islam.

The *affréteurs* engaged G. Forrester & Company of Liverpool to make the *Great Eastern* ready. She was glided on to the four-hundred-foot gridiron at New Ferry, and the hull stripped of a mat of grey weed that looked like coarse hair. A thousand artisans went to work knocking out the cable-tanks and restoring two boilers and the fourth funnel, which had been removed for cable stowage. The Board of Trade, mindful of her rough service as a cable-layer, advised the *affréteurs* she would need a thorough hull and engine survey before she could have a passenger certificate. The inspectors found a kink in the main paddle-shaft. The charterers had figured an outlay of half a million francs, but extra thousand-franc notes peeled away like artichoke leaves at the Café Anglais.

Like everyone else, the charterers had the ship's original propaganda handouts firmly imbedded in their concept of her. They enjoined Forrester's to be sure and restore the original elegant accommodations for four thousand passengers. The French were unaware that the ship had never been fitted for more than fifteen hundred. The contractor gave them what they wanted. Twenty-seven thousand yards of linen tick and forty tons of curled hair and wool went on the bill. Thirty thousand yards of linen and eleven thousand yards of towelling were added. To assure adequate mess facilities, three dining saloons were erected on the main deck, the first intimation of liner superstructure. They were decorated in gilt and silver with lemon panelling.

In this fashion Brunel's floating city at last came true, at the behest of France where his father was born, where he was educated, and whose inventive passion had nurtured his grand ideas. The French are not often thought of as the world's leading gadgeteers, but they are. Their genius for contrivance often fails, owing to lack of the capital and organization Britons and Americans line up behind an idea. The *affréteurs* even rigged steam steering apparatus, another drawing-board feature that got lost in the panic of the launching. The *Great Eastern* was the first ship to install this feature. The total bill for reconversion was £50,000. The Emperor's friends thought nothing of it. Four or five full passenger lists of American rock oil and railway nabobs would bring in a million dollars on each two-way journey and soon put this extravagant charter outlay in proper perspective.

The maiden French voyage was advertised for March 23, 1867, from Liverpool. Fitting-out and provisioning was not completed for three more days, during which time the charterers put up twelve hundred passengers in hotels. One said the French 'behaved very handsomely towards us in other respects'.

There were many distinguished passengers, including Cyrus Field, Mr. and Mrs. Alfred Cohen of San Francisco, James MacAlpine of New York, the Hon. John Rose of Toronto, and William Barber, the company director. Huge bills for reconversion awaited not only the Frenchmen but Gooch and Barber. The Telegraph Construction Company put twenty thousand pounds into the enterprise, since the passenger-carrying venture might prove to be the renascence and vindication of the *Great Eastern*. Gooch put Barber aboard to keep an eye on things, and the company director, Sir James Anderson, assumed command of the ship.

An unremarked passenger was a young French science fiction writer named Jules Verne, who had published several fanciful novels not yet translated into English, about voyages to the centre of the earth and to the moon. In order to report the *Great Eastern's* French venture, he had interrupted work on his new novel, *Vingt mille lieues sous les mers* (*Twenty Thousand Leagues Under the Sea*). The big ship was a matchless thing to Verne: he might have imagined it, had not Brunel and Scott Russell already wrought it in iron. He came aboard while the fitters were still at work on many marvels, including the new steam steering apparatus. Verne witnessed the ultimate preposterous effort of the *affréteurs* to realize Brunel's drawings:

> A small steamer, intended as a shore boat for the *Great Eastern,* came alongside. Her movable engine was first hoisted aboard by means of windlasses, but as for the steamer herself, she could not be embarked. Her steel hull was so heavy that the davits to which it was attached bent under the weight. Therefore they were obliged to abandon the steamer.

On sailing day a stiff wind forced First Officer Halpin to employ men on the capstan bars to aid the donkey engines in weighing anchor. The port bow donkey engine failed when the ten-ton anchor was part way up, placing the entire strain on the men. One of the capstan pins snapped and the anchor dropped, spinning the capstan like a top. Men were swept down and thrown in all directions, and the capstan bars flew like projectiles. They struck five men, of whom two were killed. Halpin had a narrow escape. 'This event made very little impression on board,' said Verne. 'These unhappy men, killed and wounded, were only tools, which could be replaced at very little expense.' A passenger disembarked with the dead—he had had enough of the *Great Eastern*.

At sea Verne observed the passengers at the first meal:

F

The Californians certainly distinguished themselves by their proclivities for champagne. Near her husband sat an old laundress, who had found gold in San Francisco washing tubs. She emptied a bottle of champagne in no time. Three pale, delicate-looking young ladies eagerly gobbled slices of red beef. Everyone worked away in the highest spirits; one could have fancied oneself at a restaurant in the middle of Paris. When lunch was over, the decks were filled: people bowed and spoke to each other in passing as formally as if they were walking in Hyde Park: children played and ran about, throwing their balls and bowling hoops. Corpulent Americans swung themselves backward and forwards in their rocking-chairs.

It was indeed 'a floating subprefecture'.

In the saloons three pianos and an organ sounded all day long. Verne said,

> I noticed a tall, bony woman who had marked all the notes with numbers, and the piano keys with numbers corresponding. She struck key twenty-seven, key fifty-three, and so on, perfectly indifferent to the noise around her and to some disagreeable little children who thumped with their fists on the unoccupied keys.

He watched a group of men with an 'easy-going air, their legs stretched on the sofas, and hats screwed down on their heads. They are Yankees—pure Yankees. Put two of them in a room together, and in an hour they will have profited ten dollars from each other.' There was a tall 'man of importance', a Chicago banker, 'who always carries an album under his arm, with the principal views of his beloved city'. Verne met a Peruvian honeymoon couple, Elder Obediah Hatch of the Church of the Latter Day Saints, and a Frenchman who was carrying to America thirty thousand papier-mâché dolls, which, according to the novelist, said 'Papa' with 'a very successful Yankee accent'.

Among the handful of French passengers was one of far greater celebrity than Verne—Paul du Chaillu, the first white man to observe live gorillas. He had recently returned from a trek to Ashangoland, where he had discovered a new sensation, pygmies. The explorer gave two lectures to the passengers and Captain Anderson regaled them with the story of the Atlantic cable. The steward department organized a benefit concert for the widows of the capstan victims and raised £100. Captain Anderson did card tricks, while above him, 'through the half-open hatchways', said Verne, 'might be seen the broad, sunburnt faces, and the great black hands of the sailors'. At the concert's end, when 'God Save the Queen' was announced, some Yankees prevailed on the Frenchman at the piano to strike up the 'Marseillaise'. The Americans roared the song in a perfect silence of English people. The pianist averted an awkward situation by vamping on into 'God Save', and the Queen had the last word. 'This soirée was as good as amateur soirées usually are', Verne said, 'that is to say, it was chiefly a success for the performers and their friends.'

Captain Anderson ran at low speed. His new engine parts tended to overheat and he faced strong headwinds and squalls. In the 'blink', the misty iceberg zone, Anderson had a bucket of sea water drawn every half-hour to take water temperature. A colder sea indicated that ice blocks were near and Anderson altered his course. It was the traditional method of subarctic navigation. The original *Great Eastern* directors had failed to install the pump Brunel designed for the blink zone, which would have continuously poured sea water over a thermometer on the bridge.

Elder Hatch tacked up an announcement for a lecture on Mormonism in the grand saloon. A delegation of panicky puritan ladies prevailed on Sir James Anderson to forbid it, lest their 'husbands become acquainted with the mysteries of Mormonism', Verne said. The captain improved the physical tone of the husbands by leading gymnastic exercises on deck. 'About fifty unemployed men, each armed, like himself, with a stick, imitated all his movements with strict exactitude', said Verne, who was content to watch.

The *Great Eastern* was making a weak ten knots when the cyclone came. Verne was on the bridge with the captain and Robert Halpin. They were enveloped in spray and the ship faltered. Verne reported:

The Captain was smiling as usual and the first officer laughed, and showed his white teeth, at the sight of the ship pitching enough to make one think the masts and chimneys were coming down.

Sir James refused to yield to the storm. He kept course and would not turn her head to the wind.

I was really astonished at the Captain's obstinacy. The sea swept right across the deck at the bows. I watched this grand sight; this struggle between the giant and the billows, and to a certain extent I could sympathize with the Captain's wilfulness; but I was forgetting that the power of the sea is infinite, and nothing made by hand of man can resist it.

A towering sea struck the port bow and smashed away its massive nine-foot bulwarks. Hundreds of tons of water rolled down the deck, sweeping up men and crumpling the sky-lights. A large volume fell into the ladies' saloon, but no ladies were under it. The ocean spread with wreckage. Anderson took smart evasive action to avoid fouling his paddle-wheels. Sailors went forward to clear the deck debris. Verne wrote:

Suddenly there was another swoop, more violent than the first, and the sea poured through the breach, ripped off an enormous sheet of cast-iron, which covered the prow, broke away the massive top of the hatchway leading to the forecastle, and carried off the starboard barricades like the sheets of a sail.

A red-whiskered officer arose from the flood, picked up an unconscious sailor and carried him off on his back. The others dived through the open forecastle hatch. Verne continued,

There was three feet of water in the 'tween-decks. New spars covered the sea, and amongst them were thousands of dolls which my countryman had thought to acclimatize in America. The little bodies, torn from their cases by the sea, danced on the summits of the waves.

Captain Anderson understood at last. I saw him run to the little wheel on the bridge, and the giant ship, turning like a canoe, made head toward the north, and fled before the storm. At this moment, the Captain, generally so calm and self-possessed, cried passionately—'My ship is disgraced!'

The *Great Eastern* shipped no more water, as she ran with the gale. Chief Engineer George Beckwith estimated two thousand tons of water in the holds. He put the pumps to work on 'the lagoon that had formed there'.

Sir James Anderson's *amour-propre* returned as things quieted down the next day. Entertainments and lectures were resumed. Three sailors blacked up, fastened sea-biscuit buttons on their coats, and plunked out a 'Brudder Bones' routine for the people. Men returned to the smoking-room, where gigantic gambling games had raged the way across. The sailor died who had been knocked out by the wave and was sewn in canvas with a cannonball at his feet and slid into the brine. Chips, the chief carpenter, busied his men with temporary bulwarks.

Her own-made cable had notified New York of the *Great Eastern*'s departure. When she failed to appear after eleven days, the agents fidgeted. Two more days passed without report and 'the soothsayers had begun to shake their heads and shrug their shoulders', said the *New York Times*. On the fourteenth day the Montauk lightkeeper telegraphed that she had been sighted, and the city got ready to show its emotion. Four years had passed since the *Great Eastern* had last been seen in New York. Off Fire Island the pilot came aboard. 'He wore a glazed hat, black trousers, a brown overcoat lined with red, and carried an umbrella,' said Verne. The pilot brought a bundle of newspapers and the passengers rent the package. The *affréteurs* invited everybody to have champagne on them at the farewell dinner as the great ship paddled into New York Bay.

The city greeted the ship handsomely. The war had faded into uninteresting political wrangles about carpetbaggers, reconstruction, and scallywags, and the 'Leviathan Gallop' was revived. The money panic and the cholera epidemic of 1866 that carried off five thousand residents had subsided. It was feast and forget. Among the forgotten was Customs Inspector No. 75, novelist Herman Melville, whose West Street office handled the *Great Eastern* in the North River. His 'vast toy' lowered her hooks into the Hoboken-New York link of the continental telegraph. The ship was to tear apart the cable as she weighed the anchor a week later.

Verne checked into the Fifth Avenue Hotel, and walked down Broadway to Barnum's Theatre, where he caught a play called *New York Streets*, the climax of which were a fire on stage and the appearance of 'real fire-engines, worked by real firemen'. He took a boat to Albany and a train through 'the land of Fenimore Cooper', the Mohawk Valley. 'All this theatre of the grand *épopée* of Leather Stocking, formerly a savage country, is now a civilized land,' Verne noted with a hint of disappointment. He and his travelling companion called each other Hawk's Eye and Chingachgook, and went to see Niagara Falls.

The novelist returned in time for the ship's sailing with her first four thousand Americans for the Paris Exhibition. His entire description of the return voyage consisted of, 'Twelve days later we reached Brest.' It was all Verne had the heart to say. There were only 191 passengers.

The *New York Times* adduced some Customs House figures to show the extent of the disaster. Port dues based on the *Great Eastern*'s tonnage were £1,209 and £60 more had gone to the harbourmaster. She had also to pay agent's commissions, printing, advertising, pilotage, suppliers, and clearance dues, bringing the New York cash demand to at least £2,000—half the fares she had received. The *Times* estimated that the voyage would lose about £20,000.

'Notwithstanding this unpleasant exhibit,' said the paper, 'we are assured that she will positively return to this port to fulfill the contract now being made with passengers, that she shall sail again on the 28th of May, and again on the 9th day of July.' The *Times* said the lack of passengers was due to rough weather and

the fact that the Exposition is not yet the attraction that it may
be a month hence; and the disappointment felt generally in
the slowness of her passage to this port. If she makes a good
trip out this time, there is reason to hope that the summer
traffic may in some measure realize the expectations.

As Jules Verne and the *Great Eastern* went down the bay,
it was the last time New York was to see the Wonder of the
Waves.

When the ship decanted her corporal's guard of Americans
at Brest, Napoleon's embarrassment was so grievous that the
French press tactfully omitted all mention of the voyage. In
fact, the charter affair has not been deemed worthy of mention in the history of the Second Empire. The bands struck
up and the fair was on.

The Universal Exhibition on the Champ-de-Mars centred
round a large glass and iron palace built to resemble an illu-
minating gas-tank. It contained the latest achievements of
science and art—Herr Krupp's cannon, an illustrated sylla-
bus of the advances in bacteriology, paintings by Millet and
hunks of a mysterious new metal called aluminium. The
Triumph of Machinery was displayed in the periphery of the
hall; in the inner ring there was a show of the Rise of Civiliza-
tion from the Stone Age to Louis Napoleon.

Paris was the Paris of Louis's wife, Eugénie-Marie de
Montijo de Guzman, the lady of the feathered fore-and-aft
bonnets. The city danced to the operettas of Offenbach. His
latest piece, *Bluebeard*, had given Paris its lip tune, '*La Vie
Parisienne*', and he was mounting a special exhibition musical, *The Duchess of Gerolstein*, starring Hortense Schneider,
a *vedette* who accounted it a poor week when a prince or
royal duke did not leave her a bejewelled pretty under her
pillow. The new façade of the Opera was unveiled and Baron
Haussmann's boulevards, bulldozed through medieval Paris,
were opened. The *Great Eastern*'s passengers were swallowed in ten million visitors, the first people to stroll the
glorious Champs Élysées and the Grands Boulevards. Few
of them knew Napoleon's key instructions to Haussmann, to

cut strategic routes for deploying troops against a resurge of the Communards. 'The world made a pilgrimage to the Great Exhibition and learned to recognize itself', said a student of those times.

Napoleon III entertained fifty-seven reigning monarchs and crown princes, virtually a census of the current kinghood. Among those who helped to take his mind off the *Great Eastern* were Czar Alexander I, William of Prussia, the kings of Bavaria, Portugal, and Sweden, and that young man who loved to leave home, Edward Prince of Wales. Louis also got a sultan (not the dreadful Abdul-Aziz, however), and was exploding starshells, champagne corks, and garters for him, when the disturbing news came that Maximilian I was not coming. He was a handsome Austrian *dummkopf* whom Louis Napoleon had inserted in an improvised Mexican crown while the United States was busy at war. His less than grateful Indian subjects had placed Maximilian against a wall and shot him.

Among the notables who came to the show was Prince Otto von Bismarck. The humourless soldier saw Mlle Schneider in Offenbach's frivolous military satire, and enjoyed it very much. To Bismarck it seemed the French were out of humour with soldiering, were ruled by a fool and were ready for the plucking. Bismarck's smash and grab at Sedan was only three years away, when he would take a hundred thousand betrayed Frenchmen, with the Emperor at the top of the bag. The summer of the Universal Fair was 'the sunset glory of the Second Empire'.

Chic new Seine steamers carried people to the Fair. In the Prussian restaurant a young, obscure Viennese bandmaster named Johann Strauss introduced one of his compositions that had failed in his home town, and Paris whirled to 'The Blue Danube Waltz'. *Nouveau riche* Brazilians blew in, loaded with contos, and were cleaned out by the girls of the half-world, who had been reinforced to twice normal strength by an influx of provincial talent. They provided counterpoint to one of the scholarly conventions Louis had brought to Paris, the International Medical Congress for Combating Sexual Diseases.

The lovely music in France sounded sour to Sir Daniel Gooch, who held £20,000 in unpaid fitting-bills left by Louis Napoleon's light-footed dancers. Gooch ordered Captain Anderson to bring the ship back to Liverpool, before Napoleon charged up another sou. There the crew was discharged without pay to mingle with the unremunerated fitters. The seamen marched on the Great Ship Company offices in Castle Street and made 'very insistent demands for their wages'. Sir James came out to speak to them. He expressed hearty sympathy and said they ought to take out summonses against the Frenchmen.

The crew went away and saw a solicitor, who applied in the Court of Admiralty to seize the ship on behalf of the men. Sir James advised them to cut the wage demand to the actual voyage time and offered to pay that sum from the Great Ship Company. The men said no; they had signed articles for three months and they wanted three months' wages. A purser and seaman went to the police court and obtained a summons for Sir James himself. The injured parties weren't going to chase French wisps—they went after the directors. J. W. Carr, a solicitor, formalized the new and alarming turn of affairs by handing affidavits supporting a demand on the company for £4,500, representing three months' wages for three hundred men. It reveals a man's wages in the mid-Victorian merchant navy: five pounds a month. Sir James refused to pay it. He insisted that the claim was too high.

The Master of the Court of Admiralty issued an order to the Receiver of Wrecks to seize the *Great Eastern*, and the ship was so attached. Sir James declared the men would not get a penny for acting in this way, and withdrew the offer to pay voyage time. With the ship in receivership, the directors had been dealt high cards again. Sir Daniel Gooch was busy in London. He assumed the chairmanship of the Telegraph Construction & Maintenance Company and there were big

F*

deals afoot. One was that 'a new and influential company with a large capital' was going to give the Paris exhibition trade another try. This rumour was allowed to run its very short course. Liverpool papers flouted another that Gooch was organizing a third Atlantic cable expedition. He was doing just that. In London Sir Daniel was holding full-dress *pourparlers* with Baron d'Érlanger and Julius Reuter of the French Telegraph Cable Company.

CHAPTER THIRTEEN

THE FRENCH TELEGRAPH

Paul Julius Reuter, the latest prospect for trampling by the juggernaut, was a German banker's son, a slender, fast-moving man with side-wheel whiskers and a sharp feel for the mid-century changes. In 1849 he saw the thing that beat banking. A land telegraph was strung from Paris east to Verviers and a westward line from Berlin to Aix-la-Chapelle (Aachen), leaving a ten-mile gap on the uneasy Franco-German border. Reuter figured there was money to be made by a communications shuttle through the silent zone. Accordingly he posted his wife at Aix and went to Verviers, and they exchanged messenger pigeons.

Another recent phenomenon, the metropolitan daily newspaper, was emerging on the basis of the rotary printing press and prompt publication of stock exchange and produce market reports and diplomatic news. The current round of revolutions in western Europe sharpened the demand for rapid communications between restless cities and uneasy thrones. The telegraph and the modern newspaper were interdependent; one could not have come without the other, a fact Reuter appreciated. Banking, the market, politics and commerce were all part of the wedding of electricity and paper. Reuter set out to organize German intelligence sources to provide fast exclusive reports to Paris journals. The French press was not ready for the advanced concept. Reuter took it to London, where the air was crackling with big ideas. He opened an office in the City to sell his service to stockbrokers and newspapers. The Great Exhibition year was important to Reuter. In 1851, he became a British sub-

ject and one of the best customers of the newly operating
Dover-Calais submarine cable. An earlier Channel cable had
been destroyed by a French fisherman, who hauled it in, cut
out a hunk, and sailed home to show part of a golden snake
he had found in the sea.

Reuters Ltd., founded in 1851, was the father of international press bureaus and remains the leading British
agency. In 1858 Reuter made his highest connection when
The Times bought the telegraphed text of a bragging speech
in Paris by Louis Napoleon, who was giving Whitehall the
willies with his imperial hallucinations. On this sale Reuter
built his apparatus. During the U.S. Civil War, he financed
a submarine cable from Ireland to England, which picked up
news from eastbound steamers at Cork and beat the ships to
England by a day or two. He wove a strand to Cuxhaven,
Germany, and spread his wire and pigeon capillaries over
northwest Europe. Reuter knew the value of an Atlantic
telegraph and in 1865 won a concession for a cable to be
shared with the Anglo-American Telegraph Company. Cyrus
Field, however, had the *Great Eastern*, the assistance of the
Royal Navy, and the expert Telegraph Construction Company team. His was the first cable.

Now in 1869, after the failure of the passenger charter,
Reuter found the right moment. He also held a twenty-year
concession from Louis Napoleon and had friendly allies in
the United States Senate, notably Charles Sumner of Boston.
For the first time a cable was to come ashore in the United
States: the course ran from Brest to Miquelon and St. Pierre,
the French islands off Newfoundland, and thenceforward to
Duxbury, Massachusetts, near Boston. Sir Daniel Gooch
offered the *Great Eastern*'s services for £ 1,400, plus £ 20,000
in shares of Reuter's company. Gooch was furnishing competition for the Field cables, in which he owned considerable
shares, but his personal income stood only to gain: he owned
parts of the ship, the construction company and all three
Atlantic cables. He had come far in the thirty years since
he had stood begrimed on the footplate of the wide-gauge

locomotive *The Lord of Isles*, with Isambard Kingdom Brunel.

Wreckers tunnelled through the ship, ripping out the costly French staterooms and saloons to make way for the cable. That year more than 150,000 Britons emigrated to the United States—none, of course, in the *Great Eastern*. The directors knew but one way to make her pay, by charter and shares in a cable. It covered interest and running expenses and gave the directors leverage in other firms.

Although several cable baronets were to accompany the French telegraph expedition, Sir James Anderson relinquished command to the first officer, Robert Halpin, who had been his right hand man since '65. Halpin was a barrel-shaped Irishman from Wicklow. He had blue eyes, a curly spade beard, and a staid, amused manner that was often tried by the great ship in his ten years with her, the longest service of any of her masters. Among Halpin's admirers was Jules Verne, who had sailed with him in '67: 'An active little man with a very sunburnt skin, a beard almost covering his face, and legs which defied every lurch of the vessel', Verne described him. 'A skilful energetic seaman, he gave his orders in a clear, decided tone, the boatswain repeating them with a voice like the roaring of a horse lion.' The crew knew his qualities. They remembered an occasion in '66 when the wind shifted a heavy tail-block on the starboard mainstay. Halpin sent up a man to undo the clove hitch and bring the block down. The sailor climbed the thick stay but the wind was too strong for him. He started down and lost his nerve directly over the open paddle-engine hatch. He froze there, white-faced, slipping toward a fall of eighty feet into the awful engines. Halpin called out, 'Hold on, I'm coming up'. He shinned up the stay, and clinging with one arm and leg, placed the man's legs around his neck and brought him safely down. Halpin was slightly over five feet tall and weighed 15 stone. He hated crimps, and when he signed on free men he took care of them.

To the portly Wicklow man, as much as to Cyrus Field, the

world owes the advent of international cables. Halpin was first officer on the 1865 and '66 cables; as commander of the *Great Eastern* he laid three more Atlantic cables, and repaired four in mid-ocean. He laid the Indian Ocean telegraph, a cable from Madras to Singapore and Penang, the Australian-Java and Java-Sumatra lines, the cable from Madeira to Brazil and half a dozen shorter water links. In all Halpin was responsible for 26,000 miles of ocean telegraphs. After his last cable-voyage he married a Newfoundland girl whose father, John Munn, ran the world's largest whale fishery. There is a memorial obelisk to the stout mariner in Wicklow, where his daughter was still living in 1953. Halpin's chief paddle-engineer for the French telegraph voyage was the Welsh-man George Beckwith, who had sailed as second engineer on the *Great Eastern* on her maiden voyage and was to remain with the ship during her entire career.

A French pilot was taken aboard at Portland in June, 1869, and the cable-laden ship crossed to Brest, where the *Hawk* and *Chiltern* waited in the roads with the shore end of the telegraph. Sir Daniel said 'the stupid French pilot' mistook the landfall at Ushant and they went to sea and lost a tide before they could enter the harbour. Gooch was not a Fran-cophile.

'The people of Brest still show the most profound indiffer-ence to all connected with the cable and this indifference is not assumed but most genuine', *The Times* correspondent reported as he came aboard. The Brestois may perhaps be forgiven for their negligent attitude towards the essen-tially British enterprise and its Parisian patron. Louis Napoleon had just dissolved the legislative assembly and street fighting had begun in Paris that June. The people were taking up cobblestones and the grilles around Baron Hauss-mann's chestnut saplings, the classic material of the barri-cades.

The vigilant French customs men did their duty, however. The *douane* posted two sentries at the shore end of the cable to see that no contraband was landed in France. When the

electricians came ashore, the sentries would not permit them
to take their galvanometers to the cable-hut. The test party
had to row around to the customs house and pass them
properly. The *douaniers* 'seemed not a little perplexed to
know what the galvanometers were and what to do with
them at all, but as it was necessary to do something, they relieved their minds by weighing each of the little things carefully and letting them pass', *The Times* correspondent related.

The cable-layers carried four extremely thick cable-ends
for the shoal termini at Brest, Miquelon and Duxbury. *The
Times* man hinted that they were not merely for protection
against careless fishermen. Under the latest ministry of the
artful Disraeli, the British press was all out for the big
Irish scare. Recently the last public execution in English
history had occurred, that of the Fenian Michael Barrett,
convicted of the Clerkenwall Gaol Explosion. Hangmen and
journalists were doing a propaganda job. 'The Atlantic cable
of 1865 has been broken maliciously in two places some forty
miles from the Newfoundland shore', the reporter asserted. 'It
was done at the height of the Fenian troubles and when a
rumour was spread in America that there had been a rising in
Ireland.' Why in the world Irish rebels, who enjoyed their
main foreign support in the United States, would want to de-
prive Boston and New York of glad insurrection tidings, the
analyst failed to explain. As a matter of fact, the only sabotage
of the Atlantic cables that has been traced was by an underwater earthquake half a century later.

The blasé citizens of Brest bestirred themselves when excursion trains arrived from Paris on June 19 with hundreds
of courtiers who had come to see the *Great Eastern* splice
into the shore cable. Two hundred and fifty French government officials and Paris journalists dined aboard with the
cable-knights. The Vicomte de Vougy, director-general of
the French National Telegraphs, was toastmaster. He accepted tributes to Queen Victoria and Napoleon III, and
eulogized the directors. Baron Émile d'Érlanger acknow-

ledged for the company and evacuated himself of several thousand sentiments.

The next morning in a choppy sea the escorts gathered to the *Great Eastern* to splice the shore end.

As the *Great Eastern* departed with the longest cable ever attempted—2,584 nautical miles—Sir Daniel Gooch, M.P., was worried about the vote in the House of Lords on the Irish Church Bill. His mind was soon diverted to matters at hand. At sea the testing-room reported that they were getting clear signals from Brest, but Brest couldn't hear them. The Frenchmen on board claimed a fault had been laid down. Gooch said, 'We consulted with the French engineers and got an unclear opinion from them'. Gooch and Canning predicted that the fault would work out. The French stated that they would not accept the cable.

Several hundred miles had been laid. To pick up cable and cut it out would be impossible. The tremendous length of the main line taxed the capacity of the *Great Eastern* and she had no room for spare lengths to replace defective sections. They would have to go back to Sheerness and manufacture more cable and lose a year and a lot of money. Canning ordered the ship to be stopped. Construction company officials conferred privately and Gooch emerged with an offer to extend the guarantee on the cable from thirty days to two years. The courageous decision swayed the French. The next day the fault disappeared and they obtained instantaneous two-way transmission.

Four hundred miles out the alarm gong rang. The speck of light had vanished from the galvanometer. Canning and Halpin pulled off an audacious manoeuvre. Instead of cutting and transferring the cable to the bow pickup wheel, they backed the *Great Eastern* and risked losing the cable in the propeller. By now they had a steam winch at the stern. It saved hours and reduced handling damage to the recovered section. Every foot of cable was precious. Six thousand feet were reeled in before Canning found the flaw—a small hole in the gutta percha wrapping. The Fenians were blamed.

The cablemen cut and spliced and the voyage resumed. An hour later the gong sounded again. This time it was a message from Brest that the ship's signals were dead. As Canning started to pick up, Brest telegraphed the wire was O.K. For twenty-four hours the 'wheels went whirring merrily away', while the officials caught up their sleep. They were roused by another defect. The ship and paying-out gear were reversed so promptly that the flawed section was reeled in before it reached the floor and the cablemen had the line going down again within an hour. The incident was due to another puncture in the wrapping. The Fenians were blamed again. The French were highly amused at the prevailing Celtophobia. When boiled mutton was put on the table, the French said *les irlandais* must have been sabotaging the cooking as well.

Morale improved during two days of glorious hot weather, 'more like the Mediterranean than the Atlantic', and nearly seven hundred miles went down, exhausting the fore cable-tank. The veteran cable-men swiftly carried out the complex operation of tapping into the aftertank. The ocean got deeper. The cable was settling in a depth of nearly two miles, when a squall came upon them at midnight of the eighth day out. Furniture and stores were made fast for bad weather and the *Great Eastern* rolled on. At 5 a.m. another fault was detected. Halpin ordered the engines to be reversed and ran aft with Canning to deal with the reversing cable-gear. The ship backed into a roaring following sea which shot over the stern and covered them and the pay-out gang. 'The great ship took sea after sea abaft and quivered from stem to stern in a way that startled everyone,' said a passenger. The men fought for the cable which came up slowly under alarming strain, accompanied by drenching masses of water. For two hours they struggled. The biggest of all waves arrived, and swept the men away from their holds, carrying them down the deck like chips in a millrace. Canning and Halpin found their feet and counted the men. All were safe. The cable was in danger of ripping out at any minute. Canning ordered the cable to be cut and buoyed until the storm passed.

'Barely had he given this command when a loud crack and a loud shout proclaimed that the cable had parted in the fore part of the ship.' The tarred snake undulated along 'Oxford Street', whipping its heavy tail right and left, and bore down on the brakemen who had to stay by their levers to stop it. They stood to their posts and braked it short of the pay-out wheel. Hastily they shackled the end to a buoy and lowered it into the sea. The escorts, *Chiltern* and *Scanderia*, stood by, looking 'very wretched indeed, but they managed to lay a mark buoy', said the journalist.

The furious action allowed no time to notify Brest. In the beach hut the electricians sat by a dark index and a silent key. French telegraph shares slumped acutely on the Bourse and Exchange. The *Great Eastern* hove to for forty-eight hours, awaiting the pleasure of the elements, before the buoy could be hooked and service restored. Cable shares climbed back to par.

The following day the gong struck fear anew. Halpin reversed engines and Canning's gang stood by to pick up. The watch electrician sounded the all-clear after a few fathoms were in. Brest had telegraphed, 'CLERK PUT HAND ON NAKED WIRE'. Gooch said, 'I wish we had that careless fellow. We would drum him around the ship.'"

The ship was laying the line nearly three miles into the deepest valley of the North Atlantic, when the second storm arrived on the fifteenth day. Officers and officials stayed on deck through the night, brooding over the greatest danger to their enterprise. The ship rolled heavily and the cable, 'threw itself about in a most curious way and tried constantly to throw itself into kinks and tangles'. The wire was an animate thing to them.

In the cable-tank the men danced briskly to avoid the snarling coils, which could have seized one of them, carried him up through the crinoline and battered him to death. Foul weather continued the next day. The aftertank was depleted and they spliced into the main cable-tank. The eighteenth day, July 9, was 'one of the days to be remembered aboard the *Great Eastern*'. The ship reached the tail of the Grand Banks and the cable climbed to within a mile of the surface. It was the end of the nerve-racking deep-water run.

Halpin altered course for Miquelon in a fog, and pressed on in poor visibility towards his rendezvous with the shore-end cable-layer, the *William Cory*, which was standing thirty miles out to meet him. For two days Halpin could not see the sun or stars and his compasses were suspect owing to the proximity of iron cable-wire. But he came right upon the *William Cory*. They spliced at midnight of the twenty-second day and received the French governor aboard. The next day was the eighty-first anniversary of the fall of the Bastille: eloquent messages flashed between Paris and the last remaining French colony in North America. There was no celebration aboard the *Great Eastern*, which was preparing to go home immediately. The English had no humour for this egregious French holiday. Sir Daniel Gooch was not the sort to kick up his heels in the carmagnole and sing, 'The aristocrats to the lamp-posts!'

On the voyage home the crew got up a burlesque rifle corps, which drilled on deck with brooms and handspikes to the tune of fife, accordion and bones.

The *Chiltern*, *Scanderia* and *William Cory* spun the cable to Duxbury. While they were trudging along, political gongs were struck in the States. There was a clique in the Senate which resented the landing of a foreign cable on America's shores, and demanded an all-American ocean telegraph. The English had two, now the French were getting one, and there would be no business left for a future U.S. telegraph. (Cyrus Field must have smiled to think of how many times in years past he had vainly tried to sell cable shares in the States.) The Senate had risen for the summer and the patriots declared the cable could only be landed with approval by that body. Secretary of State Hamilton Fish quelled the rising by granting permission to land the cable. Boston and Duxbury threw a rousing reception for the telegraph, which was, however, not a patch on the Boston Peace Jubilee held the previous month. That one featured a chorus of 10,371 voices, accompanied by 1,094 instruments, including anvils and dismasted church bells. War was never like that.

The original cable company charged a five pound minimum for a transatlantic message. Reuter cut the rate to two pounds. Although knighthoods had been dealt liberally to the officials of the '66 telegraph, the Privy Council suggested none for Reuter. He became Baron de Reuter in a novel manner. In 1871 he received the title from the Duke of Saxe-Coburg-Gotha, a German princeling closely related to the late Prince Consort. Queen Victoria then recognized Reuter's title and that of his heirs in Britain.

From '65 to '74 the *Great Eastern* submerged five transatlantic lines, and repaired four of them in mid-ocean. In a laconic summary of his career written late in life, Captain Halpin alludes to a repair job in 1871, which suggests a lost saga. Both the 1865 and 1866 cables had broken down in deep water. 'The repairs were completed under most unfavourable circumstances,' said he, 'owing to continued bad weather and presence of ice, and for this service the A-A Telegraph Company presented me with a cheque for £1,000.' Her cable successes permitted the *Great Eastern* a sentence in the history of the nineteenth century.

CHAPTER FOURTEEN

THE ALL-RED LINE

By 1869 the *Great Eastern* had thrice proved that long and deep submarine cables could be laid and there was urgent clamour for an ocean telegraph to India. A land wire to Bombay already existed. It had been opened in 1865 with a news flash on the fall of Richmond, the Confederate capital, and with the appurtenant bad news that cotton had declined five pence a pound on the Liverpool Exchange. It took an average of eight days to transmit a message from London to Bombay. During the Panic of '66 the Agra Bank blew up in London. The Bombay branch continued to pay out for ten days, while the telegram was on its way. In 1869 there died the celebrated Reform politician and classical scholar, Lord Derby (who once refused the throne of Greece). The news was cabled to India. It has not yet arrived.

This was clearly no way to run an Empire. The trouble with the land telegraph was the crotchets and customs of a dozen countries through which it ran. From Old Broad Street, London, the cable passed under the Channel to Paris, across Europe to Turkey, to Mesopotamia, down the Persian Gulf, and thence along the Makran coast to Karachi and Bombay. The confusion began in the Paris station, which gave priority to French domestic traffic and spiked international messages until the wire was free. Then the delayed messages were transmitted from the top of the hook down. Much the same patriotic method prevailed in middle Europe and the Balkans. In Turkey bandit tribes cut the wires, murdered telegraphists and prevented repair gangs from getting at breaks, while on the eastern frontier, Turkish officials were reluctant to pass the infidel messages at all. When the Turks were difficult, London sometimes tried the alternative Russian route which ran through France, Germany, Poland and the Russian State System to Tiflis, Teheran and to a junction on the Persian Gulf. This was a desperate resort indeed. The Russian relay operators had no English. They turned vital messages into virgin cryptograms. These pied essays were sometimes printed in the Bombay *Gazette* for laughs and to stir up demand for an ocean telegraph.

The Telegraph Construction and Maintenance Company and the newly formed British India Telegraph Company argued for an ocean cable which would not cross meddling sovereignties, but would follow the naval lifeline of the Empire and emerge from the water at British forts and colonies—Gibraltar, Malta, Alexandria and Aden fort, an 'All-Red Line', except for a station at Lisbon, which was to be the only one on foreign territory. The Portuguese monarch, Luiz, was notoriously manageable. The longest submerged section would be from Aden to Bombay, across the Indian Ocean, a distance matching the awesome span of the *Great Eastern*'s Brest-Miquelon line. The British India cable company under John Pender and the construction company led by the persevering Sir Daniel Gooch, proposed the longest cable system ever attempted, nearly seven thousand miles. The *Great Eastern* could do her share, but the promoters wanted Her Majesty's government to underwrite part of the cost. Crown dispatches would figure largely in the cable traffic.

Lord Cranborne, Secretary of State for India, refused to divert Indian revenues to the scheme. The telegraph men tried the Chancellor of the Exchequer and were turned down. There was no ardent royal Albert to bespeak their cause. Messrs. Gooch and Pender determined to take a private risk with a million-pound company. The Royal Navy threw in a frigate to make soundings in the Red Sea, where existing charts showed exactly three soundings in a thousand miles. Within a year the Red Sea was to become a steamer high-road when Ferdinand de Lesseps finished his big cut at Suez.

Tropical seas were another problem: they were full of *Teredo navalis*. What would happen to the cable when the shipworm ate its hempen cover? The cable company tried a wrapping of ground flint and mineral pitch and the tunnelling clam did not attack. But what of the billions of coral architects in the hot ocean; what would they do to the cable? This problem, too, disappeared when the cablemen found that the coral-builders agreeably covered the wire with their skeletons, adding armour that man could never have provided.

The manufacture of the cable was finished in the autumn of '69, an event marked by one of those banquets without which Victorian business ventures could not proceed. Sir Daniel was in the chair for 180 trenchermen, including a number of peers and Bull Run Russell. Lord Houghton replied to the toast to the House of Lords with a tart remark that, although Parliament had given them no money, 'when individual enterprise has done its best, the government may step in and take the telegraph out of your hands'. Parliament was debating a bill to nationalize the domestic telegraph lines, which was done the next year.

In November, 1869, the *Great Eastern*, under the command of Robert Halpin, left Portland at the head of a formation of cable-layers consisting of H.M.S. *Hibernia, Chiltern* and *Hawk*. The latter was a yachtlike racer built to run the Union blockade in the Civil War. The big ship carried 3,600 nautical miles of cable, the entire Aden-Bombay section, 5,512 tons of it, as well as 10,323 tons of fuel, cable equipment and stores. Her total displacement was 34,000 tons. She was the heaviest object ever floated, exceeding her own indicated lading and drawing thirty-four feet. Although the Suez Canal was to be opened in a few weeks, the *Great Eastern* was going all the way round the African Cape. The Canal was then too shallow for the big ship. Lloyd's had placed a very high insurance rate on her two million pounds' worth of ship and cargo.

The first day out she encountered the brig *Thompson,*

blown off course from Belfast to Plymouth, and shipping water. The giants lumbered over to the little ship and offered assistance. The skipper of the dismasted brig declined aid and the *Thompson* was last seen low in the water and pumping hard. The *Hibernia* and *Hawk* then parted for the Mediterranean, where they were to spin the cable through to the Red Sea.

The *Great Eastern* and the *Chiltern* paraded down the Salvage Coast, swung in along the Ivory and Gold Coasts, steamed through dark days of tropical lightning off the Slave Coast, and went further to sea. Three hundred miles offshore the ships paddled through the mud-green out-pouring of the Congo. At Capetown the big ship took three thousand tons of coal and struck out for India on the last day of 1869. A decade had passed since the Little Giant had launched the colossal argosy to gather the riches of the Orient. Now at last the *Great Eastern* was on her way east, to tie India to Britain by a thread.

Off East Africa she breasted the Mozambique Current, and lost the *Chiltern*. Halpin swung over to the Madagascar shore and found a northbound stream that lifted the *Great Eastern* along as much as 220 miles a day. He crossed the Indian Ocean past the Seychelles and neared Bombay after a voyage of eighty-three days from England.

The chronicler assigned to report the adventure for the combined British press waited in Bombay. He was J. C. Parkinson, who had covered the French cable voyage, another of the first-rate writers who have left us chapters of her epic. He had been travelling in the interior of India, visiting the holy fair at Allahabad, the Taj Mahal, and the sites of the well-remembered gore of the Indian Mutiny, the well at Cawnpore and the ruins of Lucknow. He had inspected a government rehabilitation camp for thuggee prisoners, one of whom obligingly showed Parkinson how to strangle a man with slight pressure on a knotted handkerchief.

Word had leaked through the land telegraph of the departure from England, but the *Great Eastern* was now unre-

ported for nearly three months. Parkinson lounged around
the new cable house on the Bombay Cotton Green, among
the boulder-like bales of fibre the railways had brought for
the steamers. The cable house was a 'serviceable little man-
sion', put together by screws so it could be taken apart and
boxed for shipping to China and Australia when the cable
unreeled to those lands. It had a thatched roof and teak-
wood Venetian blinds.

The *Great Eastern* arrived at night and anchored at sea to
await high tide. The news was telegraphed via Turkey in the
hope that it might reach London in a week or so. At dawn
the Apollo Pier was thronged with Parsee merchants, Hindu
boatmen, Muslim buggy-wallahs and English folk, come
to see the *Great Eastern* gliding slowly into the harbour to
her mooring buoy. Parkinson and several cablemen leaped
into a longboat and rowed two miles to the great ship in the
burning sun. He exclaimed, 'No! There is nothing like the
Great Eastern in all the world. No sight which preserves its
freshness in the same way. I find myself holding breath as I
draw under her bows; and then the beautiful proportions,
and the vast graceful sweep of line, elicit the old encomiums
and the old warmth.'

The ship was ghostly white. Halpin had ordered her
painted white from stem to stern in the last days out, a
colour which reduced the heat in her cable tanks by eight
degrees. She looked 'like a huge iceberg, or some mammoth
of the seal kind', Parkinson thought, as he climbed aboard.
'The first sight greeting us was a pair of grey carriage horses
taking their morning exercises composedly up and down one
side of the deck,' he said. Captain Halpin shook hands and
told the journalist, 'She insisted on stepping along these last
few weeks.'

The Bombay press chattered rhapsodically. It was the biggest event since the Mutiny, and somewhat more welcome.
Captain Halpin had learned a good deal about crowd mani-
pulation in his last years on the *Great Eastern*. He advertised
certain visiting days and assigned ticket sales to shops in the

city. The proceeds were to be a bonus for the crew upon their return to England—'on records of good behaviour'. The first day's admission was two rupees, which effectively ruled out the poor Indian, for whom this was several weeks' wages. Englishmen praised Captain Halpin's shrewdness over their sundowners at the Byculla Club: Pukkah Sahib and his lady could inspect the ship without mingling with natives. Captain Halpin also announced that lower rates would prevail on other days, to accommodate the masses.

However, no plans for the *Great Eastern* ever worked out. On the first two-rupee day, natives outnumbered Englishmen ten to one. Parkinson wrote:

> The snowy robes and peculiar headdresses of the Parsee are to be seen on all sides—on the paddle boxes, the bridge, down in the saloon, outside the cable tanks. Clustered around the enormous red buoys were the bright costumes and intelligent faces of Hindoos and Mohammedans.

A Parsee visitor told Parkinson, 'The largest vessel ever seen in Bombay used to be the *Bates Family* of Liverpool'. He gestured over the bulwarks. Below lay the *Bates Family*, a tiny paddle-wheeler tied up alongside to pass eight thousand tons of coal into the *Great Eastern*. Hundreds of coolies, men and women, heaved the coal sacks. Captain Halpin discovered that it was beyond local logistics to round up the army of coal-passers and transport them to the ship in time to begin the day's work promptly. There was nothing to do but keep the coolies aboard overnight. The ragged army bedded down on the broad deck, and prayer rugs were unrolled at sundown.

On days when the ship was closed to visitors to get work done, they came anyway. Parsee and Hindu with their women and children in resplendent saris, gold nose rings and silver anklets, looked up from boats alongside. They cajoled Captain Halpin. He usually gave in. Indian aristocrats got around the restriction by another techique. They sent the skipper embossed visiting cards, asking permission to introduce him to their families. Halpin saw no serious in-

terruption to his work in saying hello and taking tea with a
leading merchant. One such guest brought three hundred
people of various sexes and ages, including a small baby with
jewels fastened to its naked toes.

The coaling went on endlessly. The white ship was lost in
a black cloud as choking coolies passed coal. It was worst on
misty mornings, before the sun had burned away the fog.
One such forenoon was elected by the governor, Sir Seymour
Fitzgerald, for a visit with his suite. Parkinson said, 'To touch
a handle, or to sit down, was to carry away a fascimile impression in black'. As the governor and ladies disembarked
to their steam yacht, the reporter described them as 'pie-
bald'. The big ship turned sullen grey, like 'a miller who has
been up a chimney'.

One day the ship was visited by an important rajah whose
card read, 'The Chief and Bahee Sahib of Jumkhundee'. He
brought his maharani, a lady famous for her beauty and
brains. She kept a mixed Indo-European salon and rode the
European saddle. Halpin was staggered by her erudition.
When he showed her the testing room, the maharani coolly
engaged the electricians in their own argot. The lady had
crammed on electrical theory and was paying the visitors a
superb compliment. Captain Halpin gave tiffin to the Bahee
Sahib's party in the grand saloon. The rajah took Halpin's
hand and held it 'like an affectionate schoolboy' as he presented the fat little captain from table to table.

One night the cable was brought ashore and hitched to a
team of bullocks to drag it to the cable station. Ahead of the
team, gangs of coolies dug a three-foot trench, and more followed to cover the cable with earth. The workers 'exulted in
the fun,' and vented their feelings in an improvised chant.
They heaved and sang, 'Good are the cable-wallahs, great are
their names! Good are the cable-wallahs, wah, wah! Great
are the cable-wallahs, wah, wah!' The procession of men in
loincloths advanced loudly and in high humour by lantern
light towards Cotton Green. The cable-wallahs fell into the
spirit of it and joined the chant. En route they ploughed

through a sleeping British military encampment, turning out tent pegs and drowning the angry questions of the awakening soldiers. The tent fly of the commandant, General Sir Augustus Spencer, flew open and an aide emerged to rate the insolent natives. He saw white men, unmistakably English, heaving away at a tarry rope in a throng of coolies, the lot of them singing their heads off, as earth flew and bullocks snorted. He went back to the general and imparted the dreadful news that the cable roughs were fraternizing with the coolies. Before military measures could be taken the holocaust had passed on, leaving the ground level as before.

Captain Halpin was worried about the coaling operation which was going all too slowly for his timetable. The monsoon season was coming. The *Great Eastern* would have to leave before the rains. The skipper decided to appeal to his own crew to help pass coal. They were different men from the poor souls shanghaied in '61. Most of them had been aboard for several voyages and they had a pride of craft. Seagoing unions were now on the scene. No body of Englishmen who ever sailed together had a stouter fibre than the cablemen; veterans of the heartbreak of '65 in mid-Atlantic and victors of the '66 Atlantic cable and the French telegraph. They had what Walt Whitman called, 'the surly English pluck, and there is no tougher and truer'. To ask these men to handle coal was a hard test of Halpin's personal credit.

He spoke about the monsoon and he touched on their common love of the big ship and what they had been through together. Then he got down to hard cases and offered a bargain. If the men would pass coal, he would give them the last two days ashore. If it had been said by several other masters of the *Great Eastern*, a jaundiced spirit in the back of the crowd would have given an anonymous jeer that could have turned it into another *Great Eastern* 'mutiny'. The men were with Halpin. They got into the lines of benighted coolie women and passed coal. Black dust thickened around the ship. Duty officers looked like minstrels in blue and gold.

Staterooms with sealed portholes were saturated with coal
dust. The tarred cable coiled in the tanks bubbled in the
tropical heat and filled the ship with a smell that took many
sea days to wash away. Halpin's mastiff, 'Harold', licked the
dirty dew which hung in droplets from the shrouds and
bounded into 'queer rolls and gambols'. When the work was
done, the master gave every man jack two days' leave in
Bombay, although the rains were almost upon them.

India was loath to part with the great ship. The last two
days were a succession of galas running round the clock.
There was a ball at the Byculla Club, while the crew wallowed in the town. Shilling and rupee were punted at the
race track. On the eve of departure there was a party on
board for the ship's officers and the local quality. It eclipsed
all previous *Great Eastern* banquets. They toasted everything
they could think of, including the Queen, Captain Halpin and
officers, the Telegraph Construction Company, the British
India Telegraph Company, the Port of Bombay, the officers
of H.M. dockyard and the ladies. The latter toast was responded to, for some reason, by Mr. Oliphant, secretary
of the Byculla Club. The toast to the press was acknow-
ledged by two local news-hawks named Wood and Hopper,
who were so undone by the occasion that they pledged not
to slander the *Great Eastern* after she left.

When the guests were counted on the homegoing barge
at dawn, several were missing. The barge bumped through a
fleet of banana boats, carrying supine or semi-conscious *Great
Eastern* sailors and raucous merchants of fruit, vegetables,
parakeets and monkeys. The boats bobbed in the morning
swell around the great ship, exchanging crew, mislaid guests,
animals, produce and money. Parkinson almost missed his
big story. He had been on the town all night and barely made
the ship in a water taxi manned by a larcenous individual.
Parkinson brought with him an intellectual Parsee man-
servant named Sarabjee, who was to torment the Christians
throughout the cable voyage with his tolerant philosophy.
The sailing day, February 14, 1870, was blowy. A coal barge

alongside shipped water and went down as the great ship spliced on the shore end of the cable, brought up by the *Chiltern*. The cable-men sang, 'Shove her along, push her through'.

She was off for Aden at dinnertime. There were several paying passengers. When they came down to the first meal they were denied the pleasure of discovering interesting people. The ship was full of technicians. They all knew each other. 'There were no mysteries and there was nothing to find out,' said Parkinson. The Grand Saloon was full of desultory technical lingo as tricks of cable-men came to eat around the clock, amidst dimming pier glasses and flaking gilt and silver. Each officer and deadhead had a first-class cabin. In none of the accounts of the *Great Eastern* is there a description of how people lived in the forecastle and the steerage. When the ship got into trouble her chroniclers mention how terrible it must have been below, but none went down to see.

The plan of the British-India telegraph required H.M.S. *Hibernia* and *Hawk* to string the wire from Malta to Alexandria, while the *Great Eastern* brought it westward to the lower end of the Red Sea. The big ship could not be risked in the reefy and uncharted Sea of Islam. The *Chiltern* would carry the cable up the Red Sea to meet the east-bound cable-layers, and complete the telegraph from Bombay to Malta, from which a cable already extended across France. The next year an ocean wire from Malta to Gibraltar, to Lisbon and Cornwall would complete the seven-thousand-mile political-proof telegraph over which Indian colonial business could be transacted with the speed of London instructing Manchester.

The Admiralty had warned all vessels that the *Great Eastern* and *Chiltern* would cross the India Ocean slowly in close formation with the smaller ship to starboard. The *Chiltern*, an auxiliary steamship, lifted her propeller and proceeded under sail in favouring winds. Her task was to sound the bottom for the deep-laden cable ship, which moved at under six knots to avoid breaking her tarry thread. The Admiralty warning was not strong enough to curb the excitement of the ships that had not only been first to navigate Suez, but came upon the *Great Eastern* in the Indian Ocean. On her second day out the monster was sighted by Her Majesty's troopship *Euphrates* from Aden. Like Pirate Hicks, everyone on the trooper wanted to see the iron mountain that floated on the sea.

The commander of the *Euphrates* bore down on a course to cross the big ship's bows and give his people an admirable elevation view of the *Great Eastern*. Out of sight on the other side was the *Chiltern*, proceeding under sail. The big ship hid even the tips of her escort's masts. Cheering soldiers and crew lined the rail of the *Euphrates* as she crossed. Then the trooper captain saw a parallel ship bearing down on him.

The *Chiltern*'s master, Captain Edington, had seen none of this skylark. He could not reverse engines. He had none turning. The two little ships closed for the crash. Edington threw his helm hard over in a desperate manœuvre. The wind spilled out of his sails. The *Chiltern* yawned alongside the trooper, almost bumping her, as the *Euphrates* made off with bells jangling and soldiers scrambling away from the rail. The dialogue between the two Royal Navy captains has not been passed along to posterity, but fortunately the ships did not collide. If they had, the *Great Eastern* might have ground them both down far out on the ocean on a bright day. Sightseers always made trouble for the great ship.

She steamed on in a blue sea amidst flying fish which skittered like gulls along the curly waves. The cable ran off the paying out wheel with dull competence as though devices no longer needed men. The apprehensive cruise turned to tedium and dreams. The men forgot the alarm gongs swaying idly at the test room and the captain's caboose. Nothing happened in the long, torpid days except several cases of heat prostration in the boiler rooms.

One morning they went listlessly to breakfast, exhausted the cable talk, and had fallen silent in the heat, when a loud rapid drumming of metal brought them to their feet. Captain Halpin, Chief Engineer Laws of the Construction Company, and Paddle Engineer George Beckwith led a race to the testing room. The watch electrician looked up in surprise and said, 'The cable is O.K., sir.' Halpin walked along 'Oxford Street', inspecting the trough. The cable ran smoothly. He called down into the cable tank. The tank-men, hardly able to move in the heat, said all was well. Nobody had struck the gongs. Joking about the ghostly riveter, the men returned to breakfast.

The drumming continued. Halpin was about to order a general inspection when the noise ceased. A late-rising gentleman entered with his hair wet. 'Nothing beats a shower in this heat,' he said. His stateroom was over the saloon and he had been running his shower on the iron deck. Halpin requested him to breakfast punctually in the future.

The trudging cable-layers were overtaken by H.M. trooper *Jumna*, from Bombay for Aden and Suez. Courtesies were exchanged and more sightseers stored away boasts for their grandchildren. 'We'll report you all well,' Halpin's watch officer trumpeted from the paddle-box. The testing room tapped the message through the long ravelling to India. Four decades before Marconi, the *Great Eastern* owned a magic like radio and could speak across the sea through the un-reeling wire. The electricians refused to send more than two such ship hails a day. They were constantly testing the line for faults and one might appear and go undetected while the key was gossiping with Bombay. For this reason Halpin refused an offer from Reuter's Bombay correspondent to send the ship a daily European news budget.

A break in the monotony came every afternoon when the cattle pens were opened to exercise the bulls and cows along 'Oxford Street'. Goats, chickens, calves, pigs and Southdown sheep broke for freedom and were chased round and round by the merry men. Souvenir parakeets chattered and mac-aques and black langur monkeys ran up the shrouds. Captain Halpin's birthday fell on St. Patrick's Day. That was before the saint had achieved political and commercial beatification. The best the cable-men could do on the Indian Ocean was the toast, 'Prosperity to Captain Halpin and the cable!'

Parkinson had time for word-painting; as much literary inspiration is received on long voyages as in gaol, plus more scenery. He described a night at sea:

> A row of swinging lamps suggests a festal illumination. You discern the men on guard, in shadow by the wheels, or waiting in the bulwarks opposite. A group of cows and goats were lying on the deck, chewing the cud peacefully. The moon was up, but thick white clouds obscured her light, and the line of lamps over the trough made the ship look inconceivably long and dark.

One starlit night they passed an eastbound Peninsular & Oriental liner and saw women on the lighted quarterdeck. Halpin fired rockets and burned blue lights at the bow, paddles and stern, to give the ladies a thrilling picture of the *Great Eastern* and the men 'a grateful topic over this evening's grog'.

After two weeks the uneventful voyage drew to an end when they raised Sham Shan Peak and the burnt mountains of Aden. Parkinson saluted the dreary place with a parlour version of Tecumseh Sherman's gag, 'In the words of the American who said if he held property in the place unmentionable to ears polite, he should part with his Aden holding and live in Hades for choice.' What General Sherman said was, 'If I owned Hell and Texas, I'd rent out Texas and live in Hell'.

The wind was rising as the Parsee agent of the telegraph company came aboard and reported that coolies were standing by to dig the trench from Steamer Point to the cable station in the Indian general store. With him came a man the cable gang knew of old—C. W. de Sauty, electrician of the 1865 cable voyage, now technical chief in this desolate place, as though exiled for his error in mid-Atlantic. There was a high serious wind and the *Great Eastern* was pitching and rolling, threatening to tear out her lengthy Indian um-

G

bilicus. De Sauty cut the cable, sealed off the end, made it fast to two large buoys and lowered it into the sea.

The next morning the weather was too rough to attempt to lay the shore end. Halpin transferred to the *Chiltern* and toured the buoys. The escort got a hook on the first buoy and lifted it. There was no cable attached. Halpin lifted the second buoy. The Cable had broken loose from it too. The Indian telegraph was lost. De Sauty had done it again.

An inquiry was convened on the *Great Eastern*. The anguished de Sauty was reassured by the veterans. They said he had done the right thing by buoying off in the storm. They questioned the men who handled the buoys. A mishap of the stormy night had not been appreciated at the time. When the first buoy was lowered over the stern it was taken in a violent sea and carried completely through the screw well. The cablemen were pretty sure the buoy cable had become fouled in the big screw, but there had been no way to check during the gale. There must have been a heavy strain on the buoy cable, which descended two hundred fathoms to a mushroom anchor, but there was nothing that could have been done about that either. They merely hoped everything would come out right. It had not. The cable was lost and a buoy chain probably was wrapped around the propeller of the *Great Eastern*.

Robert Halpin went to the *Chiltern* and ordered a battle for the cable. The escort steamed south and then east to make a pass with a grapnel. The *Chiltern* got her six-armed fishing hook on the floor and dragged it through soft ooze and little shells. The cablemen stared at the dynamometer with hard eyes. They had carried the blasted cable around the Cape to India and trailed it all the way to Aden without a single fault; now all they could do was watch a dead index and hope the labour was not lost. Rain blew and hours passed. During the vigil good news was sent from the *Great Eastern*: the screw was not entangled. The *Chiltern* continued to grope. Halpin came down from the bridge to watch the dynamometer, which danced little maddening steps that meant nothing. Six hours passed before the indicator leaped with contact and showed a heavy stress. Twenty minutes later a loop of black cable was drawn to the bows. The Indian eel was on the hook.

Halpin dropped another mushroom anchor, and made the cable doubly fast to its buoy. He put down a flag buoy to mark the spot, in case the cable escaped again. The strain on human dynamometers slacked off as the men quit for the night. At dawn Halpin picked up the cable and a very much relieved de Sauty tapped into the raw cut and signalled Bombay. From the Cotton Green came the prompt reply,

'O.K. WHAT HAPPENED.'

They put the cable ashore beneath the volcanic buttes of Aden, 'where there is neither leaf nor shrub to break the terrible sterility'. Foremen yelled and rained blows on the trench-diggers, ragged Arab Jews in embroidered yamalgas, whose dark limbs contrasted picturesquely with the gleaming houses of Steamer Point, Her Majesty's officers in white dress, and the snowy robes of Parsees. 'The heat was terrible,' said Parkinson, 'and one envied the sailors and cable hands, whose duty was to jump from the barge into the sea, and so bring the end on shore.'

In the brooding loneliness of such a place as Aden fort many ceremonial guns were fired—sunset gun and reveille, when steamers were sighted from the lookout on Sham Shan Peak, and on imperial birthdays, but the place had never heard such salutes as the day the *Great Eastern* secured the Indian Telegraph with repeated peals of her four brass guns, to which the *Chiltern*'s gunners fired the echoes.

On a deck poster the great ship's company read the first wire news from England, via the land line to India.

CONSERVATIVE PEERS ASSUME LEADERSHIP—DISRAELI CON- VALESCENT—BISHOP OF ST. ASAPH RESIGNED—AMERICAN CORVETTE ONEIDA COLLISION 120 MEN DROWNED—PRINCE OF WALES EXAM- INED IN MORDAUNT CASE EMPHATICALLY DENIED IMMORALITY WITH LADY MORDAUNT VERDICT LADY MORDAUNT INSANE.

The great ship's people prepared to string four hundred miles of cable into the Red Sea, there to hand the splice to the *Hibernia* for a thousand-mile relay to Suez. 'The sharks have been most assiduous in their attention to the *Great Eastern*,' said Parkinson. 'When her men were busy with her screw and stern-chains close to the water's edge, monsters fourteen feet long played about them, ready to act with sportsmanlike precision in the event of a slip or fall.' She set out on a calm, close night under a sky aglitter with stars. On the bridge was 'a pilot in petticoats', the formidable Red Sea navigator, Ali Rischdi. At the volcanic island Jebbel Teer the splice was made to the *Hibernia*. Captain Halpin left the great ship for the smaller one: he was marine superintendent of the Telegraph Construction Company and had to see the line through the Red Sea before he rejoined his ship at Aden. He and Parkinson watched the *Great Eastern* putting back for Aden to wait for him. The journalist told the stocky master that he had run the big ship with 'the kindly amenities of a social gathering, the order of a factory, and the discipline of a barrack'. Ali Rischdi balanced on the bridge rail of the *Hibernia* with a big cigar in his mouth and told Halpin that his one ambition was to take the *Great Eastern* to Suez. 'Plenty water there. Very good make big ship go. I got papers.' At Daedalus they cut and buoyed the cable for the *Chiltern* which brought the link from Alexandria. Then the All-Red Line was open from Bombay to London.

The first ceremonial messages on the Indian submarine cable were sent from a party at John Pender's house in Arlington Street, London, where a miniature telegraph office was installed. Sir James Anderson was the telegrapher. Captain Halpin and Sir Daniel Gooch hung over the key as he relayed a message from the Indian Viceroy at his Simla summer palace to President Ulysses S. Grant in Washington. The President replied with a wish for

A LASTING UNION BETWEEN THE EASTERN AND WESTERN HEMI-SPHERES,

an aim that was not too ambitious in those days.

The Prince of Wales arrived fashionably late and wired the Khedive of Egypt and the King of Portugal. The latter flashed back thanks and added,

> EQUALLY I CONGRATULATE MYSELF FOR THE COMPLETION OF THE TELEGRAPH LUIZ.

The Prince sent another wire to General Grant. The Viceroy of India's wife, Lady Mayo, was invited to step up and send love to Simla. Her billet-doux deserves quotation in full:

> IN AVAILING MYSELF OF THE SUBMARINE CABLE I FEEL THE OBLIGATION WHICH SCIENCE IMPOSES UPON THE WORLD NOT ONLY DOES IT SERVE POLITICAL INTERESTS BUT ASSISTS DOMESTIC RELATIONS IN THUS ENABLING ME TO SEND YOU ALMOST INSTANTANEOUSLY AN AFFECTIONATE GREETING FROM YOUR WIFE AND FAMILY.

Before the Viceroy had time to savour his lady's greeting, Edward was on the wire again with a royal message to Simla. The guests had discovered the electric train of the century there in Pender's parlour. Anderson got an acknowledging signal for the Prince, but it proved to be from an onlooker in the Gibraltar office. In every station along the way provincial operators were plugged in. Sir Bartle Frere elbowed his way to the operator and sent a wire to his chum, Governor Sir Seymour Fitzgerald in Bombay. Five minutes later, while the Prince still awaited his reply, the Bombay operator came through with:

> SIR SEYMOUR IN BED WILL REPLY AS SOON AS HE CAN BE CALLED UP.

The commercial business had actually begun a couple of weeks earlier when the results of the Derby were flashed to Bombay in five minutes. The winner was Kingcraft.

CHAPTER FIFTEEN

SHOWBOAT

In 1874 the Telegraph Construction Company launched a custom-built cable-ship, the *Faraday,* and the *Great Eastern* became obsolete. Sir Daniel Gooch journeyed to Sheerness to his familiar cabin on the great ship. 'We sail tomorrow for Milford Haven,' he wrote in his journal,

> where we intend to lay her up. It may be a long time before I have to sail in the old ship again, as I do not know how we are going to employ her in the future. But we will not give up hope that some useful work will be found, as she is a noble ship and has done good service in the past.

Robert Halpin was in command on her valedictory voyage from London River, where the ship was made. Excited crowds of yore blackened the banks, and brass bands blew the veteran marching airs. The ship paddled wearily with her load of barnacles. Off the Lizard sixpenny steamers circumnavigated her spryly, and fishing sails crossed and recrossed her bows. It took Halpin three days to reach the Haven. He moored the wonderful ship off Milford and went down the ladder for the last time. George Beckwith stayed aboard as caretaker and tried to keep the engines in order. After a while there was no money to pay him and Beckwith put out anchor as a consulting engineer in Cardiff.

The Milford harbour board was confronted with a clumsy iron reef, blocking one fairway or another. They shunted the *Great Eastern* here and there. The owners would not remove her. Trippers came to Wales to see the sleeping monster, still by far the largest ship in the world. The locals were sick and tired of her. They circulated petitions, begging Parliament to relieve Pembrokeshire of its unwieldy lodger. Milford's patience wore out in 1876 when a Manchester engineer named Frederick Appleby was given a contract to build two big dry docks and found the *Great Eastern* plumped directly on the most desirable site for the larger dock. The pubs were full of talk that 'somebody ought to blow her up with gun-powder'.

In Appleby the ship again had summoned an imaginative engineer. He asked the townsmen not to demolish the vessel. He had an idea: What if he left the ship where she lay and built the dock around her? The *Great Eastern* was all one could ask as a platform for pile drivers. The dock could be framed close to her sides and built round her. It would save a nice sum on construction. Appleby reversed the method used in a Limehouse dry dock constructed in 1829 by sinking the twelve-hundred-ton East Indiaman, *Canton*, and putting the dock inside her. Once more the *Great Eastern's* main deck sounded with men and machines. It was like the cable days. When Appleby's splendid dock was finished, it was full of the *Great Eastern*. He opened the lock, floated the mammoth, and fastened towlines to draw her through the seaward gate. The ship was too wide to pass through.

It had taken engineers eighteen years to get around to making a dock large enough for the *Great Eastern*, only to find it slightly too small. Before the incredible joke had time to spread, Appleby's surveyors went over the problem with tape and ascertained that the ship could pass out if the paddle-boxes were removed. The dismantling operation consumed much of the money Appleby had saved. But the ship squeezed through. Then the owners notified the engineer kindly to restore the paddle-boxes, a labour that wiped out the construction economies altogether. The ship was beached near by. Appleby's dock is still in use. It is the last physical evidence of the dimensions of the great iron ship, a coffin, as it were, of a goliath long disintegrated.

Eight thousand pounds was spent on cleaning and repairs, an activity that launched more rumours and charter syndicates. A newspaper humourist said Ferdinand de Lesseps could dig the Panama Canal by steaming up the *Great Eastern* and ramming his way through the Isthmus. Proposals were made to employ the ship to remove the sewage of London, raise wrecks, to serve as a model lodging house on the Thames, or to become a smallpox hospital. A socialist soapboxer at Westminster Bridge said that, 'Mankind would be benefited if the whole of the aristocracy were shipped on board, taken out into the Atlantic, and the vessel scuttled with the whole crew'. These various ideas were equally impracticable.

In 1880 Sir Daniel Gooch gave up the ship. He resigned from the board in favour of Thomas Brassey's son, Henry. Barber continued as chairman. The next year Cunard launched the *Servia*, made of mild steel, the first advance on Scott Russell's iron plate. Although the *Servia* was little more than a third of the *Great Eastern*'s displacement, she was of interest as the first red-stacker to adopt the double hull design Brunel had put into the *Great Britain* four decades before. The *Servia* was also the first vessel with electric lights, a feature Brunel had tried unsuccessfully to install in the big ship, twenty-five years earlier. *The Times* hailed the *Servia* with an editorial that, in passing, disparaged the *Great Eastern*. Barber defended his ship. He said all her troubles stemmed from the American rock and the recent depression in shipping. The chairman said she 'is now ready to resume as a commercial enterprise' and that a lot of fellows wanted her. Barber's boom faded into an auction sale that autumn. The highest bid for the *Great Eastern*, £24,000 was not accepted.

In 1884 the municipal virus of the century, exhibition fever, struck New Orleans, seaport of the renascent South and gateway to the Mississippi. When New Orleans's condition was known in London a syndicate was formed to charter the world's biggest ship and sail her to America's biggest river and operate her as the world's biggest hotel and faro palace. The ship was invented by exhibition promoters and

they never could resist her. The Great Eastern Syndicate
Company pictured her paddling up the delta with black
brass bands crying across the bayous. The ship, like Queen
Cleopatra, did not lose allure by age, and many played her
Enobarbus.

Some of the New Orleans tale came out later before Mr.
Justice Pollock and a special jury in the Old Bailey in the
conspiracy indictment of The Queen *v.* Barber & Others.
A defendent named Pine allegedly collected £3,000 from
the Mumm's champagne people and £1,500 from Schweppe's
mineral waters for beverage concessions at New Orleans. Mr.
Justice Pollock lectured the partners and the jury found them
guilty. Sentence was deferred. New Orleans never saw the
Great Eastern. The syndicate dissolved with the announcement that the Louisiana show was 'financially unstable'.
Barber handed the hot-potato-ship to his son-in-law by the
name of Mr. King George (*sic*).

In October 1885, the ship was offered at auction again
in Lloyd's Captain's Room, Royal Exchange, London, by
order of the High Court of Justice. A few days earlier Mr
Justice Chitty, presiding, had refused a private offer of
£20,000 from Louis S. Cohen, managing director of Lewis's
('for whom no scheme is too immense'), a firm of clothiers
and drapers in the Midlands and North of England.

Rebuffed in his private bid, Louis Cohen went to Lloyd's
Captain's Room with his twenty thousand quid. The place
was crowded with idly curious persons. They laughed at the
first offer of £10,000. There were several bidders, and
Cohen was left behind at £20,500. The bidding narrowed
to fifty-pound raises, and the ship was knocked down for
£26,200 to Edward de Mattos, representing London Traders
Ltd. This company had been formed to put the *Great Eastern*
into service as a coaling hulk at Gibraltar.

Cohen ran after de Mattos as the auction broke up. He
told how David Lewis, the founder, had opened his first
modest shop in Liverpool, in the year of the great ship's
launching, and how the proprietor had raised twenty thou-

G*

sand pounds to buy the *Great Eastern* as a sentimental ges-
ture. David Lewis had died on the eve of the auction and
left Louis Cohen with the sacred duty to rescue the ship. To
the merchant's surprise, de Mattos said, 'Would you be
interested in a year's charter?' A deal was struck then and
there. Cohen departed highly gratified: he had not expended
his capital and had the vessel for the Liverpool Industrial and
Maritime Exhibition the next year. De Mattos was equally
pleased. He had been having a bad time at Gibraltar, where
local coal dealers had put pressure to bear against granting
a hulk licence. It would take some time to overcome them.
—Cohen had been warned of the folly of chartering the
Great Eastern. People said repairing her for a seaworthiness
certificate would 'cost a bloody fortune'. They told Cohen
the plates were rusted away; there was a hole below the
waterline 'big enough for a stage'; and sundry old gashes had
been plugged with bricks and mortar. 'Don't think you're
going to have the Board of Trade surveyors aboard for a
day and send them off with a banquet,' they said. A new
generation of doom-criers had arisen around the ship.

The surveyors spent a long time looking her over. A diver
took two weeks to clear filth from her stern tube and boiler
injectors. He reported the hull sound, but incredibly blan-
keted with barnacles. During her stay at Milford Haven the
biological encrustation was examined by the marine natura-
list, Henry Lee, who was keeper of octopuses at the Brighton
Aquarium. Lee was the sort of student who would travel
two hundred miles to study barnacles on an old iron bottom.
He reported acorn barnacles and mussels were six inches
deep on 52,000 square feet of iron plates. 'There were not
less than three hundred tons of living marine animals ad-
hering to her,' he said.

The Board of Trade issued the certificate and Cohen
brought to Milford a party of two hundred guests who were
to voyage to Liverpool. With them were sign painters and
several cases of deflated animal bladders, lettered with store
advertisements. Sixty Welsh firemen arrived by tug from

Cardiff. The *Great Eastern*'s new master, her tenth, was named Comyn, and, as screw engineer, Cohen hired Peter Jackson, who bristled with seven types of engine certificates. The paddle engines were not to be used.

The guests arrived and the wine was opened on April Fool's Day, 1886. Jackson laid fires in boilers which had been cold for eleven years. Passengers came down the rusting ladders and crowded in upon the oilers, as Jackson made ready to turn the engine over. James Watt's engines would not start. A guest yelled to Jackson that he should get out his extra first-class steam engineer's licence and read it to the engines. Frictional resistance was remarkable. Jackson found that he also wanted vacuum; there was an air leak in the forward starboard piston between the sluice injection valve and the condenser. Jackson showed the passengers a little bit of that which had won his certificates. He stuck a lighted candle into the seam and sealed the hole with its tallow. When the candle snuffed out inside, he had his vacuum. The engines turned over and he applied the reversing gear. It took twelve of his strong Welsh firemen twenty minutes to turn the corroded valves from full ahead to full astern.

The engines stopped three times. Jackson figured there were other air leaks. He sent a man up to hail a chum, a paddle tug skipper named Strong, who was expert on jet condensers. The tugboatman came down, dusted himself of rust flakes from the ladder rungs and looked at the screw engines of the *Great Eastern*. He turned to Peter Jackson and grimaced. Strong had never seen such a jumble of mastodon bones as the forgings of John Watt. He followed Jackson as a tourist after a museum guide. They found several leaks in the side valves and repaired them with candles. They got her going again and the engines persisted. The oilers attacked rust in the journal bearings and the engines ran up to eight revolutions per minute. The *Great Eastern* protested as they took the dampers down, but she progressed steadily backwards, a sure bet to ride down a dozen harbour-front buildings.

So thought Captain Comyn, high above on the flying bridge. He ordered 'Stop' and 'Go ahead'. The Welshmen wrestled with the valves. The *Great Eastern* trembled and the engines died. Jackson and the tugboat captain reached for all their lore, but the engines were tired. The *Great Eastern* lifted on the drastic afternoon flood tide of the Haven. Comyn was adrift. He put out anchors. The ship could not escape that day. The screw engine crew, which had been struggling for eight hours in geysers of leaking steam, fell exhausted on the hot plates. The guests climbed out.

They were unhappy. Steamer passengers start worrying at any incident that may postpone the drama of arrival, although today they do not congregate in the engine room or the bridge. Lewis's guests had not even started their diverting cruise. They sent a messenger ashore with telegrams to Liverpool, assuring their loved ones they had not yet perished at sea. Peter Jackson sent a wire to Swansea to George Beckwith, the custodian of the long layup, to come to the rescue. Jackson roused his men and they laboured through the night, caulking, overhauling steam cocks and closing split seams with wooden wedges.

Beckwith arrived in the morning and fussed over the old engines. At noon she steamed away 'under the master hand' at five knots. The Liverpudlians regained their spirits as the ship neared Great Castle Head and open water was sighted. There the *Great Eastern* quit. It was a calm evening when she hove to, but some of the passengers got the wind up. Beckwith and Jackson plumbed the engines, while Louis Cohen tried to jolly his guests. He was learning the far-distant art of the cruise social director. The engineers found three clean holes through the main steam pipe, blown out from the inside. Jackson banked the boiler fires while a blacksmith forged iron collars to seal the pipe.

Next morning George Beckwith got her going into the Channel. As land sank from sight the fire alarm rang. Wisps of smoke arose from the screw engine room. The passengers retreated to the bow in despair. Vibration had shaken loose

rotten woodwork which fell around the overheated boilers
and smouldered for a while undetected in the steamy boiler
rooms. The debris was wetted down and Louis Cohen went
round reassuring the guests. He tried to divert them from
morbid thoughts of fire and drowning by issuing the advertising balloons. He bade them inflate the balloons by mouth
and throw them into the sea. Each skin bore a message instructing the finder to write in to the store. For months after-
ward Lewis's received letters from County Down and other
distant shores. During the slow, plodding passage painters
hung over the sides, splashing away. Passengers went on the
guard-walks and squinted at what they were doing.

At the bar lightship of the Mersey the *Great Eastern* was
taken up by the tugs, *Toiler, Brilliant Star, Ranger* and
Wrestler for her journey to Sloyne Pool. Aboard the *Wrestler*
there was a cabin boy named Davey Duff, who is now Captain David Duff, O.B.E., an honour he received from George
VI for coming out of retirement to pilot American, Norwegian and French sea-going tugs which arrived in the
Mersey during the Second World War. Captain Duff wrote
this author a charming bit on the ship:

> When we arrived off the barship we put the *Eastern* to
> anchorage, to go up to Liverpool on the next day's tide. Well,
> on the day's tide on Sunday they hove up their anchor on the
> *Eastern* and the tug *Wrestler* got into position under the bow
> of the *Eastern* for them to take our hawser aboard. Whilst we
> were doing so the starboard anchor of the *Eastern* came down,
> striking the *Wrestler* on her stern, doing quite a bit of damage.

She was still too big for the ships. Captain Duff's damage
report is the last known evidence of her awkwardness. She
was still hitting them after thirty years; the *Wrestler* was the
tenth vessel she had damaged or sunk.

Captain Duff continued:

> Well about ten a.m. we started to tow the *Eastern* up the
> Channel for Liverpool. When we were passing New Brighton,
> which is at the entrance of the River Mersey, the pier heads on
> both sides were crowded with people sightseeing. We towed
> the *Eastern* up to New Ferry, that is on the Cheshire side of

River Mersey, where she was put at Anchorage on exhibition for a few month and the People were charged one shilling per head to go on Board. The Tugs done all the carrying of the People from Shore to Ship.

Captain Duff may be the last man alive who walked the deck of the *Great Eastern*.

Her arrival was a bombshell. Liverpool had not seen the great ship for eighteen years, and there was a generation awaiting the sight, but what astounded the port was not so much the ship as what had been done to her. Birkenhead, on her port side, was faced with a 21,000-square-foot iron poster with thirty-foot letters, proclaiming that 'LADIES SHOULD VISIT LEWIS'S BON MARCHÉ CHURCH STREET'. On the other side Liverpool was advised that 'LEWIS'S ARE THE FRIENDS OF THE PEOPLE'. Advertisements circled the funnels, arched across the paddle-boxes and blazed from the cabooses.

Cohen hired cleaners, painters and decorators to dress the ship for visitors. Queen Victoria was to open the Liverpool Exhibition in May and was expected to inspect once more the mammoth she had last seen a quarter of a century before. The Queen duly made her royal river progress in the ferry steamer *Claughton*, in blowing rain. The weather, or perhaps distaste for the state of the ship, caused 'a last-minute change in Her Majesty's plans'. The *Claughton* sailed past the billboard without stopping.

Due to a thirty-one-foot maximum rise and fall of tide, Liverpool uses pontoon landing stages, moored along the riverbank, for embarking and disembarking steamship passengers. The famous Prince's Landing Stage was used by ferries to the *Great Eastern*; Lewis's opened a ticket booth on the south end of Prince's Stage, near the embarkation point of transatlantic saloon passengers. As jolly excursionists from Walsall and Bootle, Oswaldtwistle and the Potteries awaited the ferries, ocean travellers stared across the barrier at people who had never taken a voyage, but loved the great ship nonetheless. In all her vicissitudes the people were loyal.

One of the visitors was Edwin Charles Lowe of Wigan,

who had seen the ship first in 1861, when she lay flag-dressed in Sloyne Pool, taking on passengers for one of her record transatlantic dashes. 'What a contrast!' Lowe wrote. 'Then she was in full bloom and a vessel of great expectations in spite of all her slanders. Now she is a mammoth advertisement. How are the mighty fallen!' He boarded the ferry with a crowd of

> hot-blooded Lancastrians, sharp of tongue, rough and ready, of uncouth garb and speech. Many of them carried the usual seaside penny cane, some displayed a *Great Eastern* medal on their breasts. The proceedings were enlivened by the strains of the dying remains of a string band.

As they drew under the great ship, Lowe thought she would have room 'to stow away a few ships like the *Umbria*, which was within a cable's length of her'. The *Umbria* was a vaunted new eight-thousand-ton Cunarder with one-fifth the *Great Eastern*'s passenger capacity.

Lowe climbed aboard and read in Lewis's guidebook:

> On this vast deck has stood our present Prince of Wales, together with his lamented father, and there is scarcely a scientific man of eminence in the civilized world who has not at some time or other hailed the privilege.

Lowe remarked,

> I will describe what these great men would have heard and seen could they have gone on that spacious upper deck when I did. 'This way, gentlemen, this way to see the greatest curiosity of the day, Bob, the Missing Link.' Then again, 'Gentlemen, you will see the African Mystery; all should see her.' Then they would have been invited to ring-throwing for knives; throwing for coconuts, Aunt Sally, and swings. They would have seen an American drinking bar, a shooting gallery and toffy stalls, a photographic studio and a camera obscura. The tank which contained 1,700 miles of cable has been converted into a music hall. The effect upon me was most saddening. We all know that life of the *Great Eastern* has been a failure, an arrow that has missed its mark. Anything I should think would be better than the life she is leading. If she cannot pay a breaking-up price, let her be decently buried beneath the wild billows of the great Atlantic. I for one will contribute to her funeral expenses.

Seafaring men went aboard and stood silent, like combat soldiers amidst a wild civilian victory celebration. They looked around the river and over the chimney pots at the green Welsh hills. Near by were moored four gallant old three-deckers, now like the *Great Eastern* fallen to strange fates. H.M.S. *Indefatigable* had become a training ship for the orphan sons of sailors. H.M.S. *Clarence* was a Roman Catholic reformatory ship, full of young Liverpool Irish 'slummies'. These spirited lads had been lately transferred to the *Clarence* after burning their previous institution to the water. H.M.S. *Akbar* was a Protestant reformatory ship. To round out this glimpse of Victorian methods of bringing up Young England, H.M.S. *Conway* was a training ship for the sons of gentlemen. Orphan, Catholic and Protestant delinquents and Young Gentlemen were hard to tell apart as they stared from the old wooden walls at the girls climbing aboard the *Great Eastern*. Beyond the ancient-men-of-war, lay a fleet of powder hulks, painted red.

A door had been cut into the fore cable tank and inside was a freak show with Bob, the Missing Link. A visitor, could not, of course, proceed along the lower deck to other parts. The *Great Eastern* was still solidly compartmented and the visitor had to climb to the main deck and down again to see each sight. The Photographic Studio, said the guide-book, was

> where the ambitious visitor may obtain his counterfeit present-ment standing upon classic soil, or rather wood, and thus be able to hand to ages yet unborn ocular proof of his having one time stood upon the decks of a ship whose name will for many generations be nearly as familiar in our mouths as that of Noah's Ark, and at once we enter the Ladies Saloon.

Why can't we have advertising writing like that today?

One of the best patronized attractions was a lithographic press, which for a copper imprinted on the visitor's own handkerchief pictures of the *Great Eastern*, Lewis's five stores and The Late David Lewis, Founder of the Firm. It retired many a handkerchief from nasal use and evidenced an ad-

vertising genius unknown to our times. Lewis's made the cus-
tomer supply the stock and pay for printing an advertisement that has been kept as an heirloom over three genera-
tions. Furthermore, on the return to shore, there was a run
on Lewis's handkerchief counter to buy replacements. Today
these handkerchiefs are regarded as museum pieces, while the
firm they advertised continues to thrive.

In the main and ladies' saloons were buffet restaurants
catered by Powell Brothers of Leamington Spa, who were
noted for hunt breakfasts. The main cable tank had become
a music hall, seating a thousand people. Here played a continuous bill of the Jungfrau Capelle, a Swiss Band of yodellers
and bell-ringers; Major Devono, a conjuror; Miss Ida Izon,
'Characteristic Vocalist'; Miss Nelly Fletcher, 'Champion
Skipping Rope Dancer'; and Smith & Orton, 'Breakneck
Knockabout Negro Comedians and Big Boot Dancers'. In the
evenings the music hall tank was cleared for public dances
'by electric light'. In the after cable tank was a side show,
featuring a trick rifle-shooting act by Captain & Kitty Man-
ard; Val Vose, ventriloquist, 'The Man with the Talking
Hand' (an early version of Señor Wences); and a contor-
tionist. Between decks several dozen pitchmen sold seashells,
souvenirs, flowers and canes. There were coconut shies, ring-
toss games and glass ball shooting galleries.

Twenty-six years before, the passengers of her maiden
voyage had discovered the circus-like rigging of the *Great
Eastern*, and the Liverpool showmen took full advantage
of it. As evening shades drew over the Merseyside, 'Beautiful
Ariel' climbed the shrouds to a long snare ruffle in limelight
beams that revealed the elegance of her limbs. Atop Tuesday
mast Beautiful Ariel grasped a trapeze and swung into the
night. Even the calliope of the steam carousel on deck was
stilled for her daring glide. 'It has no equal!' said the play-
bill. As Beautiful Ariel gained Wednesday mast, from the
afterdeck came a triumphant burst from Mr. Amer's Brass
Band of Newcastle-upon-Tyne: ('Pretty Music!'). Then came
the flyers, Louis & Elba, soaring and catching each other in

the foggy air of the masts. Crowds on shore could see the gleaming artists passing above the old ship.

Dizzied by the sight, the customers could turn immediately to the second-class refreshment saloon 'as well as one of the rapidly popularizing American bars, whereat the thirsty traveller may brighten himself up with 'A Flash of Lightning', an 'Eye Opener', or even a 'Corpse Reviver'. There was also a Gipsy Encampment aboard.

On fine nights the people danced on deck to two rousing bands from Newcastle. But the real crowd-catchers were the massive engines down in the dark interior and the *Great Eastern* her mighty self. The bands, calliope, howls of barkers and rattle of shooting galleries faded away as people went down in awe to the engine rooms, and measured their puny human size with the forgings of James Watt and Scott Russell. The biggest ship in service that year, the Cunarder *Etruria*, was less than half the bulk of the *Great Eastern*.

Ship-proud Liverpool looked at the eyesore with growing indignation. Over fifty thousand people paid a shilling admission in the first month and Whitsuntide Bank Holiday (in June) saw twenty thousand go aboard in four days. The Liverpool Exhibition didn't turn out to be much of an attraction; the *Great Eastern* stole the show. Folks from the farms, mills and potteries came to see the great ship and neglected the shoreside fair of industry and navigation. They didn't leave much money in Liverpool. Lewis's seemed to be getting it all. Shipping men resented the department store people as landlubbers exploiting the pride of Britain's ocean might. There were outcries in the clubs and wrathful letters to the press. Orthodox marine historians to this day sniff at the episode: they are not interested in the fact that half-a-million visitors had a whacking good time on the *Great Eastern* in 1886, and that as a showman and advertiser, Louis Cohen demonstrated something like genius. The critics had no practical alternative to offer.

CHAPTER SIXTEEN

LAST DAYS OF LEVIATHAN

To those who've failed in aspiration vast,
To unnam'd soldiers fallen in front of the lead,
To calm, devoted engineers—to over-ardent travellers—
    to pilots on their ships,
To many a lofty song and picture without recognition—
    I'd rear a laurel-covered monument,
High, high above the rest—To all cut off before their
    time,
Possess'd by some strange spirit of fire,
Quenched by an early death.
                           —WALT WHITMAN, 1888

As AUTUMN came the charter expired and the ship reverted
to Edward de Mattos. He did not know what to do with her.
His Gibraltar coaling enterprise had failed. The Gibraltese
definitely did not want the *Great Eastern*. A syndicate proposed to fit out the ship with ice lockers to carry 'dead meat'
from South America. But, after some newspaper noise, the
promoters vanished.

So the unlucky coal dealer became a showman. He painted
out Lewis's billboards and rented the ship's sides to a tea pur-
veyor. 'The greatest anxiety has been displayed by people in
various parts of the United Kingdom and Europe to see the
ship at their different ports, and it is the desire of the owners
to gratify as far as possible this very reasonable wish,' de
Mattos announced. It was Victoria's jubilee, a year of fêtes,
holidays, illuminations and people coming out to see the
sights.

Early in the spring of '87 de Mattos chose to gratify Dublin.

Davey Duff's tug was among those which towed her across. The owner did not trust the *Great Eastern*'s engines. The Irish had ever keened for the darling ship and had seen her only from afar in Bantry Bay, where she spliced the cables, and in the Cove of Cork when she lurched in from the storm. They demonstrated small affection for her guise as an advertisement for British tea. 'We spent a short time in Dublin'. said Captain Duff. The leavetaking was hastened by the port authorities, who feared the blundering monster's proximity to little ships which paid dues.

The *Wrestler* towed her back to Liverpool. The port defended itself with a technicality. The Birkenhead police gave notice that an application for a *Great Eastern* liquor licence would be opposed. De Mattos substituted an exhibition of arts and industries aboard, but the customers preferred mild and bitter. He decided to gratify Scotland. The ship was towed to the Clyde and moored between Helensburgh and Greenock.

The Scots received her warmly: had she not been built by Professor Scott Russell, that used to run the yard at Caird's? The builder had been gone five years. John Scott Russell died by the sea at Ventnor in 1882, 'in reduced circumstances'. An obituary termed him 'a brilliant man of versatile intellectual power, a good scholar, a clever and original speaker and a bright conversationalist'. However, 'a certain lack of stability or business capacity had hampered his success in life'. He had built only one ship after the *Great Eastern*, an original design, to be sure, and the first of its type, a train ferry that ran across Lake Constance from Germany to Switzerland. The other noteworthy work of his unproductive later life was a colossal sheet iron dome for the 1873 Vienna Exhibition, which was 'among roofs what the *Great Eastern* is to ships'.

Ever since his ruin, Scott Russell had been intent on his apologia. He collected his builder's models, drawings, waveline hulls and theoretical papers and gave them to the Science Museum in South Kensington. This same Museum has a log of John Scott Russell which awaits a literate en-

gineer who will take up the material and restore the Little
Giant's partner to his rightful place in mechanical engineering. As their ship was moored in the Clyde, Brunel was
forgotten in Kensal Green, Scott Russell was a mouldering obscurity, and the wonder of the seas was a living
shame.

By now the Clydeside was the shipbuilder of the world.
Four out of five steamers afloat flew the red duster and the
Scots were building most of them. In 1858 'a Clyde chip' had
advised Brunel he should have built on the Clyde and now
steamship companies had come around to the idea. The first
real rivals of the *Great Eastern* were shaping at Harland &
Wolff's yard, two White Star Line keels, laid by the only
financial arrangement that could assure the success of ships
in Brunel's class. For the first time a navy shared construction costs in consideration of designing a merchant ship as
an auxiliary cruiser. Navies had, of course, devolved from
merchant ships, which had fought the major naval battles
since Salamis. Drake beat 'the mighty sea castles of the
Hildalgos' with merchantmen. The Royal Navy had taken
the further step of adopting a commercial ship before she
was laid down.

The first White Star liner was the *Teutonic*, 556 feet long
and half the displacement of the *Great Eastern*. The Admiralty paraded her at a fleet review in 1889. It was the con-
summation of a plea *Great Eastern* stockholders had pressed
on the naval lords, in '58 and on U.S. Navy Secretary Gideon
Welles in '61.

When dour autumn rains came to the Lowlands of Scotland, the sightseers dwindled away. De Mattos published a
poster:

TO BE SOLD AT PUBLIC AUCTION on Thursday 20th October 1887
at 12 O'Clock, at the Brokers' Saleroom, Walmer Building,
Water Street, Liverpool, if not previously disposed of by private
treaty, THE CELEBRATED, WORLD-RENOWNED, MAGNIFICENT, IRON
PADDLE AND SCREW STEAMSHIP 'GREAT EASTERN', as she lies in
the Clyde. Lately steamed from Dublin to Liverpool and then

to the Clyde with her screw engine, which is 1,600 h.p. nominal; paddle engines are 1,000 h.p. nominal. She has lately been painted and decorated.

The victorious bidder was a Mr. Craik, who mentioned £26,000. Craik was de Mattos' manager. It was the owner's bid to prevent sale for a lower sum. Rain and mist enveloped the lonely mammoth as she lay idle and unwanted at Greenock. The owners tried to pump up fresh journalistic speculation, but it was too late for printing new prospectuses and lovely share certificates. The ship had beaten them all.

A month after the melancholy fifth auction, de Mattos received an offer of £16,000 from Henry Bath & Sons. He sold the ship instantly, lest the buyer entertain a second thought. London Traders Ltd. was the seventh operating company to lose on the *Great Eastern*. The stockholders were paid off at a heavy loss.

Henry Bath & Sons were metal dealers of Liverpool, London and Swansea. They were in the unsentimental business of breaking ships. The company executives, Messrs. Morrice and Greer, set out immediately to organize dismantling operations. They entrained to Barrow-in-Furness and talked to the Royal Navy harbourmaster, Captain Barnett, about putting the ship into Ramsden Dock to break her up. The newly built dock was long enough and had a gate a hundred feet wide. By removing the paddle wheels she would fit. Morrice and Greet continued to Greenock to survey the *Great Eastern* for her metal values.

They gazed upon their big possession and the sight stole their reason. They began mooning to each other about removing the old engines, installing new ones and making her pay in the cattle trade, or perhaps in carrying bulk petroleum. They went back to Barrow to arrange for a refit in Ramsden Dock. Captain Barnett saw the fever in their eyes and refused to let them have the dock.

With the spell upon them the new owners announced that they would return the *Great Eastern* to Liverpool under the power of her propeller alone. They engaged a temporary

crew of a hundred 'runners', casual seamen who sail a ship
on its last voyage to the scrapping yard. Escorted by the
steamer *Stormcock*, the great ship left the Clyde on a fair
day, August 22, 1888. She made barely four knots. It was decided to take a tow cable from the *Stormcock*.

Coming down the Firth of Clyde past Ailsa Craig the
weather frowned and a wind came up. It increased in force
and the *Great Eastern* fell to rolling heavily. The screw lost
its bite in the waves. The *Stormcock*'s master did all he could
to hold the tow, but the big ship broke the cable. The escort
could not come near the heaving monster to pass another.
The runners clung for their lives as the *Great Eastern* leaped
helplessly adrift: She galloped four hours in her last storm.
The wind died and the tow was regained. It took three days
to reach the Mersey.

Liverpool grimly watched the big ship resuming her place
on the New Ferry gridiron. Gossip had it that 'there was still
hope for her use'. The city howled. The *Great Eastern* baby,
Jimmy Paton, who was now a flourishing manufacturer,
gathered the emotions of the port in an electrifying challenge: if the dishonour to his father's name and his birthplace
were not stopped immediately, Paton would personally blow
up the *Great Eastern* with gunpowder. Glasses were raised
in the clubs and ordinaries to the civic champion. Nobody
thought what it would cost for sufficient gunpowder, how
many explosions it would take to immolate the great ship, or
what would happen to the window lights and chimney pots
of Liverpool and Birkenhead while Jimmy was performing
his bounden duty. Paton had no intention of violence. It was
a *beau geste* and what everybody wanted to say.

Henry Bath & Sons announced that the *Great Eastern*
would be broken up on the grid. There were misgivings to
the decision. Scrapping the *Great Eastern* would be a project
five or six times as large as any break-up ever attempted, and
would risk an investment as large as building a good-sized
steamer. It was reckoned that two hundred men could break
the ship in a year at a cost of £20,000 in addition to the

£ 16,000 paid for her. It would not be easy to emancipate investors and cure the great ship fever for once and all. Some said the job would never pay, and Bath & Sons would lose less money by towing her to the deep sea and opening the cocks.

The *Great Eastern* mothered another innovation in shipping practices when Bath & Sons announced that on November 21 they would auction the parts before dismantling her. Previously scrappers paid for a vessel and speculated on returns. An extraordinary crowd of bidders attended the three-day sale, many from foreign countries. Her copper fittings brought £ 3,000, gun metal £ 4,400, brass fittings £ 4,000, lead more than £ 4,000, and the Trotman patent anchors £ 300. Her 30,000 plates and 3,000,000 rivets went for £ 25,000. The total proceeds amounted to £ 58,000. At last somebody had made her pay! Bath & Sons stood to make a 35 per cent profit. It was almost as much as Brunel said she would return in the trade to Trincomalee. However, to collect the bonanza, the shipbreaker still had to dissemble the parts within his timetable.

The aged and failing Sir Daniel Gooch read of the auction in the London *Standard* and wrote in his diary:

It looks like the last of the grand old ship, the *Great Eastern*. I would much rather the ship was broken up than turned to base uses. Poor old ship, you deserved a better fate.

At the auction were many persons unknown to the scrap metal traders and chandlers. The strangers asked for single items from the wholesale parcels and bid heatedly and high for bells, wheels, panelling, lamps and furniture. It was the debut of collectors of Greateasterniana, who were to project her crowd fervours into the future. A public house at New Ferry obtained walnut panelling for a bar buffet. A Cheshireman bought one of her wheels, now owned by C. C. Bennett of Northwich. Another wheel went to William Thomas, a stationary engineer for the Garston Copper Works. Thomas also got a dining-room bell, which is still shown in Garston. Fans bought the allegorical panels from the grand saloon and

her binnacle which looked like a small temple and was sur-
mounted by a brass British lion with his forepaw atop the
globe. One of her brass saloon lamps has been handed down
to Nigel Kennedy of Lower Bebington, Cheshire. Captain
Halpin's nephew was there to enlarge the ex-skipper's great
ship souvenirs at Tinnakilly House, Wicklow. This collection
was given by the captain's daughter Miss Belle, to the Maritime Institute of Ireland in 1953. J. S. Paton, son of the *Great
Eastern* baby, owns an engraved *Great Eastern* teapot and a
water jug, one of those that contained no ice water on the
Cape May cruise.

The master stroke of the souvenir hunters silenced the
scrap dealers in wonder. A mistress of Miss Hockley's Boarding School at West Kirby, Lancashire, bought the captain's
mahogany deck caboose from under the flying bridge with
its gold and white panelling and its wraiths: Harrison going
to be drowned, Vine Hall playing the flute, Kennedy grinning at the icebergs, Paton bowing to Mary Lincoln, Walker
studying Hamilton Toyle, Anderson awakening to the test-
room gong, and Robert Halpin dangling the baby with the
jewelled toes. The caboose was re-erected on the grounds of
Miss Hockley's School as a children's clubhouse.

Yet they appear, the mortal reminders of the *Great Eastern*.
One of Goering's pilots hit an old house in Bristol and, in
that eruption of plaster dust and paper which is a bombed
house, were found £6,000 in shares of the Great Eastern
Steam Navigation Company. The certificates were neatly tied
in tape with a note signed 'Rowland Brotherhood', who wrote
he bought them because 'Mr. Brunel has been such a good
friend to me'.

The breaking-up began on the first day of 1889, a month
short of thirty-one years after the launching, a good old age
for a capital ship. So many workmen and visitors used the
Liverpool ferry that it was renamed 'The Great Eastern and
Rock Ferry Line'. The workers removed the interior fittings
on schedule, but the well-found hull defied them. More than
half the shipbreaker's income and all his profit lay in the

double iron hall. The oxyacetylene torch had not yet appeared. The men worked the rivets loose by hammering on plate, driving chisels under the heads, and sawing and smashing away. It was soon evident that more effort was required to remove a rivet than it had taken to drive it a generation before.

In October, 1889, Sir Daniel Gooch died, survived by the Great Eastern which was taking Henry Bath & Sons for one of her famous rides. The ship challenged a generation of mechanical minds. The final problem was how to take her apart. Bath & Sons solved it with the invention of the wrecker's big iron ball. A derrick was erected over the ship and a stationary steam engine raised a heavy iron ball to a spur. It was released by a trigger. The impact shocked two shires and arrested gossip, deals and assignations. But it started the rivets. The awful repeated crashes of that ball eclipsed any noises Jimmy Paton could have made with the gunpowder plot and introduced neuroticism to Cheshire. Life was a torment for families living near the gridiron.

The side plates were shed, and after eighteen months the men reached the double bottom. The work was harder there and they worked long, bitter, bruising days to uproot the cells. Mr. J. M. Lamb recounted to the author a memory of standing on Prince's Landing Stage one day in 1890 when the Rock Ferry boat came in. 'Off it came a rough gang of men, all shouting and cussing. A little man was laying down the law, and I, being nine years old, was very frightened. I asked Papa what those men wanted. Said my Papa "They are vexed because they cannot earn their salt". When I got home I asked my mother what it was when a man cannot earn his salt. Papa began laughing and told Ma that shipbreakers working on the Great Eastern had gone on strike. They were paid by the ton, and had got down to the keelson.' It was the last 'mutiny'.

One day they were breaching a compartment in the inner shell on the port side, when a shriek went up that stopped all work and ran wildly through the port and country. One who hurried to New Ferry to see it was David Duff. He wrote me:

> They found a skeleton inside the ship's shell and the tank tops. It was the skeleton of the basher who was missing. Also the frame of the bash boy was found with him. And so there you are, sir, that is all I can tell you of the *Great Eastern*.

In 1899, forty-one years after the ordeal of the Isle of Dogs, a longer vessel was launched, the 704-foot White Star liner, *Oceanic*. She was smaller in displacement by six thousand tons. The first ship to exceed Brunel's came in 1906, when Cunard launched the successor to the presumptuous *Great Eastern*. The name of that ship was *Lusitania*.

INDEX